Wolcott H Littlejohn

The Constitutional Amendment

Or, The Sunday, the Sabbath, the Change, and Restitution

Wolcott H Littlejohn

The Constitutional Amendment
Or, The Sunday, the Sabbath, the Change, and Restitution

ISBN/EAN: 9783744746519

Printed in Europe, USA, Canada, Australia, Japan

Cover: Foto ©Lupo / pixelio.de

More available books at **www.hansebooks.com**

THE CONSTITUTIONAL AMENDMENT:

— OR —

THE SUNDAY, THE SABBATH,

THE

CHANGE, AND RESTITUTION.

A DISCUSSION BETWEEN
W. H. LITTLEJOHN, SEVENTH-DAY ADVENTIST,
AND THE
EDITOR OF THE CHRISTIAN STATESMAN.

STEAM PRESS
OF THE SEVENTH DAY ADVENTIST PUBLISHING ASSOCIATION,
BATTLE CREEK, MICH.:
1873.

Entered, according to Act of Congress, in the year 1873, by the

S. D. A. P. ASSOCIATION,

In the Office of the Librarian of Congress, at Washington.

PREFACE.

As it has been thought best that the following articles, which, with the exception of the Replies and Rejoinders, have already been published in the *Christian Statesman*, the *Sabbath Recorder*, and the *Advent Review*, should have a still wider circulation, it has been at last decided to present them to the public in the form of the present volume.

The occasion of their first appearance was as follows: Within the last few years, a party has been organized in this country, whose especial aims are the amendment of the Constitution, so that the names of God and Christ may appear in it; the recognition in the same instrument of the Bible as the fountain of national law; the securing of the reading of the Bible in the common schools; and the enforcement by law of the observance of Sunday, as the Christian Sabbath. Slowly, but steadily, the friends of this movement are bringing it to the public notice and enlarging the circle of its active supporters. A single glance at the existing state of affairs reveals the fact that, at no distant date, the issues which these men are making up will be the ones over which contending parties will wage fierce contest. Already the press of the country, by the drift of events which they find themselves incapable of controlling, are compelled, almost daily, to record transactions which are not only calling the attention of the people to a conflict which is both imminent and irrepressible, but which are also continually adding fuel to a flame which even now burns with a fierceness and volume indicative of its future scope and power.

In view of these facts, the writer of the subjoined articles, while taking no particular interest in party politics, merely as such, nevertheless felt a profound conviction that the time had come, in the providence of God, when Christian men should offer a solemn protest against a state of affairs which, while ostensibly inaugurated in the interest of the kingdom of Christ, will ultimately prove most destructive of religious liberty. This, he therefore attempted to do, purely from the stand-point of the Bible. Through the courtesy of the editor of the *Christian Statesman*, which paper is the organ of the amendment party, the first seven of the following communications were permitted to appear in the columns of that periodical. Subsequently, the editor of that paper felt it incumbent upon him to take issue with what was thus published, and to answer the same in a series of editorial articles. To these again, the author of the original communications published a series of rejoinders, in defense of the positions assumed by him in the outset, and in controversion of those of the reviewer. These articles, the replies of the editor, and the rejoinders thereto, having been grouped together in the present volume, are offered to a candid public for serious consideration.

The reader will readily perceive that the whole discussion turns upon the Sabbath question. Fortunately, also, he will discover that the ground covered in the debate by the respective disputants is that generally occupied by the classes of believers whom they represent. Leaving him, therefore, to decide for himself as to which of the views presented has the sanction of the divine mind, the writer of the present preface can do no more than to give expression to his earnest desire that the God of all truth will vouchsafe his Spirit for the illumination of every mind which comes to the consideration of this subject with an honest purpose to ascertain his will in the matter under consideration.

W. H. L.

Allegan, Mich.

CONSTITUTIONAL AMENDMENT.

ARTICLE I.

One of the marked features of our time is the tendency toward the discussion of the Sabbath question. Nor can this subject be treated with more indifference in the future than it is at the present. Agitation, ceaseless, unrelenting, excited, and finally severe, is rendered certain by the temper of all the parties to the controversy. On the one hand, the friends of Sunday observance are dissatisfied with the laxity of the regard which is paid it, and are loud in their demands for statutory relief; denouncing upon the nation the wrath of God, in unstinted measure, should their petition be set at naught. On the other hand, the enemies of the Sabbath institution, in all of its phases, are becoming bold in their protestations against a legalized Sabbath, as something extremely oppressive and inexpressibly intolerable in its very nature.

In all parts of the country, activity characterizes the camps of both these contending hosts. Everywhere the elements of strength—hitherto unorganized, and inefficient to the accomplishment of great results because of that fact—are being brought out and employed in effective service.

Cincinnati, Chicago, New York, Boston, San Francisco, in their turn, become the theaters where the skirmish lines of future combatants, on a larger scale, are brought into occasional collision. The ordinary appliances of dinners, processions, national and State conventions, city, town, and district societies, are rapidly becoming the order of the day, while those who are brought within the range of their influence are stimulated and aroused, on the one hand, by earnest appeals to the Bible and religion, and on the other, to natural rights and individual conscience. So far has the matter now proceeded, so much has already been said, so fully has the contest been opened, that retrogression means defeat to either the one or the other party. And as to compromise, this can never be attained, from the fact that the position from which both parties are now seeking to emerge is that of toleration. Why, says the ardent advocate of the Sunday law, it is not sufficient that I observe the day of rest with strictness and fidelity in my own family. I owe a duty to the public; I am a member of a great Commonwealth, which God treats as a personality, and if I do not see to it that the statute laws of the land are in harmony with, and enforce the requirements of, the law of God, this nation, like all others which have ignored their obligation to legalize and enforce his will in matters of this nature, will be devoted to a ruin for which I shall be accountable, and in which I shall be a sharer. Moved by such considerations as these, his purse is open and his labors untiring for the accomplishment of that which now appears to him to be in the line of both individual interest and religious duty.

Again, his neighbor across the way being, perhaps, of the free-thinking order, and an ardent admirer of the complete separation of Church and State, wonders that he has so long consented to that abridgment of his personal liberty which has been made by statutory provision, and which has hitherto compelled him to surrender much of what he calls natural right to the whims and caprices of those with whom he differs so widely on all questions bearing upon the relation of man to his God. Henceforth, says he, I pledge my means, my influence, and my untiring effort, to a revolution which, if need be, shall shake society to its very center, rather than to consent to the legalized perpetuation of an instituion which requires on my part an acknowledgment of a faith which I have never held, and of doctrines which I detest.

Of course, all do not share alike, either in the enthusiasm or the animosity which characterizes certain individuals when entering upon a conflict like the one in question. In every party is found more or less of the aggressive and the conservative elements. Especially is this true in the incipient stages of its history. Some men are necessarily more earnest than are others in everything which they undertake. Some are bold, headlong, defiant; others, cautious, slow, and timid. One class leaps to its conclusions first, and looks for its arguments afterward; the other moves circumspectly, and, while it gives a general assent to the desirability of results, finds a world of trouble in deciding upon what means ought to be employed in securing them. One is forever foaming because of delay, and fears defeat as the result of hesitation; while the other protests against too rapid and ill-considered action.

Such is, at present, the condition more especially of the positive side of the Sunday movement in this country. The strong men and the weak men, the resolute men and the undecided men, are struggling for the mastery of the policy in the camp. One sort discovers no difficulties in the way of immediate and complete success. Lead us to the front, say they, our cause is just, and all that is necessary to success is the courage and inspiration of battle. But hold, say the others, not too fast; public sentiment is not prepared for the issue. And besides, we are not so clear in our minds as are you respecting the lengths to which this controversy should be carried, and the line of argument which ought to be pursued. Why, say the first, what need can there be of more delay? Nothing is more manifest than the means which we ought to employ for the accomplishment of our purpose. Our work is simply that of enforcement. Has not God said in so many words, in the decalogue, "Six days shalt thou labor, and do all thy work: but the seventh day is the Sabbath of the Lord thy God: in it thou shalt not do any work"? Is not this language explicit? Is it not a part of that law which nearly all Christians acknowledge to be binding? Do we not enforce the observance of the remaining commandments by statutory provision? And is it not equally clear that this should be treated in like manner? Why delay, then? Why not move upon the enemy's works with the inspiring battle-cry of "God in the Constitution?" Why not at once clamor for the amendment of that instrument, and for the passage of statutes by which the better observance of the Christian Sabbath can be secured? Give us these, and our victory is won. Our Sunday mails, and trains, and travel, and public amusements of every name and nature, can be removed at a single stroke. As a result, the nation will stand higher in the estimation of God; and the people, having acknowledged his supremacy, will have taken a long step in the direction of final renovation and conversion.

But wait, says another, not too fast in matters of so great moment. Please bear in mind the fact that this contest is to be one of words and arguments. Your danger is that of underrating the capacity and intelligence of our opponents. If you expect to meet them successfully, it must be by a logic which will bear criticism and examination.

As an individual, I am by no means certain that the Bible authority for our movement is so clear and abundant as you seem to imagine.

The law which you quote in justification of our course is truly a Sabbath law, and its import is unmistakable; but, unfortunately, instead of making for our cause, it is diametrically opposed to your efforts, and plainly declares that the *seventh day* of the week is the Sabbath of the Lord, whereas you are unmistakably occupying before the world a position no less awkward than that of insisting that the first, and not the seventh, is the one which should be enforced by legal enactment. While, therefore, I am in full sympathy with the general purposes of this movement, I am convinced that, before we shall succeed, we must rest it upon a different basis than the fourth commandment. So far as my individual preferences go—in order to avoid the difficulties which lie along the line of Scripture justification for our conduct—I suggest that we rest it upon the broad principle of social necessity, relying for our success upon the generally conceded fact that *rest* upon one day in seven is indispensable to the well-being of individuals and communities.

But, says a third party, while I agree with you in condemning the proposition that the fourth commandment, as originally given, furnishes us warrant for the observance of the first day of the week, I can never consent to the idea of its unconditional repeal; for without it in some form we are entirely without a Sabbath law; a condition of things which would be deplorable indeed. I therefore conclude that that law has been brought over into our dispensation, and so far changed as to adapt it to the enforcement of the observance of the first day of the week, agreeably to the example of Christ and the apostles. With this view, I can safely predict power and triumph for the grand scheme upon which we have entered. Give us a Sabbath of divine appointment and backed by a sacred precept, and victory is certain. But so sure as we lower the controversy to one which is merely corporeal in its nature and results, and pecuniary in its considerations, defeat is written upon our banners, since you have taken from us all the inspiration of the contest, and dried up the very springs of our enthusiasm and courage.

What the final result of such discussions will be, there is little room for doubt. That a revolution is fairly inaugurated in the minds of the people, it is now too late to question. What remains to be done, therefore, is simply to execute the grand purpose for which it has been instituted.

That this cannot be accomplished by a merely negative policy, has been illustrated too many times in history to require further demonstration. Men, having once entered the field of conflict, universally become less and less scrupulous in regard to the means employed to secure the desired object. In the primary meetings of a great movement, the voice of the conservative may be listened to with attention and respect; but should he give expression to the same prudent counsel upon the battle field, when the sword of the enemy is red with the blood of his compatriots, his utterances would be silenced in a storm of indignation such as would threaten his very existence, and consign his name to the list of those whose fidelity was at least questionable, and whose sympathy with the common foe was far from being impossible.

So, likewise, with the half-way men in this incipient struggle, which is about to throw open the gates of controversy upon one of those religious questions which, above all others, is sure to be characterized, first, by uncharitableness, and finally, by bitter hate and animosity. With each advancing month, their hold upon the confidence of their associates will grow less and less, and the counsels of their party will come more and more fully under the control of those positive, nervous spirits, who are swept along by convictions so deep and strong that they will bear down everything before them.

Nevertheless, candid reader, it is by no means certain that there may not be much of truth in the positions assumed by the more moderate men in the existing issue. At all events—since we have not as yet entered into that impassioned state of the public mind from which calm deliberation is banished by the necessity of immediate action—let us pause here for a moment, and carefully weigh the correctness of the suggestions presented above.

Is it worth the while to enter the lists in the approaching struggle, in order to secure the results proposed?

I say proposed, because, of course, the result is as yet more or less uncertain; nevertheless, we incline to the opinion that the end desired will be substantially realized, so far as appearance is concerned. Yet this will not be brought about in a moment, nor will it be accomplished without a hard fight. It must, from the very necessity of the case, be a contest which will enter, divide, and distract families, and which will alienate a large portion of the community from the other. But, with a united and well-drilled ministry, on the one hand, backed by the compact organization of their respective churches, and opposed by a heterogeneous mass of discordant elements, there can be little doubt as to final success.

First, then, let us suppose that the policy inaugurated shall be that of the class represented above as desiring to strip the subject of its religious garb, and to array it in the habiliments of mere policy and temporal considerations. Are the benefits reasonably to be expected from such a course such as would warrant the enthusiasm now manifested by the advocates of the proposed reformation? We believe not. In fine, so certain are we of it, that we should not hesitate to predict immediate and perfect paralysis to their efforts, so soon as they should inscribe this doctrine upon their banners. How many of the gentlemen in question are really so profoundly interested in the social status of the working-man that their zeal in his behalf could be wrought up to the point of sacrificing time and money, and of devoting voice and pen to the mere work of giving him a septenary day of physical rest? What satisfaction would be afforded them by the reflection that, as the result of legal enactment, the carefully appointed police in our great cities should be able to meet each other on the boundary lines of their respective beats, on the morning of Sunday, with the accustomed salutation, All is quiet! and cessation from labor is complete in all parts of the great metropolis? Who would highly prize a coerced rest of this sort? What particular gratification would be afforded to the religious world, as they gather, in their costly churches, by the thought that the great mass of the people were quietly sleeping, or lazily lounging in the various places of their retirement? Certainly there is nothing in such a state of things which offers results sufficiently desirable either to reward them for the great sacrifices with which it would be necessary that they should be purchased, in the first instance, or to secure that patient continuance in vigilant perseverance which would be required to insure the perpetuity of an order of things at once so compulsory and so precarious. We say, therefore, that to rest the contest upon this issue would be simply to falsify the facts. It is not the physical consideration of rest, in any large degree, which animates the mind and strengthens the resolve of those engaged in the newly organized reform. No; there is something behind all this. The informing soul, that which electrifies, stimulates, and nerves to action, is the profound conviction that this is a religious movement; that which is sought is the honoring of God by the observance of a Sabbath such as is found in his word. If this be not so, if the higher idea of Christian worship as the primary one is not paramount in this matter, then the whole thing is a farce, from beginning to end. Not only so; if what is sought is merely the improvement of bodily condition, then the plan suggested is, in many cases, far from being the best which might be offered. Take, if you please, our over-populated cities, with the dense masses of human beings who are there crowded together, under most unfavorable circumstances, many of them perishing for lack of pure air, and others pale and sickly for want of exposure to the vivifying rays of the sun, which is continually shut out from their gaze by the massive piles of masonry by which they are inclosed; who will not say that, leaving the spiritual out of consideration, and setting aside the idea of the sanctity of the day, it would be a blessing incalculably greater for them, should provision be made whereby this should become to them a day of recreation, while wandering amid flowers, and over hills, and through groves, instead of one in which, either from necessity or choice, they should still perpetuate the confinement which has already nearly proved fatal in their cases?

ARTICLE II.

Turning from the secular phase of this subject, let us regard it for a moment from the religious stand-point.

Is there anything in the purpose itself which is worthy of the cost at which alone it can be realized? In other words, since the object aimed at is ostensibly that of bringing the nation up to the point of a general regard for the first day of the week as a Sabbath, would such a result be one which should be profoundly desired?

We reply that this will depend altogether upon circumstances. In this case, as in the first, mere cessation from labor on that day, which is not prompted by a regard for the will and approval of Jehovah, could afford no relief to a nation, which is seeking to avert divine displeasure since there is no element in the act itself calculated to recommend it to the favor of Heaven. To illustrate: The individual sentenced to solitary confinement in the State's Prison is precluded from the possibility of laboring on the Sunday; will any one therefore argue that there is any merit in his inaction on that day? Again: The heathen nations, in common with the majority of the Christian world, have many of them regarded the Sunday as a sacred day; should we presume, therefore, that they are looked upon by the Almighty more complacently on this account? You answer, No; and urge, as a reason for this reply, that they have been engaged in a false worship, and have not been actuated by any regard for the true God. Where, then, is the line? Manifestly, right here: The men who honor God by the keeping of any day must be prompted by the conviction that they are doing it in strict and cheerful obedience to a divine command.

Here, then, is the crucible in which we will try the metal of this modern movement. If, when their grand design shall be accomplished—as the result of many labors and toils—and, even though before their purpose is attained, it shall be found necessary for them to reach their object through a conflict intensely bitter and impassioned on the part of the opposition, we shall witness the spectacle of a nation bowing submissively to the *law* and *will* of *God* in the humble and fervent observance of a weekly rest of *divine appointment*, it will be the grandest triumph which history has recorded. No treasure of gold —we were about to say no sacrifice of life— would be too great a price to pay for so glorious a victory. Let it be understood, however, that this must be a voluntary and intelligent worship on the part, at least, of the mass of the people.

But will this be true, should our friends compass the great object of their ambition? Let us inquire once more after their intentions. What is it they advocate? The answer is, A universal regard for the first day of the week, as the Sabbath of the Lord.

But what is the authority upon which the majority of them rest their argument for the proposed observance? Is it merely pecuniary advantage? No, say they, it is out of a sincere regard for the God of Heaven, and a conscientious desire to fulfill his law. But this implies religious duty. So far, so good. It also clearly sets forth the fact that God has a law, and a Sabbath which it enforces. The appeal, therefore, must inevitably be to that law, as the proper instrument from which to instruct the people.

To that they must be brought, again and again. Its import must be patiently taught, its sacredness must be thoroughly inculcated. Let them but be satisfied by *sound logic* that the divine statute is explicit in its demands for a strict observance of the first day of the week, let them be thoroughly educated into the idea that they are under its jurisdiction, and let them be instructed that this whole movement proceeds upon this religious conviction, and you have laid a foundation which will uphold a structure of imposing dimensions and enduring character, the cornerstone whereof is the fear of God, and an acknowledgment of his presence in the affairs of men. But how is it in the case in question? Is the commandment of a nature such as to support, in every particular, the tenets presented by the reform under consideration? This is really the vital point. Let it speak for itself. It is the fourth of the decalogue which is urged. "Remember the Sabbath day, to keep it holy. Six days shalt thou labor, and do all thy work; but the seventh day is the Sabbath of the Lord thy God: in it thou shalt not do any work, thou, nor thy son, nor thy daughter, thy man-servant, nor thy maid-servant, nor thy cattle, nor thy stranger that is within thy gates: for in six days the Lord made heaven and earth, the sea, and all that in them is, and rested the seventh day: wherefore the Lord blessed the Sabbath day, and hallowed it." If this is not a Sabbath law, then there is none in existence; for, *mark it*, this is the only instance in all the Scriptures in which it will be claimed by any one that we have a positive command for the observance of the Sabbath. So far, therefore, as the first day of the week is concerned, its friends have this advantage, that, if they but succeed in resting it upon this commandment, their labor is ended; for it—*i. e.*, the commandment—has no rival. All that is needed, consequently, is a clear, pointed exegesis showing that the day in question is the one, the observance of which the divine Lawgiver has required. But, unfortunately, such an exegesis would be beset with difficulties. To begin with, Who shall be able to harmonize the declaration which the commandment contains in these words, "The *seventh day* is the Sabbath of the Lord thy God: in it thou shalt not do any work," with the utterance of those who, on the contrary, say that the *first day* is the Sabbath of the Lord, and must be observed as such? The divine Lawgiver—as if determined that there shall be no room for debate in regard to the day which he had in his mind—has identified it in a manner such as to leave no room for dispute. In the first place, he announces his willingness that six days of the week should be devoted to secular employment, "Six days shalt thou labor, and do all thy work:" then follows the disjunctive, "but —the seventh day is the Sabbath of the Lord thy God: in it thou shalt not do any work." Here it is made plain that it is the "Sabbath of the Lord" upon which we are to rest. Again, passing over the intermediate space, we come to the close of the commandment, in which he sets forth three important transactions by which that was constituted the Sabbath, and by which it may ever be recognized. He says, "For in six days the Lord made heaven and earth, the sea, and all that in them is, and rested the seventh day: wherefore the Lord blessed the Sabbath day, and hallowed it." That is, the day which we are to keep as the Sabbath of the Lord is the one upon which he *rested*, which he *blessed*, and which he *hallowed*. Therefore, before the first day of the week can, with any show of reason, be kept in fulfillment of this commandment, *i. e.*, before it can be regarded as the "Sabbath of the Lord," it must be shown that, at some time, God has rested upon it, blessed, and hallowed it. But this would be a difficult task; for not only are the Scriptures silent, so far as the affirmation of this fact is concerned with reference to the first day of the week, but, on the contrary, they positively declare that it was the very day upon which Jehovah *entered upon the stupendous undertaking of making a world*. Should additional evidence be required on this point, *i. e.*, that the last day of the week, and not the first, is the one which Jehovah intended to sanctify, we have but to cite the intelligent reader to the fact that Moses, the prophets, the Lord himself, the holy women after his death, and the whole Jewish nation—in whose language the decalogue was given—are, and have been, unanimous in placing this construction upon the Sabbatic law.

Should any, however, perceiving the dilemma into which they are thrown by the effort to enforce their view in the use of the law, as it was originally given, seek relief in the position that it was so far amended in the days of Christ as to admit of the substitution of the day of his resurrection for that of God's rest at the end of creation week, we reply, If such a fact can be clearly made out, it would certainly furnish the very help which is needed just at this juncture, and without which confusion must inevitably characterize the movements of those who feel the necessity of a Sabbatic law for the keeping of Sunday.

Let us, therefore, carefully investigate this most important point. Is it true that the Son of God did so change the phraseology of the commandment of the Father that, from his time forward, its utterances have not only justified the secularizing of the last, but have also enforced, by the penalty of eternal death, a strictly religious regard for the first day of the week, on the part of both the Jewish and the Gentile world? Now this, if accomplished, was no trifling affair, and could not have been done in a corner; since it involved the guilt or innocence, the life or death, of countless millions of men and women, whose condemnation in the day of Judgment for the violation of Sunday sanctity would turn, of necessity, upon the words of one who both had the power to change, and had brought the knowledge of that change clearly before them. Certain it is, therefore—since God does not first judge, and legislate afterward—all the light which is necessary for the proper elucidation of this subject is now to be found in his written word. To this, then, we turn; and with a profound conviction that the language of Christ was true in its largest sense, "If any man will do his will he shall know of the doctrine,"—we inquire, Where is it stated, *in so many words*, that God made the amendment in question?

Should the response be returned, as it certainly must be, that such a statement is not to be found within the lids of the Bible, we answer that this is a concession which, most assuredly, will greatly embarrass our friends in the proposed reform. Sagacious men will not be slow in discovering its bearing upon the subject, and it will be very difficult to explain such an omission to the satisfaction of cautious and reflecting minds. Should it be suggested, however, that—notwithstanding the fact the change has not been set forth in so many words—it has nevertheless occurred, and is therefore binding, we answer: Although the transaction upon the face of it, to say the least, would be a singular one, if an alteration has really been made, the next thing to be ascertained is its precise nature. We have already seen that the first law was very explicit in its statements; and all are conversant with the fact that to it was given the greatest publicity, and that it was uttered by the voice, and written by the finger of God, under the most imposing circumstances. Now, if Christ—whose power to do so we shall not question here—has really undertaken the task of adding to, or taking from, this most sacred precept, will some one furnish us with an *authentic copy* of the statute, as amended ? Now this is a reasonable and just request. To declare simply that a change has occurred, without making known precisely what that change is, is but to bewilder and confuse. Conscious of this fact, the State is always extremely careful to give to its citizens—in the most public manner—every variation which is made in its enactments, lest the loyal man should be incapable of proving his fidelity by obedience, or the disloyal justify his violation upon the plea of necessary ignorance. Shall man be more just than his Maker ? Shall Christ—who, in every other respect, has, in matters of duty, furnished us with line upon line, and precept upon precept—be found, at last, upon this most important point, to have been unmindful of the highest interests of his followers? Most assuredly not. He that never slumbereth nor sleepeth, He that knoweth the end from the beginning, He who hath said, " Where there is no law there is no transgression," has certainly never required his people to occupy a position in the face of their enemies so extremely embarrassing as that in which they would be compelled to ignore the plainest dictates of reason and Scripture, by seeking to condemn in the world a practice which is not necessarily immoral in itself, and against which there is no explicit denunciation of the Bible. Who, then, we inquire again, will furnish us from the sacred page the precept so remodeled as to meet the exigences of this case? Is it *larger* or more *condensed* than before? Does the first clause read, "Remember the Sabbath day, to keep it holy?" If so, it is well. Is the second in order expressed in these words, "Six days shalt thou labor, and do all thy work?" This, again, is good. But how is it with the third, "The seventh day is the Sabbath of the Lord thy God: in it thou shalt not do any work?" Here, unquestionably, the change must begin. Who among us, therefore, can produce the divine warrant for a reading of this passage which shall make it harmonize with the keeping of Sunday? Who dare declare, upon his veracity, that he has ever discovered in the sacred word an instance in which it has been so rewritten as to read, "But the *first* day is the Sabbath of the Lord thy God: in it thou shalt not do any work?"

Furthermore, passing over the instructions in regard to sons, daughters, servants, the stranger, etc., what has the pen of the divine remodeler done with the *reason* of the commandment as found in the words, "For in six days the Lord made heaven and earth, the sea, and all that in them is, and rested the seventh day: wherefore the Lord blessed the Sabbath day, and hallowed it?" Has that been stricken out altogether? Or, is there a glaring inconsistency in the remodeled statute, by which it is made to state that the *first* day of the week, instead of the *seventh*, is now the Sabbath of the Lord our God, because of the fact that, in the creation of the world, God rested upon, blessed, and hallowed, the latter? These are weighty questions. Upon them, virtually, turns the issue of an amended law. For, to amend, is so to change or alter as to vary the duty of a subject; and if no one is capable of informing definitely and particularly in regard to the precise variations of the phraseology, then, of course, no one is able to decide just how far our course of action should deviate from what it has been hitherto, in order to meet the demands of the divine will as now expressed, in a rule which has never been seen, and which no hand would venture to trace with any claim to exactitude. Who, then, we inquire again, is sufficient for this task? Not one among the millions of Protestants who are so earnestly clamoring for the sanctity of the day in question will seriously lay claim to the ability to perform that which would at once elevate him to a position—in view of the relief which it would bring to thousands of troubled minds—more exalted than that of any saint or martyr who has ever lived.

Nor is this all; behind all this pretentious claim for an amended law are very many indications of a wide-spread conviction—though undefined and hardly recognized by the individuals themselves—that the fact upon which they place so much stress is, after all, one in regard to which there are serious doubts in their own minds. As an illustration of this, we have but to call attention to two things. First, on each Lord's day, so-called, thousands of congregations—after devoutly listening to the reading of the fourth commandment of the decalogue, word for word, syllable for syllable, letter for letter, precisely as it was written upon the table of stone by the finger of God—are in the habit of responding with solemn cadence to the utterances of the preacher, "O Lord, incline our hearts to keep this law." Now this prayer means something, or nothing. It is either an expression of desire, on the part of those employing it, for grace to enable them rightly to observe the commandment as it reads—seventh day and all—or else it is a solemn mockery, which must inevitably provoke the wrath of Heaven. These people, therefore, judging from the most charitable stand-point, are witnesses—unconscious though they may be of the fact—of a generally pervading opinion that the verbiage of the fourth commandment has not been changed, and that it is as a whole as binding as ever. Second, nor is it simply true that those only who have a liturgy have committed themselves to this idea. It is astonishing to what extent it has crept into creeds, confessions of faith, church disciplines, and documents of a like nature. But among the most striking of all evidences of its universality, when properly understood, is the practice of nearly all religious denominations of printing, for general distribution among the Sunday-school scholars, verbatim copies of the decalogue, as given in the twentieth chapter of Exodus. Yet this practice would be a pernicious one, and worthy of the most severe censure, as calculated to lead astray and deceive the minds of the young, if it were really true that this code, in at least one very important particular, failed to meet the facts in the case, as it regards present duty.

In view of these considerations, a change of the base of operations becomes indispensable. A commandment, altered in its expressions so as to vary its import, and yet no one acquainted with the exact terms in which it is at present couched—and all, in reality, being so skeptical upon the point that even its most ardent advocates reason as if it had never occurred—would certainly furnish a foundation altogether insufficient for the mighty superstructure of a great reform, which proposes, ere the accomplishment of its mission, to revolutionize the State.

ARTICLE III.

Where, then, shall we turn for relief? There is one, and but one, more chance.

Acknowledging that the law, as originally given, will not answer the purpose, and that its amendment cannot be made out with sufficient clearness to warrant the taking of a stand upon it, we turn, for the last time, to examine a position quite generally advanced; namely, that of Sunday observance inaugurated, justified, and enforced, by the resurrection and example of Christ. Is it true, then, that such is the fact? Have we, at last, found relief from all our difficulties in the life and career of no less a personage than the divine Son of God? Let us see.

The point of the argument is briefly this:—

Our Lord—by rising from the dead, and by his practice of meeting with his disciples on that day—both introduced, and made obligatory upon his followers, the necessity of distinguishing between the first and the remaining days of the week, as we would between the sacred and the profane. Now, if this be a case which can be clearly made out, then we are immediately relieved in one particular; that is, we have found authority for the observance of the Sunday. But how is it as it regards the seventh day? This, we have seen, was commanded by God the Father. The obligation of that command is still recognized. Now, consequently, if Christ the Son has, upon his own authority, introduced another day immediately following the seventh, and clothed it with divine honors, is it a necessary inference that the former is therefore set aside? To our mind, it is far from being such. If God has a law for the observance of a given day, and Christ has furnished us with an example for that of another also, then the necessary conclusion is, that the first must be kept out of respect for God the Father, and the last through reverence to Christ the Son. Three facts, therefore, must be clearly made out, or our situation is indeed one of perplexity.

First, it must be shown, authoritatively, that the resurrection effected the change which is urged, and that the practice of Christ was what it is claimed to have been.

Second, that that practice was designed to be exemplary; in other words, that what he did in these particulars was of a nature such that we are required to imitate it.

Third, it must also be shown that he not only sanctified the first, but, also, that he secularized the seventh day of the week.

But can this be done? Let us see. First, then, we will consider the matter of the resurrection. Now, that it was an event of surpassing glory, and one ever to be held in grateful remembrance, there is no room for dispute among Christians. But shall we, therefore, decide that it must of necessity be commemorated by a day of rest? This would be assuming a great deal. It seems to us that it would be better, far better, to leave decisions of such importance as this entirely with the Holy Spirit. Protestants, at least, warned by the example of Roman Catholics, should avoid the danger of attempting to administer in the matter of designating holy days; since, manifestly, this is alone the province of God. Hence, we inquire, Has the Holy Ghost ever said that the resurrection of Christ imparted a holy character to the day upon which it occurred? The answer must, undeniably, be in the negative. No such declaration is found in the Holy Word. Nor is this all; even from the stand-point of human reason, every analogy is against it. It were fitting that, when God had closed the work of creation, and ceased to labor, he should appoint a day in commemoration of that rest. The propriety of such a course, all can see. But, on the contrary, is it not equally manifest that to have remained inactive on that glorious morning, when the Son of God had burst the bands of death, and the news was flying through all parts of the great city of Jerusalem, "Jesus has risen to life again," would have been a condition of things wholly out of the question? Both the enemies and the friends of Christ—the one class stimulated by hate, and the other released by the mighty power of God from the overwhelming gloom and crushing despondency of three terrible days—were, by the very necessities of the case, moved to action by an energy which would cause them to overleap every barrier and to break away from every restraint. Everything, everywhere, animated by the new aspect which affairs had suddenly assumed, demanded immediate, ceaseless, and untiring activity. And such it had. From the early morning, until far into the hours of the succeeding night, scribe and Pharisee, priest and Levite, believer and unbeliever, were hearing, gathering, and distributing, all that could be learned of this most mysterious event. We say, consequently, that so far is it from being true that the day of the resurrection is one which should be hallowed, either exactly or substantially as that of the decalogue, the very opposite is the fact; and, if it were to be celebrated at all, every consideration of fitness demands that it should be done by excessive demonstrations of outward and uncontrolled joy, rather than by quietude and restraint.

Passing now to the other branches of the subject, we inquire, finally, What was there in the *example* of Christ and the apostles which in any way affects the question? If they are to be quoted at all upon this subject, it is but reasonable that their history should be examined with reference both to the seventh and the first day; for, if precedent, and not positive enactment, is to be the rule by which our faith is to be decided, in a point of this significance, it is at least presumable that the historic transactions by which this question is to be determined will be ample in number, and of a nature to meet and explain all the phases of the subject. That is, the Gospels and the Acts of the Apostles—covering, as their history does, a period of about thirty years—will afford numerous and conclusive evidences that both Christ and the apostles did actually dishonor the old, and invest with peculiar dignity and authority the new, Sabbath. First, we inquire then, Is there, in all the New Testament, the record of a single instance in which Jesus or his followers transacted, upon the seventh day of the week, matters incompatible with the notion of its original and continued sanctity? The answer is, of necessity, in the negative. The most careful and protracted search has failed to produce a single case in which the son of Joseph and Mary departed in this particular from the usages of his nation, or in which his immediate representatives, during the period of their canonical history, failed to follow, in the most scrupulous manner, the example of Him of whom it is said that, "as his custom was, he went into the synagogue on the Sabbath day, and stood up for to read." (Luke 4:16.) Nor is this all; it is a remarkable fact, and one well calculated to stagger the investigator at the very threshold of his researches into the data for the modern view, that, whereas the Sabbath is mentioned fifty-six times in the New Testament, it is in every instance, save one (where it refers to the annual sabbaths of the Jews), applied to the last day of the week. So far, therefore, as the negative argument is concerned, which was based upon the presumption that the claims of the old day were constructively annulled by the appointment of a new one, its force is entirely broken by the record, which, as we have seen, instead of proving such an abolition, is rather suggestive of the perpetuity of the old order of things. Hence, we turn to the positive side of the subject.

How do we know that Christ ever designed that his example should produce in our minds the conviction that he had withdrawn his regard from the day of his Father's rest, and placed it upon that of his own resurrection? Did he, in laying the foundation for the new institution—as in the case of the Lord's supper—inaugurate the same by his own action, and then say to his disciples, As oft as ye do this, do it in remembrance of me? Did he ever explain to any individual that his especial object in meeting with his followers on the evenings of the first and second Sundays (?) after his return from the dead was designed to inspire in the minds of future believers the conviction that those hours, from that time forward, had been consecrated to a religious use? If so, the record is very imperfect, in that it failed to hand down to us a most significant fact. I say significant, because, without such a declaration, the minds of common men, such as made up the rank and file of the immediate followers of Christ, were hardly competent to the subtile task of drawing, unaided, such nice distinctions. How natural, how easy, by a single word, to have put all doubt to rest, and to have given to future ages a foundation, broad and deep, upon which to ground the argument for the change.

But this, as we have already seen, was not done! and after the lapse of eighteen hundred years, men—in the stress of a situation which renders it necessary that they should obtain divine sanction, in order to the perpetuity of a favored institution—are ringing the changes of an endless variety of conjectures drawn from transactions, which, in the record itself, were mentioned as possessing no peculiar characteristics, which should in any way affect the *mere time* upon which they occurred.

Let us, therefore, with a proper sense of the modesty with which we should ever enter upon the task of deciding upon the institutions of the church, when there is no divine precept for the guidance of our judgment, examine for ourselves. As we do this, it will be well, also, to bear in mind the fact that our prejudices will be very likely to lie entirely upon the side of life-long practice and traditionary inheritance. In fact, nearly every consideration, political, financial, and social, will be found, if not guarded with the strictest care, wooing us to a decision which—though it might dishonor God, and do violence to the principles of a clear, natural logic—would exempt us, individually, from personal sacrifice and pecuniary loss.

ARTICLE IV.

First, then, we suggest that it would be well to collate all the texts in the New Testament in which the first day of the week is mentioned. They are as follows: "In the end of the Sabbath, as it began to dawn toward the first day of the week, came Mary Magdalene and the other Mary to see the sepulcher." Matt. 28:1.

"And when the Sabbath was past, Mary Magdalene, and Mary the mother of James, and Salome, had bought sweet spices, that they might come and anoint Him. And very early in the morning, the first day of the week, they came unto the sepulcher at the rising of the sun." Mark 16:1, 2.

"Now when Jesus was risen early the first day of the week, he appeared first to Mary Magdalene, out of whom he had cast seven devils." Mark 16:9.

"And they returned, and prepared spices and ointments; and rested the Sabbath day, according to the commandment. Now upon the first day of the week, very early in the morning, they came unto the sepulcher, bringing the spices which they had prepared, and certain others with them." Luke 23:56, and 24:1.

"The first day of the week cometh Mary Magdalene early, when it was yet dark, unto the sepulcher, and seeth the stone taken away from the sepulcher." John 20 : 1.

"Then the same day at evening, being the first day of the week, when the doors were shut where the disciples were assembled for fear of the Jews, came Jesus and stood in the midst, and saith unto them, Peace be unto you." John 20:19.

"Upon the first day of the week let every one of you lay by him in store, as God hath prospered him, that there be no gatherings when I come." 1 Cor. 16 : 2.

"And upon the first day of the week, when the disciples came together to break bread, Paul preached unto them, ready to depart on the morrow; and continued his speech until midnight." Acts 20 : 7.

Doubtless the reader is not a little surprised, provided he has never given his attention to the subject before, at discovering the meagerness, so far as numbers at least are concerned, of the passages alluded to above. Nevertheless, let us take the data thus furnished, and from them endeavor to derive all the information which they can legitimately be made to afford. At first glance, it will be discovered that six of the passages of Scripture under consideration relate to one and the same day, which was that of the resurrection. Written as they were from five to sixty-two years this side of that occurrence, and penned by men who were profoundly interested in everything which was calculated to throw light upon matters of duty and doctrine, we would naturally expect that they would seize these most favorable opportunities for instructing those whom they were endeavoring to enlighten in regard to the time of, and circumstances connected with, the change of the Sabbath. Let us observe, therefore, how they discharge this most important responsibility. It will not be urged by any that John 20:1, and Mark 16:9, furnish anything which in any way strengthens the Sunday argument. The statements which they contain are merely to the effect that Mary Magdalene was the one to whom Christ first presented himself, and that she visited the tomb very early in the morning. Neither will it be insisted that the declaration found in Matt. 28:1, and Mark 16:1, 2, and Luke 23:56, and 24:1, afford any positive testimony for the sanctity of the first day of the week. On the contrary, we think that every candid person will concede that the bearing which they have upon the subject is rather against, than favorable to, the case which our friends are so anxious to make out. To illustrate: In Matt. 28:1, we read that "in the end of the Sabbath, as it began to dawn toward the first day of the week, came Mary Magdalene, and the other Mary, to see the sepulcher." Again, in Mark 16:1, 2, the same general fact is stated, with the simple variation that, instead of the expression, "in the end of the Sabbath," are substituted the words, "when the Sabbath was passed," while in Luke 23:56, and 24:1, it is declared that these things transpired on the first day of the week, the context carefully setting forth the fact that the women had "rested upon the Sabbath, according to the commandment," and that it being past, they came to the sepulcher, bringing with them the spices which they had prepared.

Now, putting all these things together, what have we learned? Manifestly, the following facts: First; when the events transpired which are set forth in these scriptures, there was a Sabbath; since it is stated, by way of locating them in point of time, that the Sabbath had ended before the affairs spoken of were transacted. Secondly; that the Sabbath, to which reference was made, was the seventh day of the week, since it preceded the first, and was that of the commandment. Thirdly; that, if the first day of the week was a Sabbath, as is now claimed, the women were ignorant of it, since it is clear that they did not go to the tomb on the seventh day to embalm the body, because of its being holy time; whereas, upon the first day of the week their scruples were gone, and they came to the sepulcher, bearing their spices with them, to accomplish a work which they would not have regarded as legitimate on the Sabbath. Fourthly; that the seventh day was not only the Sabbath at the time mentioned, but also that, according to the convictions of the historians, it was the

Sabbath at the time of their writing—since they apply to it the definite article "*the;*" whereas, if there had been a change of Sabbaths, it would have been natural to distinguish between them in the use of explanatory words and phrases, such as are now applied, as, for instance, "the Jewish Sabbath," "the Christian Sabbath," &c., &c. Fifthly; that, while Matthew, Mark, and Luke do, in every instance cited above, honor the seventh day of the week in the most scrupulous manner, by applying to it the Bible title of the Sabbath, they do, nevertheless, make mention of the day of the resurrection in each case, in the same connection, in the use of its secular name, "the first day of the week." A slight which is utterly inexplicable, provided the latter had really put on a sacred character; since, that being true, it was much more important that its new claims should be recognized and inculcated by those who could speak with authority, than it was that they should perpetuate the distinction of a day whose honors had become obsolete. Having now examined five of the six texts under consideration, there remains but one more to occupy our attention. This reads as follows: "Then the same day at evening, being the first day of the week, when the doors were shut where the disciples were assembled for fear of the Jews, came Jesus and stood in the midst, and saith unto them, Peace be unto you." John 20:19. Here, again, we are struck with the manifest disposition on the part of John, in common with the other evangelists, to avoid the application of any sacred title to the first day of the week. Twice, in this chapter, he makes mention of that which is now regarded as the "Queen of days," but in both instances, he avoids, as if with studied care, attaching to it any denomination by which its superiority over other days should be indicated. How perfectly in keeping, for instance, it would have been with the facts as they are now claimed to have existed—as well as with the interests and desires of millions who have since lived—had he in the text before us so varied the phraseology of the first clause that it would read as follows: "And the same day at evening, being the *Christian Sabbath*, when the disciples were assembled," &c. This, however, he did not do, and we inquire of the reader, right here, concerning his *motive* in omitting that which now appears to us so desirable, and which would have been perfectly legitimate were the views of our friends correct. Did he intentionally omit an important fact? Was it left out because of an oversight on his part? Or, would it be safer to conclude that perhaps, after all, the difficulty lies, not with the apostle, or with the Holy Spirit, which dictated his language, but with the theory, which seems to be out of joint with his utterances?

Nevertheless, as it is still urged that, in the absence of a positive declaration, this, the only remaining text, does furnish abundant evidence of the sacred regard in which the day of the resurrection was held—since it gives an account of a religious meeting held upon it, manifestly for the purpose of recognizing its heavenly character—let us examine more critically into the nature of the claims which are based upon its record. That those with whom we differ should be tenacious in their efforts to rest their cause very largely upon the account found in John 20:19, is not at all surprising. It is the only chance, as we have seen, which is left them of basing their argument upon a passage of Scripture which relates to the day of the resurrection. So far as 1 Cor. 16:2, and Acts 20:7, are concerned, it will not be disputed by any that their testimony is merely collateral evidence. If Sunday has become the Sabbath, it was by virtue of transactions which occurred immediately in connection with the rising of Christ. In other words, it was on the third day after the crucifixion that Christ, if at all, began to impress upon the minds of his disciples the Sabbatic character which had already attached to, and was henceforth to continue in, the day which saw him a conqueror over death and the grave.

Nay, more; if the change occurred a all, it must have dated from the very moment that the angel descended, the guard was stricken down, and the Son of God, glorified, came forth. This being the case, from that time forward it would naturally be the effort of Christ to produce in the minds of his followers the conviction of this most momentous fact. Every action of his would necessarily be—if not directly for the purpose of imprinting the peculiar sacredness of the hours upon those by whom he was surrounded—at least of a character such as to impart no sanction either to a deliberate, or even an unintentional disregard, on the part of any, of their hallowed nature. Hence, our friends, seizing upon the fact that he met with them while assembled together in the after part of the day, have endeavored to clothe the incident with great interest, and have largely elaborated their arguments to show that this was not an accidental occurrence, but rather partook of the nature of a religious meeting, Christ himself honoring these instinctive efforts on the part of the disciples to act in harmony with the spirit of the hour, by his own personal presence.

Before we sanction this view of the subject, however, let us give our attention for a moment to the manner in which the previous portion of the day, then closing, had up to that point been spent. Certain it is, that Jesus had not, during its declining hours, been suddenly moved by a newly created impulse for the accomplishment of an object which had been just as desirable for twelve hours as it was at that moment. Sunday sanctity had already become a fixed fact, and its knowledge as essential to the well-being of the disciples in the morning, as at the evening. We naturally conclude, therefore, that the very first opportunity for its disclosure would have been the one which Christ would embrace. This was afforded in his conversation with Mary. But, while there is no evidence that it was imparted, it is at least presumable that she was left entirely ignorant of it.

The second occasion was presented in that of the journey of the two disciples from Jerusalem to Emmaus, a distance of seven and a half miles. Jesus walked with them and talked with them by the way, reasoned with them about the resurrection, made as though he would have gone farther, discovered himself to them in the breaking of bread, and disappeared, leaving them to retrace the seven and a half miles to the city, with no word of caution against it on his part. Nay, more; his marked approval of the propriety of the act might properly have been inferred from the fact that he himself accompanied them in the first instance, in the garb of a wayfaring man; at the same time acting the part of one who was so far convinced of the rectitude of his own and of their action, that he was ready to continue his journey until night should render it impracticable. (Luke 24: 28.) Following these men now, as they retrace their steps to the city from which they had departed, and to which they were now returning—manifestly all unconscious that they were trespassing upon time which had been rescued from that which might properly be devoted to secular pursuits—let us observe them, as they mingle once more with their former companions in grief. How does it happen that they are congregated at this precise point of time? Is it because they have at last discovered the fact that it has been made in the special sense a proper day for religious assemblies? If so, whence have they derived their conviction? Certainly not from Mary, or the two disciples just returning from Emmaus. Assuredly, also, not from Christ himself.

But, again, is it not really from an induction on their own part, by which they have themselves discovered the fitness of making the day of resurrection also that of worship? Listen a moment. Hear their excited remarks as, at this juncture, they are joined by the two. Do you catch these words, "The Lord is risen indeed, and hath appeared to Simon"? (Luke 24:34.) Does not this establish the fact of their confidence in the previous report? Unfortunately, the historian adds, "Neither believed they them." Here they are, then, manifestly still doubting the very fact which some have thought they were convened to celebrate.

But, again, what is the *place* of their convocation? Unquestionably, neither the temple nor the synagogue. The record states that where they were assembled, "the doors were closed for fear of the Jews." Evidently, they were in some place of retirement and comparative safety, hiding away from the fury of a people who, in their madness and cruel hate, had crucified even the Lord of glory. We ask again, Where were they? Let Mark explain. Certainly he is competent to the task. When describing the very transaction we are considering, he says: "Afterward he appeared to the eleven as they sat at meat, and upbraided them with their unbelief and hardness of heart, because they believed not them which had seen him after he was risen." Mark 16:14. Here, then, is the clue to the whole matter. It was not a religious meeting, because they were in a frame of mind to be censured, rather than applauded, because of unbelief. It was merely the body of the apostles, gathered in their own quarters for the purpose of partaking of an evening meal, where they were in the habit of eating, and drinking, and sleeping—and where, at this time, they kept particularly close, because of the perils which surrounded them on every hand. That this is true, is further sustained by two additional considerations.

First; it was a place where Christ expected to find meat, and where he requested such for his own use, and was supplied from their bounty with broiled fish and an honeycomb, which, the record states, "he took and did eat before them." (Luke 24:41–43.)

Secondly; that they were in possession of just such a rendezvous, is clearly stated in John 20: 10, where, speaking of Peter and John when going from the sepulcher, it says, "They went away unto their own home." A few days later, Luke declares (Acts 1:13,) that when they came in from the ascension, they "went up into an upper room, where abode both Peter, and James, and John, and Andrew, Philip, and Thomas; Bartholomew, and Matthew, James the son of Alpheus, and Simon Zelotes, and Judas the brother of James."

Thus, by a natural and easy combination of the facts brought to view by the inspired penman, the whole matter has been reduced to a simple transaction, such as might have been repeated many times during the forty days, and such as—in and of itself—fails to disclose any evidence that the occurrences narrated, either necessarily or presumptively, afford the slightest justification for the supposition that Christ himself either designed, or that the apostles might legitimately conclude that he intended, by joining them under these familiar circumstances, to authorize one of the mightiest innovations upon the practice of ages which the world has ever seen.

ARTICLE V.

Nor is this matter at all relieved by the statement found in John 20:26, that after eight days, Thomas being present, he appeared unto them a second time under similar circumstances. For even should we grant that this was on the next Sunday evening—a matter in which there is, at least, room for a difference of opinion—the subject is merely complicated the more, so far as the view of our friends is concerned, since here a second opportunity, and that a most excellent one, for calling the attention of the disciples to the new character which a once secular day had assumed, was entirely neglected. In this also, as in the first instance, the conversation was of a nature to show that the object of the interview was to give additional evidence (because of the presence of Thomas) of the re-animation of the body of Christ, without any reference to its effect upon the character of the day upon which it occurred. But such silence, under *such* circumstances, in regard to so important a matter, is in itself conclusive evidence that the change claimed had not really taken place. Furthermore, it will not be urged that more than two out of the five first-days which occurred between the resurrection and the ascension were days of assembly. Had they been—as it had been decided, according to the view of those urging the transition, that the Sunday should not be hallowed by positive declaration, but simply inaugurated by quiet precedent, then the presumption is, that this precedent, instead of being left upon the insufficient support of two Sabbaths out of five, would have been carefully placed upon the whole number. Nor would the precaution have ended here. In a matter vital in its nature, certain it is that the honest seeker after truth would not be left to grope his way through a metaphysical labyrinth of philosophic speculation in regard to the effect of certain transactions upon the character of the time upon which they occurred; or the bearing of certain meetings of Christ and the apostles upon the question as to whether Sunday had assumed a sacred character, when at the same time his perplexity was rendered insupportable by the fact, that the historian states, that like meetings occurred on days for which no one will claim any particular honor.

Take, for instance, the meeting of Jesus with the apostles at the sea of Galilee (John 21), while they were engaged in a fishing excursion. Assuredly, this did not take place on Sunday; else, according to the view of our friends, they would not have been engaged in such an employment. Just what day it was, no one is able to decide; but all agree that its character was in no way affected by the profoundly interesting interview which occurred upon it between the Master and his disciples. If it were, then there is at least one holy day in the week which we cannot place in the calendar, since no one can decide whether it was the first, second, third, fourth, fifth, or sixth.

If, however, you would have a still more forcible illustration of the fact that religious meetings, were they never so solemn, can in nowise alter the nature of the hours on which they occur, let me call your attention to the day of the ascension (Acts 1). Here is an occasion of transcendent glory. If the statements in the sacred narrative of events, which transpired during its hours, could only be predicated of either one or the other of the first-day meetings of Christ with his disciples, it would at least be with an increased show of reason that they could be woven into the tissue of a Sabbatic argument. Here are found many of the elements essential to the idea of religious services, of which the instances in question are so remarkably destitute.

In the first place, those who followed our Lord to the place of meeting were intelligent believers in the fact of his resurrection.

In the second place, the assembly was not confined to a mere handful of individuals, seeking for retiracy within an upper room where they were in the habit of eating, drinking, and sleeping; but it transpired in the open air, where Jesus was in the habit of meeting with his followers.

In the third place, the congregation was made

up of persons whom the Holy Spirit had thus brought together for the purpose of becoming the honored witnesses of the resurrection and ascension of Christ.

In the fourth place, it was graced by the visible forms of holy angels in glistering white, who participated in the services.

In the fifth place, Jesus himself addressed them at length, lifted up his hands to heaven, and brought down its benediction upon them, and in the sight of the assembled multitude, steadily and majestically rising above them, he floated upward, until a cloud received him out of their sight.

In the sixth place, it is said, in so many words, that the "*people worshiped* him there."

Now, suppose, for the sake of the argument, that some modern sect should endeavor to transform our unpretending Thursday, which was really the day of the ascension, since it was the fortieth after the resurrection, into one of peculiar dignity, claiming, in defense of their position, the example of Christ, and urging that the course which he pursued could only be satisfactorily explained on the ground that he was laying the foundation for its future Sabbatic observance, how would our friends meet them in such an emergency? Deny the facts, they could not, for the record is ample. There would, therefore, be but one alternative left.

If transactions of this character are of a nature

such that they *necessarily* exalt the days upon which they occur to the rank of holy days, then Thursday is one, and should be treated as such. No line of argument, however ingenious, could evade this conclusion, so long as the premises in question were adhered to. Planting himself squarely upon them, with the consent of modern Christendom, the advocate of the newly discovered holy day, finding the record perfectly free from embarrassments in the nature of transactions which would appear to be incompatible with the notion that everything which Christ and his apostles did was in harmony with his view, if possessed of that skill and ability which has marked the efforts of some modern theologians in such discussions, could weave a web of inference and conjecture almost interminable in its length.

All the facts connected with the meeting could be expanded, and turned over and over, and exhibited from innumerable stand-points, so as to yield the largest amount of evidence possible. Having dwelt at large upon everything which was said and done at Bethany, he might return with the solemn procession to the great city. Having done this, he would not fail to call our attention to the fact that they did not conduct themselves in a manner such as men might have been expected to do under the circumstances on a common day, but that, on the contrary, impressed with the sacredness of the hours which had witnessed the glorious ascension of the Son of God, they immediately repaired to a place of assembly, manifestly for the purpose of continued worship. Again, scrutinizing with polemic eye every syllable of the history, in order to extract from it all the hidden testimony which it might contain, his attention would be arrested by these words, "A Sabbath day's journey." Immediately, he inquires, Why employ such an expression as this—one which occurs nowhere else in the sacred volume? Certainly it cannot be the result of accident. The Holy Spirit must have designed to signify *something* by such a use of the term in the connection under consideration. A Sabbath day's journey! What importance could be attached to the fact that the particular point from which Christ ascended was no more than a Sabbath day's journey from Jerusalem? The expression is not sufficiently definite to designate the precise spot, and must, therefore, have been employed to express some other idea. What was it? Undeniably, it was introduced into this connection because of the *nature* of the *time* on which the journey occurred. It was a *Sabbath day*, and, as such, it was important that succeeding generations should not be left to infer from the account given, that it was a matter of indifference to the Lord how far travel should be carried on such an occasion; but, on the contrary, that he was jealous on this point, and that the expression in question was employed to show that the procession of Christ's followers, and Christ, himself, bowed reverently to the national regulation respecting the distance to which it was proper for one to depart from his home during the continuance of holy time.

But this line of argument, though plausible in itself, and superior in fact to that which is many times used to support the tottering fabric of first-day observance, would not, we fancy, persuade an intelligent public to introduce a new Sabbath into their calendar. The verdict which even those with whom we differ would be compelled to render would be that which both reason and piety would dictate; namely, that the fatal defect in the logic was the want of a thus saith the Lord.

Passing now from the first six of the eight texts which relate to the first day of the week, let us give to 1 Cor. 16:2, and Acts 20:7, a consideration of sufficient length only to enable us to assign to them the proper place which they should occupy in this controversy. While it will be observed that they present the only mention of the first day of the week after leaving the gospels, and while it is remembered that they are separated from the occurrences there narrated by the space of twenty-six years, it is a remarkable fact that the first of them, if not in itself clearly against the conception of Sunday sanctity, at least, affords no strength for the argument in its favor. It reads as follows: "Upon the first day of the week let every one of you lay by him in store, as

God hath prospered him, that there be no gatherings when I come." 1 Cor. 16 : 2.

Now, bear in mind that the inference here is, that the gatherings spoken of were to be made in the assemblies of the Corinthians, the presumption following that, as they must have been in the habit of convening on the first day of the week, the apostle took advantage of this fact in order to secure the desired collections for the saints at Jerusalem. You will observe, consequently, that the postulate, or assumed point in the discussion, is that the Corinthians were at the church, or place of meeting, when the "laying by," which was ordered above, took place. If, therefore, this be not true, the whole logical superstructure which rests upon it necessarily falls to the ground.

Let us inquire after the facts. Does the apostle say, Let every one of you lay by himself at the church? or, does he command that his prorata donation should be placed in the contribution box of the assembly? We answer: There is not a word to this effect. Nor is this all; the very idea of the text is diametrically opposed to this notion. Before the contrary can be shown to be true, it will be necessary to demonstrate that which is absurd in itself; namely, the proposition that what an individual has voluntarily placed beyond his own reach and control by putting it in a common fund, can, at the same time, be said to be "laid by him in store."

Furthermore, Mr. J. W. Morton, a gentleman who has given the subject mature reflection and careful investigation, by a comparison of the different versions and the original, has demonstrated the fact that, if properly translated, the idea of the passage is simply that, for the purpose of uniformity of action, and to prevent confusion from secular matters when the apostle himself should arrive, each person should lay by himself *at home* the amount of his charities according to his ability. We give the following from his pen: " The whole question turns upon the meaning of the expression, ' by him;' and I marvel greatly how you can imagine that it means, ' in the collection box of the congregation.' Greenfield, in his lexicon, translates the Greek term, ' by one's self; *i. e.*, at home.' Two Latin versions—the Vulgate, and that of Castellio—render it, ' *apud se*,' with one's self, at home. Three French translations, those of Martin, Osterwald, and De Sacy, *chez soi*,' at his own house, at home. The German of Luther, ' *bei sich selbst*,' by himself, at home. The Dutch, ' *by hemselven*,' same as German. The Italian of Diodati, ' *appressio di se*,' in his own presence, at home. The Spanish of Felipe Scio, ' *en su casa*,' in his own house. The Portuguese of Ferrara, '*para isso*,' with himself. The Swedish, ' *nær sig sielf*,' near himself. I know not how much this list of authorities might be swelled, for I have not examined one translation that differs from those quoted above."—*Vindication of the True Sabbath*, p. 61.

The simple fact is, therefore, that while the text in question yields no proof that Sunday was then regarded as a day of convocation, it was one which might be encumbered with matters which would necessarily call attention to the pecuniary affairs of individual Christians, and so avoid the necessity of their giving thought to such things when Paul himself should arrive; thereby preventing delay on his part, and leaving them free to devote their whole time to the consideration of religious themes. Thus much for 1 Cor. 16:2.

ARTICLE VI.

Advancing now to the remaining scripture, which is found in Acts 20:7, we append its words as follows: "And upon the first day of the week, when the disciples came together to break bread, Paul preached unto them, ready to depart on the morrow; and continued his speech until midnight." By reading that which immediately follows the above, we shall learn the following facts: First, that here is indeed a record of a religious meeting upon the first day of the week (verse 7). Second, that it was held in that portion of the day when the darkness prevailed, since it was necessary to employ many lights (verse 8). Third, that Paul preached unto them, and that, while he was speaking, Eutychus fell to the ground; and Paul, having restored him to life, returned to his labor (verses 7–11). Fourth, that he broke bread, or administered the Lord's supper (verse 11). Fifth, that he preached until break of day (verse 11). Sixth, that Luke, and the other disciples, preceding him, sailed the vessel to Assos (verse 13). Seventh, that Paul, having preached all night, until the dawning of the day, crossed the country on foot, stepped aboard of the vessel, and went on his journey toward Jerusalem (verses 13, 14). Now let it be borne in mind, that Troas was a city on the west coast of Asia, located at the base of a peninsula, on the opposite side of which lay the city of Assos; distant about nineteen and a half miles in direct line from the former place. Let it also be remembered that the promontory in question, projecting as it did into the sea for some miles, made it necessary for a vessel, passing from Troas to Assos, to traverse a much greater distance, and to consume more time than one would be compelled to do in passing from one of these points to the other by the overland route. This explains the reason why Paul, who was exceedingly anxious to spend all the time he could with the brethren, consented to perform the journey on foot; thus being enabled to spend several additional hours with them, while Luke and his associates were toiling to bring the boat around the headland to the place of the apostle's final embarkation.

Returning now to the consideration of the meeting in question, it becomes important to know just when it was entered upon. Did it answer to what we would call a Sunday-evening meeting? If so, then Paul resumed his journey on Monday morning. But, before we give an affirmative response to this question, would it not be well to inquire in relation to the system for computing time which ought to be followed in this case? We moderns have generally adopted that of the Romans. With it, beginning the day, as it does, at midnight, we would naturally answer the interrogatory above in the affirmative. Should we do this, however, we should unquestionably fall into a grievous error. The days of the Bible commenced invariably with the setting of the sun.

That this is so, the following quotation from the American Tract Society's Bible Dictionary is sufficient to demonstrate: "The civil day is that, the beginning and end of which are determined by the custom of any nation. The Hebrews began their day in the evening (Lev. 23 : 32); the Babylonians at sunrise, and we begin at midnight." Art. Day, p. 114.

Reasoning, therefore, upon this hypothesis, the bearing of the text is immediately reversed. As the meeting was held in that portion of the first day of the week in which it was necessary that lamps should be lighted, it follows that it commenced with the setting of the sun on Saturday evening, and continued until daylight on what we call Sunday morning. It is consequently clear that we have at last found one first day in the Scriptures, the first half of which was observed in a manner compatible with the idea of its being regarded as a Sabbath. But, as a Sabbath day is twenty-four, and not merely twelve, hours long, it is indispensable that those who seek to avail themselves of the record before us, should be able to establish the point that there is nothing in it which would go to show that the remaining portion of the day was devoted to purposes, and employed in a manner, irreconcilable with the hypothesis of its sanctity. Can they do this? Let us see. Would it be legitimate for believers at the present time to traverse on foot a distance of nineteen and a half miles between the rising and the setting of the sun, on the first day of the week, in order to pursue a journey toward a point of destination hundreds of miles in the distance? Would it be admissible for others, prosecuting the same journey, to weigh anchor and hoist sail in a friendly port, and coast along the shore for a much greater distance?

Who, among the friends of Sunday observance at the present time, would venture to answer these questions in the affirmative, without putting on the record some qualifying or explanatory clause? We hazard the assertion that few of them, conscientious as we believe many of them are, would be willing, by such a response, to place themselves on the category of those who, to say the least, may have very lax views in regard to what may be done upon holy time. And yet this is precisely the situation in which Luke has left Paul, himself, and his associates, before the generations of Christians who were to follow them.

We ask, therefore, again, Can it be true that the great apostle to the Gentiles, standing as a representative man in the great work of transferring the religious world from the observance of the seventh, to that of the first, day of the week, and this not by positive precept, but, as it is claimed, simply by precedent and example, should have allowed himself to throw that example, as in the case before us, against the very work which he was seeking to accomplish? In other words, is not the obvious import of the text such that the average reader, with no favorite theory to make out, and a mind unbiased by the effect of education and early training, would naturally come to the conclusion that Paul and the disciples with him, and those from whom he parted at Troas, looked upon the day of that departure as but a common one?

We believe that if any other meaning can be drawn from the history before us, it will be reached through constraint, and not through the easy process of obvious reason. It is useless to talk about inability to control the vessel, and the urgent necessity of occupying every hour in order to reach Jerusalem in time for the feast. So far as the first of these points is concerned, if it were well taken, is it not to be presumed that, for the vindication of the course pursued, and for the benefit of posterity, it would have found a place in the sacred record? And as to the matter of limited time, the question of twelve hours longer or shorter, was immaterial in a journey of the length of the one under consideration. Besides, upon following the account as given, we we have from Luke himself that, before they reached their destination, they stopped at Tyre for seven days (chap. 21 : 4), and at Cesarea, many days (chap. 21 : 10), and yet had ample time to accomplish their object in reaching Jerusalem before the feast.

We say again, therefore, that these considerations, in the absence of any allusions to them in the context, are simply gratuitous, or, at least, are far-fetched. The narrative still remains. The great fact that Paul and his followers did travel upon the first day of the week is made conspicuous, and the only legitimate conclusion to be drawn therefrom is that which alone harmonizes with the consistency of Paul's life and that of his brethren, as well as the wisdom and beneficence of the great God, namely: That he did so because of his conviction that it was a day which might properly be devoted to labor and travel. With this understanding, the story is relieved of all embarrassment, and becomes a simple and highly interesting account of a meeting convened on the first day of the week, because of the approaching departure of a beloved brother and apostle, and rendered also worthy of record by the miracle which was performed upon Eutychus. But with such a decision, our labor is ended, and with it the whole theory in regard to the Sabbatic character of Sunday is exploded; for, not only does the scripture which we have been investigating fail to yield the doctrine which it was supposed to contain, but, on the contrary, it presents Paul as standing emphatically against it. This being true, it belongs to a faith which he never proclaimed, and which, consequently, was associated in his mind with that which should not be received, though it were "preached by an angel from Heaven."

Nevertheless, that we may not appear to have overlooked the two remaining texts, which are generally quoted as affording additional proof of the distinguished regard in which the first day of the week was held, we turn our attention for a moment to Acts 2 : 1, and Rev. 1 : 10.

As it regards the first of these scriptures, the claim is, that the outpouring of the Spirit occurred with reference to a divine disposition to honor the day of the resurrection. To this we reply, first, that if this were so, it is a remarkable fact that there is nothing in the connection to show it. The name of the day, even, is not so much as mentioned. The inspired annalist, were this supposition true, would most assuredly have given prominence to an idea which, it is claimed, was the governing one in the mind of the Spirit, in order to enable succeeding generations to extract from the facts narrated the true moral which they were intended to convey. But mark his words. Is the declaration, "When the first day of the week was fully come"? If so, we might say that this day was foremost in his own mind, and in that of the Spirit.

But such was not his language. On the contrary, his statement is, "When the day of Pentecost was fully come." Hence, it was the day of Pentecost, or the great Jewish feast, which is here made to stand out conspicuously upon the sacred page. If, therefore, we are to decide that the transaction in question was intended to hallow any particular twenty-four hours, undeniably they were those within which the Pentecost fell. But those did not occur regularly upon the first day of the week, nor was the institution one of weekly recurrence. It was annual in its return, transpiring one year upon the first, and perhaps the next year upon the second, and so on, through every, day of the week. To reason, consequently, that, because it happened to take place at this time upon Sunday, the fact is necessarily significant of a change in the character of the day, is altogether inconclusive.

That were a cheap logic indeed, which would argue that the Pentecost, which was mentioned expressly, and the return of which was waited for with patience, was in no-wise affected, illustrated, or perpetuated, by the outpouring of the Spirit upon it, whereas, a septenary division of time—not thought worthy of mention by its peculiar title—was thenceforth rendered glorious. Stand together, however, they cannot; for, if it were the Pentecost which was to be handed down in this way to those who should come after, then it would, of necessity, be celebrated annually, and not each week; but, if it were the first day of the week which alone was made the object of divine favor, then why wait until the arrival of the great annual Sabbath at the end of the fifty days? Why was not some other first day taken—say one of the six which had already occurred between the resurrection and that time —in this manner avoiding the possibility of confusion as to which event was thus honored?

Should it be replied that the Spirit could not be poured out until the great antitype of the fifty-day feast had been met in Heaven, we answer: Then it was *this* event, and not the resurrection, which furnishes the occasion for the remarkable demonstrations which were manifested before the people. We repeat again, therefore, that from whatever stand-point we look at the text, it is the *Pentecost*, and not the first day of the week, to which, if to anything, it attaches special importance. This is further demonstrated by the fact that it is to this hour a matter of grave discussion between theologians whether the day of Pentecost, at the time under consideration, did really fall upon the first day of the week or upon some other. Leaving to them, therefore, the delicate and arduous task of adjusting questions of this nature—which are neither important in themselves, nor easy of decision—we hasten to glance at Rev. 1:10. It reads as follows: "I was in the Spirit on the Lord's day, and heard behind me a great voice, as of a trumpet."

Here is something which certainly has a bearing upon the subject. The language employed is of thrilling interest. Says the apostle, "I was in the Spirit on the Lord's day." This being uttered about A. D. 95, determines the point that God has a day in this dispensation, and also proves that he has but one; since the language would be very indefinite were there two or more days of such a nature. But by what system of reasoning is the conclusion reached that this must of necessity be the first day of the week? Assuredly, it can only be by inference. If it can first be proved that the day of the resurrection has, by divine authority, been anywhere styled the "Lord's day," then the point is unquestionably gained. When those words were penned, more than sixty years had passed since it is claimed that Sunday had been clothed with divine honor. The whole canon of the New Testament, save the gospel of John, had been written within that time. Ample opportunity had been afforded for the work of placing upon record the sacred appellation which was to be given to that period of time, which, having been separated from everything of a secular nature, had been elevated to the dignity of a holy rest. But had this ever occurred? The facts are briefly these: The first day of the week, as we have seen, being mentioned eight times in the New Testament, is always spoken of as plain first day of the week; John himself, writing his gospel after the appearance of the Apocalypse, everywhere applies to it this unpretending title. Whenever the term Sabbath is used, on the other hand—as we have seen that it is fifty-six times in the New Testament—it is applied, with one exception, to the Sabbath of the commandment, or the seventh day of the week.

In view of these facts, take a common man, without bias or predilection, one, if you please, who has never heard of the controversy in question, place in his hands the Bible without note or comment, let him read the following texts which confessedly refer to the seventh day of the week, and we think the verdict which he would render would be decidedly in favor of the venerable Sabbath of the Lord; of which it is true, as it is of no other day, that he has again and again claimed it as his own. The italics are our own. "If thou turn away thy foot from the *Sabbath*, from doing thy pleasure on *my holy day;* and call the Sabbath a delight, the *holy of the Lord*, honorable; and shalt honor him, not doing thine own ways, nor finding thine own pleasure, nor speaking thine own words; then shalt thou delight thyself in the Lord." Isa. 58 : 13, 14.

"But the seventh day is the *Sabbath of the Lord thy God:* in it thou shalt not do any work :" "for in six days the Lord made heaven and earth, the sea, and all that in them is, and rested the seventh day; wherefore the Lord *blessed the Sabbath day, and hallowed it."* Ex. 20 : 10, 11.

"And he said unto them, The Sabbath was made for man, and not man for the Sabbath; therefore the Son of man is Lord also of the Sabbath." Mark 2 : 27, 28.

If such a decision be a just one, however, where are we in the matter under examination? What has become of the modern Sabbath reform for which we have been seeking justification in the word of God? First, we sought to place it upon the commandment; this, we found to be out of the question. Second, we investigated the claim of an amended law; that, we discovered to be entirely without authority, and against even the conviction and practice of the very men who urged it. Third, we turn, as a last resort, to the precedents of Bible history; these, we found, so far as they affect the question at all, to be overwhelmingly against a movement which, while it claims to be in the interest of the God of Heaven, is confronted by the following astounding facts:

First, the day whose observance it seeks to enforce by statute law is one, the keeping of which, God has never commanded. Second, Christ has never commanded it. Third, no inspired man has ever commanded it. Fourth, God himself never rested upon it. Fifth, Christ never rested upon it. Sixth, there is no record that either prophets or apostles ever rested upon it. Seventh, it is one upon which God himself worked. Eighth, it is one which, during his lifetime, Christ always treated as a day of labor. Ninth, it is one upon which, after his resurrection, he countenanced, by his own personal example, travel upon the highway. Tenth, it is one upon which the two disciples, in going to and returning from Emmaus, traveled a distance of fifteen miles. Eleventh, it was on that day that Paul walked from Troas to Assos, a distance of nineteen and one-half miles. Twelfth, it was on that day that Luke and his associates passed from one to the other of these places by a longer route, working their vessel round the promontory.

That all these things could be true, and yet our friends be right in the supposition that they are engaged in a work which commands the approval of Heaven, is too absurd to require further discussion. A movement pushed forward in the face of these facts may succeed, so far as political success and legal enactment are concerned, but when the logic for its Scriptural character is scrutinized as closely as it will be before it shall plant its banners upon the capitol of the nation, all conscientious convictions in regard to its heavenly birth will give place to an inspiration, the source of whose strength will be found in the superiority of party drill, and the overwhelming power of mere numbers. Who shall say that the God of Heaven has not permitted it to come to the surface for the very purpose of calling the attention of honest men and women, as it only could be done by the debate which will arise in controversy, to the scantiness of that Sunday wardrobe by which, as with it our friends attempt to clothe a favorite institution, we are so forcibly reminded of the bed and covering spoken of by the prophet Isaiah: The first of which was "too short to stretch one's self upon," and the last, "too narrow to wrap one's self within?" So sure as investigation is provoked upon this subject, so certain is it that, sooner or later, thinking men and women will discover—as we have already done in this article—that there is indeed a crying demand for a Sabbath reform. Not one, however, which rests merely upon the power of Congressional enactment, and Presidential sanction, but one which shall find its authority in the highest of all laws, and which shall have the approval of the King of kings and Lord of lords.

ARTICLE VII.

The conflict is finally open. The spirit of inquiry has lifted itself in the nation; and all eyes will be turned toward the Bible, as really the only source from which can be derived authority for a Sabbath reform which shall be worthy of the name.

Commencing with its opening pages, they will trace the Sabbatic narrative until they have been able to verify the following summary of history and doctrine:—

1. The Sabbath, as the last day of the week, originated in Eden, and was given to Adam, as the federal head of the race, while he yet retained his primal innocence. Proof: "And on the seventh day God ended his work which he had made; and he rested on the seventh day from all his work which he had made. And God blessed the seventh day, and sanctified it; because that in it he had rested from all his work which God created and made." Gen. 2:2, 3.

2. That, though the history of the period, stretching from the creation to the exodus, is extremely brief, it is manifest, even from that period, that the good of those ages had not lost sight of it; since the children of Israel were acquainted with its existence thirty days before reaching Mount Sinai. "And He said unto

them, This is that which the Lord hath said, To-morrow is the rest of the holy Sabbath unto the Lord; bake that which ye will bake to-day, and seethe that ye will seethe; and that which remaineth over lay up for you to be kept until the morning." Ex. 16 : 23. "Six days ye shall gather it; but on the seventh day, which is the Sabbath, in it there shall be none." Ex. 16 : 26.

3. That God, unwilling to commit the interest of so important an institution to the keeping of tradition, framed a command for its perpetuity, which he spoke with his own voice and wrote with his own finger, placing it in the bosom of the great moral law of the ten precepts: "Remember the Sabbath day, to keep it holy. Six days shalt thou labor, and do all thy work; but the seventh day is the Sabbath of the Lord thy God: in it thou shalt not do any work, thou, nor thy son, nor thy daughter, thy man-servant, nor thy maid-servant, nor thy cattle, nor thy stranger that is within thy gates: for in six days the Lord made heaven and earth, the sea, and all that in them is, and rested the seventh day; wherefore the Lord blessed the Sabbath day, and hallowed it." Ex. 20 : 8–11.

4. That this law has been brought over into our dispensation, and every jot and tittle of it is binding now, and will continue to be, so long as the world stands. "Think not that I am come to destroy the law or the prophets; I am not come to destroy, but to fulfill. For verily I say

unto you, Till heaven and earth pass, one jot or one tittle shall in no wise pass from the law, till all be fulfilled. Whosoever, therefore, shall break one of these least commandments, and shall teach men so, he shall be called the least in the kingdom of Heaven; but whosoever shall do and teach them, the same shall be called great in the kingdom of Heaven."—JESUS, Matt. 5 : 17–19. "Do we then make void the law through faith? God forbid; yea, we establish the law."—PAUL, Romans 3 : 31. "Wherefore the law is holy, and the commandment holy, and just, and good." Romans 7 : 12. "If ye fulfill the royal law according to the scripture, Thou shalt love thy neighbor as thyself, ye do well; but if ye have respect to persons, ye commit sin, and are convinced of the law as transgressors. For whosoever shall keep the whole law, and yet offend in one point, he is guilty of all. For he that said, Do not commit adultery, said also, Do not kill. Now if thou commit no adultery, yet if thou kill, thou art become a transgressor of the law."— JAMES, Jas. 2 : 8–11. "Whosoever committeth sin transgresseth also the law; for sin is the transgression of the law. And ye know that he was manifested to take away our sins; and in him is no sin. Whosoever abideth in him sinneth not; whosoever sinneth hath not seen him, neither known him."—JOHN, 1 John 3 : 4–6.

5. That, agreeably to this view, Christ—of whom it is said, "Thy law is within my heart"

—was a habitual observer, during his lifetime, of the Sabbath of the decalogue. "And he came to Nazareth, where he had been brought up; and, *as his custom was*, he went into the synagogue on the Sabbath day, and stood up for to read." Luke 4:16. "If ye keep my commandments, ye shall abide in my love; even as I have kept my Father's commandments, and abide in his love." John 15:10.

6. That the women, whose religious conceptions had been formed under his teachings, carefully regarded it. "And they returned, and prepared spices and ointments; and rested the Sabbath day, according to the commandment." Luke 23:56.

7. The Lord instructed his disciples that it would exist at least forty years after his death, since he taught them to pray continually that their flight, at the destruction of Jerusalem, which occurred A. D. 70, might not take place on that day. "But pray ye that your flight be not in the winter, neither on the Sabbath day." Matt. 24:20.

8. That the great apostle to the Gentiles was in the habit of making it a day of public teaching. "And Paul, as his *manner was*, went in unto them, and three Sabbath days reasoned with them out of the Scriptures." Acts 27:2. "And he reasoned in the synagogue every Sabbath, and persuaded the Jews and the Greeks." Acts 18:4.

9. That, in the year of our Lord 95, John still

recognized its existence. "I was in the Spirit on the Lord's day, and heard behind me a great voice, as of a trumpet." Rev. 1:10.

10. That God has never removed the blessing which he placed upon it in the beginning, or annulled the sanctification by which it was at that time set apart to a holy use.

11. That, in perfect keeping with the above propositions, it is, equally in the New with the Old Testament, scores of times denominated the Sabbath; and that, while God, and Christ, and prophets, and apostles, and inspired men, unite in applying to it this sacred title, they never, in any single instance, allow themselves to speak of any other day in the week in the use of this peculiar appellation.

12. That it is not only to continue during the present order of things, but that, in the new earth, clothed in all the freshness and beauty of its Edenic glory, creation, more than ever before, will be the subject of devout gratitude, and weekly commemoration on the part of the immortal and sinless beings who shall worship God therein forever. "For as the new heavens and the new earth, which I will make shall remain before me, saith the Lord, so shall your seed and your name remain. And it shall come to pass, that from one new moon to another, and from one Sabbath to another, shall all flesh come to worship before me, saith the Lord." Isa. 66: 22, 23.

Putting all these facts together—connected, consistent, and unanswerable as they are—men will discover that a great departure has taken place from the original practice of the church, and against the explicit command of God. Should they ask, as assuredly they will, when, and by whom, it was inaugurated, it will not be a fruitless effort on their part to obtain needed information. God has made ample provision for the instruction of those who would do his will, and for the condemnation of those who refuse so to do. Referring to prophecies given centuries ago, mapping out beforehand the history of the world, they will find the prophet Daniel—while describing the work of the "little horn," which arose among the ten horns of the great and terrible beast, and which little horn nearly all Protestant commentators agree in applying to the papal church—stating of it, by way of prediction, that it should "wear out the saints of the Most High, and think to change times and laws," and that they should "be given into his hand until a time and times and the dividing of time." (Dan. 7: 25.) Consulting history, they will discover that, so far as the saints are concerned, these terrible words have been so completely fulfilled that this power has actually put to death, in one way or other, at least fifty millions of the people of God.

Again, perceiving, as they will readily, that the "laws," which this presumptuous power should blasphemously claim to be able to change, are the laws of God, what will be their astonishment at learning, from the representatives of this great oppressive system—which alone has extended through a period sufficiently long to cover the "time, times and half a time," or the 1260 years of Daniel's prophecy—that it actually boasts that it has done the very work in question. Nay, more; what limit can be put to their surprise when they find these men absolutely pointing with exultation to the practice of the Christian world in the observance of Sunday, as an evidence of the ability of the Roman Catholic church to alter and amend the commands of God! That they do this, however, in the most unequivocal terms, will be abundantly proved by the following quotations from their own publications:—

"*Question.* Is it then Saturday we should sanctify, in order to obey the ordinance of God? *Ans.* During the old law, Saturday was the day sanctified; but *the church*, instructed by Jesus Christ, and directed by the Spirit of God, has substituted Sunday for Saturday; so we now sanctify the first, not the seventh, day. Sunday means, and now is, the day of the Lord. *Ques.* Had the church power to make such a change? *Ans.* Certainly; since the Spirit of God is her guide, the change is inspired by the Holy Spirit."
—*Cath. Catechism of Christian Religion.*

"*Ques.* How prove you that the church has power to command feasts and holy days? *Ans.*

By the very act of changing the Sabbath into Sunday, which Protestants allow of; and therefore they fondly contradict themselves by keeping Sunday strictly, and breaking most other feasts commanded by the same church.

"*Ques.* How prove you that? *Ans.* Because, by keeping Sunday, they acknowledge the church's power to ordain feasts, and to command them under sin; and by not keeping the rest by her commanded, they again deny, in fact, the same power. —*Abridgment of Christian Doctrine.*

"It is worth its while to remember that this observance of the Sabbath—in which, after all, the only Protestant worship consists—not only has no foundation in the Bible, but it is in flagrant contradiction with its letter, which commands rest on the Sabbath, which is Saturday. It was the *Catholic church* which, by the authority of Jesus Christ, has transferred this rest to the Sunday in remembrance of the resurrection of our Lord. Thus the observance of Sunday by the Protestants is an homage they pay, in spite of themselves, to the authority of the church."— *Plain Talk about Protestantism of To-day,* p. 225.

Instinctively anticipating some providential mode of escape from the terrible consequences of that great apostasy, out of which the religious world has for centuries been endeavoring to work its way, conscientious men and women will catch the notes of warning which for twenty-five years have been sounding through the land, in these words: "Here is the patience of the saints: here are they that keep the commandments of God, and the faith of Jesus." Rev. 14:12.

Inquiring into the origin of the message which is thus being given to the world, they will find that, for a quarter of a century, God has been calling attention to the subject of his law and his Sabbath, and that a denomination of earnest men and women, but little known as yet among the learned and mighty of the land, have been devoting themselves with zeal and a spirit of self-sacrifice to the tremendous task of restoring God's downtrodden Sabbath to the hearts and judgments of the people. They will find, also, that these persons have not entered upon this labor because they anticipated an easy and speedy victory; nor, indeed, because they ever believed that the great mass of mankind would so far shake off the trammels of tradition and the fear of reproach as to be able to venture an unreserved surrender to the teachings of the Bible; but simply because they saw in it that which was at once the path of duty, and that of fulfilling prophecy.

Having accepted Dan. 7:25, in common with the religious world, as applying to the papacy, and learning, as the result of investigation, that the days of the great persecution were to reach from the decree of Justinian (A. D. 538,) giving authority to the Bishop of Rome to become the corrector of heretics, to A. D. 1798—when the pope was carried into captivity, having received a wound with the sword agreeably to Rev. 13 : 10 —these students of God's word at once perceived that the next thing in order would be the completion of the restitution, which had begun in the taking away of his ability to put the saints to death, by a work equally called for in the inspired prediction; namely, that of rescuing from his hands the "times and laws" which he thought to change. Or, in other words, that the effort of the pope to remove the Sabbath of the Lord from the seventh to the first day of the week should be made to appear in its true light; namely, as the work of a blasphemous power which had held the world in its grasp for centuries.

But, while they were clear in those convictions which led them in 1846, under the title of Seventh-day Adventists, to claim that they were fulfilling the prophecy of Rev. 14: 9–12, they discerned that the same facts which brought them to this conclusion also compelled the conviction that theirs was to be the road of persecution: hardship, and privation. They read in Rev. 12: 17, in these words, "The dragon was wroth with the woman, and went to make war with the remnant of her seed, which keep the commandments of God, and have the testimony of Jesus Christ," the history of the last generation of Christians; and saw that, in God's inscrutable providence, it was to be their fortune to be the object of diabolic hate, because of the commandments of God and the testimony of Jesus Christ, to which they cling with determined perseverance.

Once more: In studying the 11th to the 18th verses inclusive of the 13th chapter of the same book, they saw that—if their view of the work which was assigned them was correct—that portion of the Scriptures was applied to the United States of America, and indicated that this country was to be the theater of a mighty contest between those who "keep the commandments of God and the faith of Jesus," and the government under which they live, from which they could only be delivered by the coming of Christ. This view they unhesitatingly proclaimed. For twenty years, they have announced it as a part of their faith. When they first declared it to be such, they brought upon themselves ridicule and contempt, for, humanly speaking, every probability was against them. The government was ostensibly republican in form, and professedly tolerant to the very extreme, in all matters of religious opinion. The Constitution had even provided that "Congress should make no law respecting an establishment of religion, or prohibiting the free exercise thereof."

Nevertheless, so firm were they in the conviction that they had the right application of the prophecy, that they unhesitatingly walked out upon their faith; and for a fifth of a century they have talked it, and published it everywhere, notwithstanding the odium it has brought upon them. Lest we might appear to be drawing upon our own imagination in a matter of such importance, we append the following extracts from their works. The words in parentheses are our own, and serve to explain that which a larger quotation from the context would make clear of itself:

"When the 'beast' (the papacy) had the dominion, all in authority must be Catholics. The popular sentiment then was that none should hold offices in the government, except they professed the Catholic faith. The popular religion at that period was Catholicism. They legislated upon religious subjects, and required all men to conform to the popular institutions and dogmas of the papacy, or suffer and die. The image must be made in the United States, where Protestantism is the prevailing religion. Image signifies *likeness;* therefore Protestantism and Republicanism will *unite;* or, in other words, the making of laws will go into the hands of Protestants, when all in authority will profess the popular sentiments of the day, and make laws binding certain religious institutions (*i. e.*, Sunday observance, &c.), upon all, without distinction."—*Advent Review and Sabbath Herald,* Vol. 6, No. 6, 1854.

"It seems to me, even to look at the subject in the light of reason, that a conflict must in time come between commandment-keepers and the United States. This, of course, will lead those who find that they cannot sustain their Sunday institution by argument to resort to some other means."—*Advent Review and Herald,* Vol. 10, No. 11, 1857.

"When all concur upon this question (Sunday-keeping), except a few who conscientiously observe the fourth commandment, how long before their constancy would be attributed to obstinacy and bigotry? And how long before the sentence would go forth, as it did in the days of Pliny, 'that for this, if for nothing else, they deserved to be punished.'"—*Review and Herald*, Vol. 19, No. 15. (*a*.)

How changed the political sky to-day from what it was when these words began to be spoken! Now, thoughtful men are pondering whether, after all, these things may not be so. They see a powerful organization looming up in the country, which appends to the call for their conventions the names of some of the most influential men in the land. They hear them declaring in so many words, that what they are determined to do is to sweep away the constitutional barrier between them and a coerced observance of Sunday, so that all may be compelled to regard it as sacred. What we want, say they, and what we are determined to have, is such an amendment of the Constitution, 1. That it shall recognize God and Christ; 2. That it shall enable us to secure the reading of the Bible in the common schools; 3. That we may be enabled to enforce the better observance of the Christian Sabbath, *i. e.*, Sunday.

(*a*) For further information upon this subject, the reader is referred to "The Three Angels' Messages" and the "United States in Prophecy," published at the *Review and Herald* Office, Battle Creek, Mich.

These declarations, a few years since, would have appalled every lover of constitutional liberty. Every man and woman imbued with a proper sense of the genius of our institutions would have been struck with horror at the very thought of pursuing the course in question. But a change has come over the spirit of the land. Steadily, the advocates of a day which has no authority in the word of God are drifting where all before them have done who have sought to maintain a human institution upon the claim of divine authority. It is idle for them to say at this stage of the proceedings that they propose to regard the rights of those who have conscientious scruples on this subject. God has said that the matter will culminate in oppression; nay, even though this were not so, reason itself would prove that this would be the case. Without questioning the sincerity of the men who at the present make these statements, we appeal to that very sincerity for the evidence that this matter will end just where the Seventh-day Adventists have claimed that it would.

They have convinced themselves that they are called of God to a mighty work. They believe that they have a noble mission. They are men of mind and nerve. But, when a few months shall have revealed the insufficiency of their logic, when Seventh-day Baptists and Seventh-day Adventists shall have confronted them with a plain "Thus saith the Lord," against their favorite scheme, they would be more than human if—refusing to yield to arguments which they cannot answer—they should continue to look with complacence upon the very men who, after all, will prove to be their most formidable antagonists in the great conflict. In fact, it would be a denial of both nature and history to say that they would not at last come to regard them in the light of enemies of God, really more worthy of condemnation and coercion than those who were simply unbelievers in any Sabbath at all, and so incapable of standing before the systematic effort which they have set in motion. (b.)

But, candid reader, the facts are before you, and between us and these events there will be ample time for calm reflection, and deliberate decision. Where do you choose to stand in this final conflict between the venerable Sabbath of the Lord and its modern papistic rival? Will you keep the commandments of God, as uttered by his voice and written by his finger? or will you henceforth pay intelligent homage to the man of sin, by the observance of a day which finds its authority alone in the mutilated form of the commandments, as they come from his hand? May God help you to make a wise choice.

(b) Persons desiring to investigate this question still further, by addressing the author of these articles, will receive by mail, without charge, a tract in which he has discussed at length a branch of this subject merely alluded to in this communication.

EXPLANATORY REMARKS.

IMMEDIATELY on the publication of the foregoing articles in the *Christian Statesman*, the editor of that paper announced his purpose to review them in the columns of that periodical. This purpose he subsequently carried out in the publication of eleven communications, in which various strictures were offered upon the positions taken by me in my original contributions. I immediately requested the privilege of replying to these criticisms in the columns of the *Statesman*, so that those who had read my argument in the beginning, and the replies of the editor of the *Statesman* thereto, might have an opportunity to see the relative strength of the positions occupied by that gentleman and myself tested in fair and open debate. My petition, however, was denied, and I was compelled either to remain silent or seek elsewhere for an opportunity to make my defense. Fortunately, at this juncture, the columns of the *Advent Review*, which is the organ of the Seventh-day Adventists, were freely offered me for the purpose in question, and in them the Replies of the editor of the *Statesman*, and my Rejoinders thereto, have since been published. To these Replies and Rejoinders, as they appeared therein, the remainder of the present volume is devoted. To them, the reader is earnestly invited to give his most serious attention, since they present, side by side, the lines of argument usually employed for and against the Sabbath of the Lord. W. H. L.

REPLIES AND REJOINDERS.

Reply of the Editor of the Christian Statesman.

ARTICLE ONE.

SEVENTH-DAY SABBATARIANS AND THE CHRISTIAN AMENDMENT.

WE have given not a little space to the argument against the Christian Amendment of our National Constitution from the stand-point of the advocates of the seventh-day Sabbath. This argument, in brief, is this: The proposed amendment, in its practical working, is intended to secure the better observance of the first day of the week, as the civil Sabbath. But the Bible, the revealed law of God, it is affirmed, contains no warrant either for individual or national observance of the first day of the week. The amendment, therefore, it is maintained, should not be favored, but earnestly opposed, by those who acknowledge the supreme authority of the law of the Bible.

This, it will be seen at a glance, is no argument against the principle of the proposed amendment. On the other hand, it bases itself on that very principle, viz., that it is the bounden duty of the nation to acknowledge the authority of God, and take his revealed word as the supreme rule of its conduct. The argument, therefore, instead of being directed against the amendment itself, is directed almost entirely against that interpretation of the divine law of the Scriptures which fixes the Christian Sabbath on the first day of the week. We consented to admit to our columns a short series of brief articles presenting an argument against the amendment. Pressing the lines of courtesy and fairness far beyond the limits of our agreement, we have, in fact, admitted many long articles, the burden of which has been to show that there is no warrant in the word of God for the observance of the first day of the week as the Sabbath of divine appointment. We shall expect equal generosity from the journals of our seventh-day Sabbatarian friends.

The amendment proposed is in substance as follows: An acknowledgment of God as the ultimate source of all power and authority in civil government; of Jesus Christ as ruler of nations; and of the Bible as the fountain of law, and the supreme rule of national conduct. Let this be distinctly borne in mind. We have here a clear assertion of the very principles for which the seventh-day Sabbatarian most strenuously contends.

Just here, we would take occasion to say that even if the proposed amendment contained an express acknowledgment, in so many words, of the first-day Sabbath, and if the argument for the seventh-day Sabbath were a perfect demonstration, there would still be, on that account, as matters actually stand in our land at present, no valid objection against such explicit Constitutional acknowledgment of the first day.

Suppose a company of the advocates of the seventh-day Sabbath, going forth as missionaries, should discover, in a distant sea, an island inhabited by a people in many respects highly civilized, possessing a portion of the Bible, and observing one day in seven, say the fourth day of the week, as a day of rest and worship of the true God, and acknowledging it as such in their Constitution of government. Suppose that in the same island should be found a large and active minority, thoroughly infidel and atheistic, striving in every way to overturn the Sabbath. The missionaries, perceiving much room and opportunity for doing good to the people, settle among them, and seek, among many things, to change the Sabbath to what they regard as the proper day. In what way would they attempt to accomplish this? Would they permit themselves for a moment to be classed with the infidel and atheistic opponents of the Sabbath? Would they not stand side by side with those who defended the Sabbath observances of the country against the attacks of immoral and unbelieving enemies of all Christian institutions?

If these missionaries were advocates of the first-day Sabbath, and we were of the number, for our part, this is what we would do: We would practice for ourselves the observance of what we are persuaded is the Christian Sabbath. We would multiply and scatter abroad copies of the entire Bible, and seek to convince the people and the nation that God's law requires the observance of the first day. In the meantime, confident that, by the blessing of the Head of the church, the circulation of the divine word and the proclamation of its truths would at length change the conviction of the islanders, we should say to them: "Do not cease to observe a day of rest and worship. To have one such a day in every seven is right. Do not blot out its acknowledgment from the Constitution. You need its legal safe-guards. True, there is no divine warrant for the observance of the fourth day of the week instead of the first. But a fourth-day Sabbath is better than no Sabbath at all. We will help you to preserve from the assaults of our common enemies the observances of the Sabbath, that you may have them to transfer, as we urge you to do, to the first day of the week." Would the advocates of the seventh-day Sabbath do otherwise, except in substituting the seventh day for the first? And now let us take the actual, corresponding case in our own land. The great mass of Christians here, as elsewhere, regard the first day of the week as the Sabbath of the Lord. Admit, for the sake of the illustration, that they have no better ground for their opinion than the islanders mentioned above. Is it not right for them to have a day of rest and worship? Is it not right for them to observe one such a day in seven? Is it maintained that, because the day is not the proper one, there is and can be nothing right about these Sabbath observances? Then, if all is wrong, it must be better to have no Sabbath at all, and utterly secularize the week. This, our seventh-day friends cannot and will not admit. They gladly testify that our first-day Sabbath, poorly as it may be observed, is infinitely to be preferred to the unbroken current of the worldliness of the week. A Sabbathless week; successive rounds of equally secularized days, marked, if marked at all, by the recurrence of unusual worldly gayety and dissipation; this is what infidelity and atheism would give us for the existing Sabbath. Do the friends of the seventh-day Sabbath desire any such substitution? Their argument against the proposed amendment on the ground that it expressly or impliedly contains an acknowledgment of the first-day Sabbath, is, that it will enforce existing Sabbath laws, and strengthen first-day Sabbath observances. But is it not better to do this than accept the dread alternative? Even from this point of view, then, we claim for the proposed amendment, what in some cases it has actually, and, we believe, most consistently, received, the approval and support of seventh-day Sabbatarians.

But we return to the form of the proposed amendment. It expresses, as it should, only the most fundamental principles. It asserts the duty of the nation to acknowledge God in Christian relations. It recognizes the Bible as the fountain of the nation's laws, and the supreme rule of its conduct. Now, if we were among either the first-day or the seventh-day missionaries, in the case of the islanders already referred to, such a national acknowledgment of the authority of the Bible is just exactly what we would desire. If the islanders had this principle, as has been supposed, incorporated into their written Constitution, we could ask for nothing more advantageous for our missionary work. If they had it not, and certain citizens were laboring to secure its insertion by an amendment of the instrument, we would most assuredly accord these laborers our heartiest encouragement and support. We should suspect ourselves of prejudice, or rather of a deficiency in good common sense, if we found ourselves inclined to pursue an opposite course. Believing that God's law requires the observance of another day than the fourth, how could we reasonably do anything else than co-operate and rejoice in the work of leading such a people to acknowledge the supreme authority of that law, and to register their purpose in the fundamental instrument of their government, to adjust all national affairs according to its requirements?

And now, what can be said of our seventh-day Sabbatarian brethren? Are they not inconsistent? They proclaim the duty of the nation to acknowledge "the highest of all laws." So far, we are agreed. They maintain that the Bible is that law. Here, too, we are at one. And yet they—not all of them, we are happy to state—oppose a movement which aims to secure in the organic law and life of the nation a sincere, reverent, and obedient acknowledgment of the authority of the Bible—an acknowledgment which forecloses discussion on no question on which Christians or others may differ, but which brings the final appeal in all national controversies to the tribunal of the unerring word of God.

The inconsistency of this attitude of opposition to the Christian Amendment cannot but create unfavorable presumptions in regard to the soundness of judgment of any who may occupy it. An attack from so weak a point, upon the Constitutional acknowledgment of the Christian Scriptures, it will be generally felt, does not betoken a very formidable assault upon the Sabbath of the Christian church. And yet, notwithstanding this, to our mind, exceedingly unfortunate connection, we would bear cheerful testimony to the fact that the articles we have inserted, so far as they are an argument against the first-day Sabbath, and this is manifestly the point which the writer had principally in view, contain a clear, calm, courteous, and attractively written presentation of one side of a very important subject. We shall present the other side of the question in succeeding issues of this journal.

REJOINDER, BY W. H. LITTLEJOHN.

"SEVENTH-DAY SABBATARIANS AND THE CHRISTIAN AMENDMENT."

WE have debated for some time in our own mind the propriety of attempting an answer to the strictures, if such they may be called, upon our articles on the Constitutional Amendment. Having decided, however, that they contain a show of logic which might deceive the careless reader, we have at last determined to give them a notice commensurate with the importance they assume, if not from their intrinsic merit, at least from the distinguished source whence they emanate.

Before doing this, we take pleasure in acknowledging the generosity of their author in allowing us to discuss in the columns of his paper the subject from a stand-point of a nature calculated to dampen rather than stimulate the ardor of his readers in the work in which, with him, they are engaged. From the outset, we have discovered no disposition to take any advantage by which the full effect of what we had to say might in any way be lessened. On the contrary, attention has several times been called to our communications, as being worthy of perusal by all.

Having said thus much in reference to the treatment we received at the hands of the editor of the *Statesman* up to the time of the completion of the publication of our articles, we shall be pardoned for expressing our surprise at finding ourselves, in his first reply, standing somewhat in the attitude of one who had taken advantage of indulgence shown him to present a line of argument different from that proposed at the beginning.

It is possible that we have mistaken the design of the statements to which we allude. This we hope may prove to be the case; for, so far as we are concerned, individually, we have covered the precise ground which we designed to at the first. If the editor of the *Statesman* has found himself disappointed, either in the nature or the length of the argument, he is to blame, and not we.

1. Because, so far as the matter of length is concerned, we stated to him that we should leave that entirely " with his magnanimity, convinced that he would not cut us short in our work so long as what we had to say was pointed, gentlemanly, and of such a nature as to bear forcibly upon the question at issue between us."

2. As it regards the scope of the articles, we stated, unqualifiedly, that we should treat the subject from the stand-point of an observer of the seventh day, appealing to the Bible for our authority. Nor were we content with declaring our plan of opposition by *letter*, but we went so far as to give, in the caption of our articles themselves, an outline of the order in which we should treat the subject. It was as follows: " The Constitutional Amendment; *or*, the Sunday, the Sabbath, the Change, and the Restitution." In it, as will be observed, is exactly set forth the manner

in which we discussed the propriety of the amendment; (1) Showing the emptiness of the claims of the Sunday. (2) The force and obligation of those of the seventh day. (3) The manner in which the change of days occurred, and (4) The work which God has inaugurated for the purpose of bringing about the Restitution.

Thus much by way of personal acknowledgment and explanation.

We turn now to the criticism proper upon our argument.

First, there is an attempt to state the positions which we assumed to prove.

In reply, it is sufficient to say that it is deficient in one very important particular. That particular relates to our proposition that God himself has inaugurated a movement *entirely outside of, and opposed to*, the Constitutional Amendment party, for the purpose of bringing about a Sabbath reform in his own way. For proof of this, we appeal to our last article in full. It is, to say the least, not a little remarkable that the editor of the *Statesman* should have overlooked this point in our communications, since a perception of it would have saved him the perpetration of the great mistake which he has made, as we shall see hereafter.

Secondly, It is intimated that the proposed amendment is not necessarily connected with the Sabbath question; and that, therefore, observers of the seventh day should unite with those of the first in securing its passage, which, being done, the differences between them could be settled at leisure.

Now we confess to not a little surprise that such a position should be taken by a gentleman of so much candor and penetration as the editor of the *Statesman*. Have we then been deceived up to this point ? Is it true that Sunday observance has not heretofore been represented as something of vital importance to the nation, to be secured, and only secured, by the alteration of the Constitution as proposed ? Have these gentlemen not been really in earnest when they have appealed to the strong love of the people for the strict observance of what they have been pleased to call the Sabbath, in their endeavors to arouse them to the significance of their movement ? If they have not, then they are unworthy of public confidence, and should henceforth be cast down from the leadership of a great party, which boasts, not only its morality, but also its Christianity.

Let us see, then, whether the amendment, which is now in their hands, is, or is not, by their own confession, to be employed in the interest of Sunday observance.

That the *Christian Statesman* is a fair exponent of the opinions and intentions of the leading spirits in the movement for the amendment, we think no one will have the hardihood to deny. What it advocates and favors, then, is destined to stand or fall with the triumph or defeat of the men who speak through it. Turning to the prospectus of the identical copy of the *Statesman* which contains the criticism which we are reviewing, we find the following statement: "The design of this paper, as its name suggests, is the discussion of the principles of civil government in the light of Christianity. It has been established to advocate the proposed Religious Amendment to the Constitution of the United States. At the same time, it will aid in maintaining all existing Christian features in our civil institutions, in particular, laws against the desecration of the Christian Sabbath," &c.

We might pause here, but, in a matter of this importance, let us make certainty doubly certain.

It was *strange* that the writer should have made the assertion which he did, with the prospectus from which we have quoted before him. It is *passing strange* that—as if guided by a Providence which had doomed him to make a complete exposure of his real sentiments, although in so doing his own consistency should be involved— he should, within two weeks from the penning of the above assertion, go back upon the files of his periodical for two years, and reprint, by way of *emphasis*, according to his own statement, the following editorial, which forever settles the point that he believes and knows that the amendment and Sunday-keeping are destined to be joined together in a common victory. As the reader peruses this editorial, let him bear in mind the fact that it is not the effusion of an excited and exasperated man, but the expression of a deep and settled conviction which has once found utterance, and which so perfectly expresses the real sentiments of its author that, after years of deliberate reflection, he felt the truth of what he had said so forcibly that he was constrained to give it fresh utterance. Let him also note the fact that the italics are not our own, but those of the editor. We regret that we have not space to give it in full, and invite those who can do so, by all means to turn to the copy of the *Statesman* which contains it, and read it for themselves.

"Time for the meeting of Congress, * * * Two years ago we printed the following telegram, dated at Washington, on Sabbath, Dec. 4, and commented on it in the following terms, which we now emphatically repeat: 'The trains yesterday and *to-day* brought large accessions to the number of Congressmen and visitors already here, and *by to-morrow morning* it is expected that nearly every Senator and member will have arrived.' Thus the fact is heralded over the whole country that a large number of the members of the National Congress openly and wantonly indulge in common travel on the Sabbath. * *
* * And there are other reflections suggested by their conduct.

"1. *Not one of those men who thus violated*

the Sabbath is fit to hold any official position in a Christian nation. * * * The interests of a nation can never be safe in the hands of Sabbath-breakers, and every one of these Congressmen has done that for which, if our laws were right, he ought to be impeached and removed.

"2. *The sin of these Congressmen is a national sin,* because the nation has not said to them in the Constitution, the supreme rule for our public servants, 'We charge you to serve us in accordance with the higher law of God.' These Sabbath-breaking railroads, moreover, are corporations created by the State, and amenable to it. The State is responsible to God for the conduct of these creatures which it calls into being. It is bound, therefore, to restrain them from this, as from other crimes; and any violation of the Sabbath, by any corporation, should work immediate forfeiture of its charter. And the Constitution of the United States, with which all State legislation is required to be in harmony, should be of such character as to prevent any State from tolerating such infractions of fundamental moral law.

"3. Give us in the National Constitution the simple acknowledgment of the law of God as the supreme law of nations, *and all the results indicated in this note will ultimately be secured.* Let no one say that the movement does not contemplate sufficiently practical ends."—*Christian Statesman,* Vol. 6, No. 15.

Now let it be borne in mind that the question at issue is one of *practical bearing*, and not of mere technical distinction. We are not splitting hairs as to what *consistency would demand* under certain circumstances; but the matter in dispute is, Is it not in the highest degree probable that a party, represented by men who express, beforehand, sentiments like those contained in the above editorial, would, when having vaulted into the seat of power, attempt the coercion of all into a strict observance of the Sunday? Is not the line of argument employed above that which would *compel them to this action*, since it is there insisted that God holds the nation and the State responsible for any dereliction in duty in this direction? Furthermore, is it not *promised*, in so many words, that if the amendment is carried, the end desired shall be secured by statutes so relentless that all offending corporations shall have their charters taken away, and by a public opinion so uncompromising that no man who presumes to violate the Sabbath law shall be thought worthy of any position of trust?

Thirdly, Waiving, for the time being, the point that the Sunday and the amendment stand together, it is urged that, though they do, this should not prevent seventh-day observers from supporting the latter, since it is better to submit to Sunday laws than to have the nation pass into the hands of atheists.

Before debating this proposition at length, it

will be well to bear in mind that what I have said in the *Statesman*, as well as what I now say, is spoken simply with reference to one occupying the position of a Seventh-day Adventist.

So far as our Seventh-day Baptist friends are concerned, we have no disposition to hold them responsible for the views which we, as Adventists, hold. But so far as it regards our relation to this subject, it is materially affected by these considerations. A failure to discern this has led the gentleman into very absurd positions. When he attempts to make a *Seventh-day Adventist conscience*, he must form it upon a *Seventh-day Adventist model*. Before he can do this, all his bright visions of a temporal millennium and good days to come, must vanish into thin air. To say, as he does, that common sense would teach him to pursue a certain line of conduct, is one thing; to say that, did he occupy the position which we hold, common sense would teach him to do the same thing, is another, and entirely different, thing. Let it be borne in mind, therefore, that we are not now discussing the proposition whether we *ought to be Seventh-day Adventists*, but, taking the ground which he has *chosen*, whether, *as Adventists*, we ought to support the proposed amendment. This being done, we are ready to inquire, What is the peculiar faith of the people in question?

We answer, 1. They believe that Jesus Christ

is about to come in the clouds of heaven. 2. That they represent a body of believers which the Lord is raising up in order that they may lift the standard of his downtrodden law and Sabbath, as one around which those who will be ready to hail him at his appearing, though few in numbers, will ultimately be gathered. 3. That, in the light of prophecy, those who thus break away from the errors of the papacy are in danger of persecution, not from infidels and atheists, bad as they may be, but from those who, in the guise of religion, shall, without warrant from God, endeavor to enforce by statute law the observance of a day which finds no authority in the word of God, but has for its support simply the *dictum* of the man of sin. 4. That the very body of men whose appearance in this country they have for twenty years so confidently predicted, as being the ones who should do the work in question, have actually appeared, and are inaugurating the campaign which is very soon to be waged with unrelenting fury against those who keep the commandments of God and the faith of Jesus.

All these features of their faith were shadowed forth in our communications in the *Statesman*.

With this understanding, how utterly empty and infelicitous is the logic of our friend. Take, for example, his chosen illustration of the islanders. There is in it hardly a single point *appropos* to the case in hand.

1. The island to which the missionaries are supposed to go is one in which, according to his statement, the fourth-day Sabbath is already acknowledged as such in their Constitution of government, and therefore carries with it the sanction and authority of statute law; whereas, with us there is no such Constitutional acknowledgment.

2. In the case of the islanders, their mistake in the selection of the day is evidently attributed wholly to ignorance, since they were in possession of only a *part* of the Bible, and their remedy was to be found in furnishing them with copies of the complete work; but our opponents, on the contrary, are in possession, and have been from childhood, of the Scriptures in full. Nor can the ministry, who are leading the movement in question, plead ignorance of the line of argument by which the seventh-day Sabbath is supported, since, for at least two hundred years, it has been iterated and reiterated, until their familiarity with it and their complete rejection of it is proved, not only by what they say, but also by what they do. Instance the fining and imprisonment, at sundry times, even in this country, of men who, having conscientiously observed the seventh day, have attempted to enjoy the privilege which God has given them, both by precept and example, of working on the first day of the week.

3. In the case cited, the infidel minority is

supposed to be on the point of mounting the throne of power, and of sweeping away every vestige of the Sabbath institution; whereas, in our case, as seen above, the danger which threatens the people of God in these last days, is not to be apprehended alone from those who scoff at God and the Bible, but from those who, according to Paul, having "a form of godliness," shall "deny the power thereof." In other words, who, while accepting the Scriptures, if you please, shall disregard their explicit statements, as in the case of the commandments, substituting in the place of the seventh day, which God has styled his Sabbath, the first, which he has never claimed as his own, nor enjoined on any man.

With this statement of our views, further remark is uncalled for. We think that even our reviewer will now perceive that, before he could bring us to accept as logical the proposition numbered three, above, it would be necessary for him to overturn the very foundations of the system of truth which we now hold. This, however, we fancy is a task which our opponent, judging from the line of argument which he has thus far pursued, would not undertake with much prospect of success, until he has become more thoroughly conversant with the scope and nature of the work in which we are engaged.

Fourthly. It is suggested that we are in danger of being classed with infidels and atheists.

So far as this peril is concerned, we simply

remark that it is generally found to be best in the long run to do right for the sake of right, regardless of what men may say concerning you, leaving the result with God. The individual who would desert sound principles because some wicked man or set of men might, for the time being, be confounded with him, is destitute of true morality. Besides, in the matter in question, who is it from whom Seventh-day Adventists need apprehend that such an erroneous impression will receive publicity? We trust not from our friend, because, in the article in question, he frankly acknowledges their devotion to the Bible in its strict construction.

Is it, then, from the infidels themselves? Well, if it should be, we think we can undeceive them. I will tell you what we will do. Whenever they attempt to "fawn upon us overmuch," we will preach to them the *law of God, Sabbath and all*, and my word for it, they will themselves shortly draw a line of demarkation between them and us, so broad and distinct that all who are not willfully blind will have no difficulty in discerning it; for it is a remarkable fact that it is as true now as it formerly was, that the "carnal mind is not subject to the law of God, neither indeed can be." The infidel of the present day hates that law with a hatred, the intensity of which is only equalled by that of the large body of first-day observers—we are happy to say not of the *Statesman* school—who have abolished the ten commandments in order to dispose of one of them, and whose special delight seems to consist in berating the law which David pronounced "perfect," and Paul declared to be "holy, just, and good."

Finally, we submit that when it can be shown, 1. That God would be better pleased with a nation having a Constitution which contained his printed name, while wielding the whole power of that Constitution against the only Sabbath which he has ever commanded, than he would be with one which—while his name would fail to appear in its fundamental law—was nevertheless administered in the interests of civil and religious liberty; and 2. That the best method of converting atheists is one by which they would be exasperated by fines and imprisonments inflicted in the name of the God of the Bible for the desecration of a day which they know that it nowhere commands; and 3. That it would be reasonable to expect that men should, by their votes, elevate to place and authority those who are destined to put manacles upon their wrists, and padlocks upon their tongues; then, and not till then, can Seventh-day Adventists be expected to support an amendment which, though in many respects desirable, will inevitably be employed against God, his people, and his law.

STATESMAN'S REPLY.

ARTICLE TWO.

THE SEVENTH DAY NOT OBSERVED BY THE EARLY CHRISTIAN CHURCH.

HAVING shown in our last article that seventh-day Sabbatarians, to be consistent with themselves in appealing to the Bible as of supreme authority, should be among the earnest friends of the Religious Amendment, we come now to consider their argument against the first-day Sabbath.

On many points dwelt upon in the articles we have published, there is no difference of view. We believe that the Sabbath was instituted, not in the wilderness, for Israel; but in Eden, for mankind. We maintain, also, that the law of the Sabbath is an essential part of the great moral code of the ten commandments, spoken by God's voice amid the awful manifestations of Sinai, and written by the finger of God on tables of stone as a law of perpetual obligation for the whole human family. These, and other points admitted on both sides, need not occupy time and space in this discussion. We are concerned here, and now, simply with the transfer of the Sabbath from the seventh to the first day of the week. Our readers have had before them an argument, of considerable length, to show that God never authorized a change of day. We proceed to prove that the transfer was made by divine authority and approval.

In doing this, we shall first have to inquire into the facts of history. We shall have to ask,

Was the observance of the seventh-day Sabbath, acknowledged as binding up to the resurrection of Christ, continued by the apostles and the early church after that event? Was any other day substituted by them in its place? For an answer to these questions, we must appeal to *facts*. We make our appeal to the records of the New Testament. A careful and thorough examination of these authoritative records shows conclusively that *the seventh day was not observed as the Sabbath after the resurrection of Christ by the apostles and the early church.*

It is admitted on all hands that Christ himself, before his death, and his disciples, up to the time of his resurrection, kept the seventh day holy. It is also admitted on both sides that after the resurrection the apostles and other followers of Christ kept holy one day in seven. While they abounded daily in the work of the Lord, the seventh-day Sabbatarians will concede with us that there was still one day marked out from the rest of the week as sacred time. What day was thus distinguished? Was it the seventh, otherwise known as the Sabbath? Let us see.

The word Sabbath occurs in the New Testament, after the close of the gospel history, twelve times. In two of these instances, viz., Acts 20: 7, and 1 Cor. 16: 2, the word means "week," and not the seventh day, as also in a number of instances in the gospels. In Acts 1: 12, the word is used to indicate a certain distance. The term is employed in two other places, viz., Acts 13: 27, and 15: 21, in incidental reference to the service of the Jewish synagogues. In Colossians 2: 16, Paul mentions the seventh-day Sabbath only to deny the obligation of its observance. This important passage will be considered farther on. There remain, then, six instances, two of them in regard to one and the same day and meeting, in which the word is found in accounts of gatherings for religious purposes on that day, the seventh of the week. These meetings were as follows: 1. At Antioch, in Pisidia, Acts 13:14; 2. At the same place, the next seventh day, Acts 13:42, 44; 3. At Philippi, Acts 16:13; 4. At Thessalonica, Acts 17:2; and 5. At Corinth, Acts 18:4. At Thessalonica, there were three Sabbaths, and at Corinth, every Sabbath, it may be inferred, for several weeks, thus marked by religious meetings. We are informed that Paul went into the synagogue at Thessalonica on the Sabbath, or seventh day, "as his manner was." And, accordingly, particularly during his first and second, or his more properly termed, missionary tours, as distinguished from his journeys in revisiting churches already organized, we may unhesitatingly infer that there were other similar meetings on the seventh day, as at Salamis, Acts 13:15; at Iconium, Acts 14:1; and at Ephesus, Acts 18:19, and 19:8.

And here we note the fact that *in not a single one of these instances was the meeting a gathering of Christians*. In no case was it the assembly of the members of a Christian church for worship. In every case, these meetings on the seventh day were in Jewish places of worship, all in synagogues regularly occupied by Jewish assemblies, except that at Philippi, which was at a *proseucha*, a Jewish place of prayer out of the city by the river's side. In every instance, it was a gathering of Jews and Jewish proselytes, with the addition of a greater or lesser number of

Gentiles, the sight of a crowd of whom at Antioch, the second day of meeting in their synagogue, excited the jealousy and rage of the Jews. And in these gatherings, in every case, Paul labored *as a missionary*, glad to avail himself of every opportunity to proclaim the saving truths of the gospel of Christ.

Can any intelligent and candid reader of the inspired records fail to understand the narrative of Paul's missionary work? He was sent forth "to turn sinners from darkness to light." As he himself states at Antioch, addressing the Jews: "It was necessary that the word of God should first have been spoken to you." His "heart's desire and prayer to God for Israel was that they might be saved." Accordingly, wherever he went, he was found going to them on the seventh day in *their* places of worship, not in Christian houses of prayer; meeting with them in *their* assemblies, not in assemblies of professed followers of Christ. Just as a Christian missionary, in modern times, going to a heathen land, would avail himself, if possible, of the customary assemblies of the residents, whatever day they might keep holy, so Paul and his fellow-missionaries availed themselves of the seventh-day assemblies of the Jews, that from among them, as well as from among the Gentiles, they might gather out an *ecclesia*—a body of followers of the Lord Jesus, in whom Jew and Gentile should be one.

The question, therefore, still remains to be answered: Which day of the week did the church at Jerusalem, existing at the time of Christ's ascension, which day did the apostles in their relations with this church, which day did the churches, organized and established by the apostles, and under their example and divine authority, observe as a holy day, a Sabbath to the Lord? In all the references to the seventh day, or Jewish Sabbath, there is not, as we have seen, a particle of evidence that that day was thus observed.

On the other hand, there is positive testimony that the very congregations or churches of Christians, organized at the places where Paul performed missionary labor on the seventh day, ignored that day, and in its stead observed another day of the week as holy time. For example, at Corinth, "as his manner was," Paul went first to the Jews and preached to them in their synagogue, the word of God, *reasoning with them*, and persuading them and the Greeks to accept of Christ. Then, when the Jews opposed themselves and blasphemed, he shook his raiment, and said unto them, "Your blood be upon your own heads; I am clean: from henceforth I will go unto the Gentiles." So he left the synagogue and the Jews, not the city, and entering into the house of Justus, received Crispus, the chief ruler of the synagogue, with all his house, and many of the Corinthians, as converts into the Christian church. Here we have the church of Corinth. Which day of the week did it observe as the Sabbath of the Lord? the seventh? Though Paul "continued there a year and six months, teaching the word of God among them," there is not a word more about seventh-day services. This, it is true, would be merely negative, if it were all. But this is not all. In Paul's direction to this same church, a few years later, he makes clear and certain, what before was probable, that their stated day for religious services was not the seventh, but the first, day of the week. 1 Cor. 16:2. The plain and most explicit teaching of this passage will be fully considered hereafter.

Again, when Paul entered into the synagogue at Ephesus, and reasoned with the Jews (Acts 18:19), and, because he could not tarry long at this time, soon returned again, and met the objections of disputatious Jews for the space of three months (Acts 19:8), his labors as a missionary are said to have been in the synagogue, no doubt on the Sabbath of the Jews, or the seventh day. But once more separating the Christian converts from the unbelieving and blaspheming Jews, and forming the Christian church of Ephesus, he continued there in incessant labors for two years. And now we hear no more of seventh-day assemblies. This, again, may be said to be merely negative, as we hear of no special honor put upon any day. But we have not done with this. Passing the last years of his life in this city of Ephesus, the apostle John writes of "the Lord's day," known and observed by the Christians among whom he dwelt. That this holy day of the early church, called the Lord's day, was not the seventh, but the first, is shown by the most satisfactory historical testimony, which will be adduced in full in its proper connection.

Once more. When Paul came to Troas to preach Christ's gospel, and a door was opened to him of the Lord (2 Cor. 2:12), whether it was on his first very brief visit (Acts 16:8), or more probably in going over "those parts," on his way from Ephesus to Macedonia (Acts 20:2), he no doubt, "as his manner was," went into the synagogue and reasoned with the Jews. A congregation of Christian disciples was formed, and the apostle departed for Greece. After an absence of some months, Paul returns to Troas, and with his companions remains there seven days, departing again on the second day of the week. Whether he departed on the first or second, however, the fact remains that, during his abode of seven days at Troas, there was one seventh day. Do we hear of any religious meeting on that day? Did the disciples then assemble for divine service? Let us hear the record: "We abode seven days. And upon the first day of the week, when the disciples came together to break bread, Paul preached unto them, ready to depart on the morrow." The seventh day is passed by. The day for the assembling of the Christian disciples is not the Sabbath of the Jews. Another day has taken its place. This most explicit instance at Troas of ignoring the seventh day, and honoring another in its place, as the stated day for the religious services of Christians, abundantly confirms, if confirmation were needed, the conclusions already reached in the instances at Corinth and Ephesus.

Thus the *facts* of the records of inspired history conclusively prove that the seventh day was not observed by the apostles and early Christians as their sacred day of divine worship, or the Sabbath of the Lord. We might add here that the testimony of all the earliest Christian writers, who received from the apostles and the companions of the apostles the institutions of the Christian church, is full and explicit to the same effect. But we shall hear their evidence for the first day, and thus also against the seventh, in good time.

It will now be in place to consider how apostolic precept corresponds with apostolic example, and that of the churches, in regard to the seventh day. Colossians 2:16, a most important passage, making particular mention of the seventh-day Sabbath, yet singularly overlooked by seventh-day Sabbatarians, now claims our attention for a moment. Judaizing teachers, so busy everywhere throughout the early church, had been at work among the Christian disciples at Colosse. They had been insisting upon the observance of the seventh day as the Sabbath of the Lord. One would think that some of these men had come down to our time and learned to use very good English. We refer these representatives of an ancient, but not honorably mentioned, class for instruction to the apostle's words to the Colossians: "Let no man judge you in meat or in drink, or in respect of a holy day [literally, *of a feast*], or of the new moon, or of the Sabbath days;" *i. e.*, of yearly, monthly, or weekly Jewish celebrations. We do not wait to examine the parallel passages in Gal. 4:10, and Rom. 14:5, where the obligation of Jewish observances, including the seventh-day Sabbath is denied, and where, in the latter case, to make the argument even stronger, the toleration of these observances as a weakness is considerately advised. Surely, it is no wonder that seventh-day Sabbatarians seem not to be aware of the existence of these portions of the divine word! It cannot be pleasant to be made to feel that, like the Judaizers of old, they bring themselves under the sharp rebuke of the inspired apostle by judging Christians in respect of the seventh-day Sabbath.

We will now sum up this part of the discussion: Admitting that the Sabbath was instituted in Eden for mankind; that it is of perpetual obligation; that it was observed by Christ himself before his death, and by his disciples until his resurrection, as by the Jews of old, on the seventh day of the week; we have gone on to see that the apostles and the early church, still having one stated day each week as a holy day, did *not* continue the observance of the seventh day. We have seen that the seventh day, after the resurrection, is mentioned only in connection with assemblies, in Jewish places of worship, of Jews, Jewish proselytes, and, in some instances, a larger or smaller addition of Gentiles, among all of whom the apostle labored as a missionary for the conversion of souls, and the formation of Christian congregations, or churches. We have found that no instance can be adduced of the apostles in their relations to Christian churches, nor of assemblies of Christian disciples, meeting to observe the seventh day as the Sabbath of the Lord. On the other hand, we have found them ignoring the seventh day and honoring another, in perfect harmony with the apostle Paul's rebuke of Judaizing teachers who insisted on having Christian disciples observe the seventh day, and his condescending toleration of their weakness.

A REJOINDER.

"THE SEVENTH DAY NOT OBSERVED BY THE EARLY CHRISTIAN CHURCH."

It is, we confess, with some degree of embarrassment, that we attempt the answering of the second article from the pen of the editor of the *Statesman*, in reply to the argument which we presented in the columns of that paper. Our difficulty does not arise from any confusion into which we have been thrown by the superior logic of our opponent; it consists, rather, in knowing just where and how to commence the work.

So far as statements are concerned, they are numerous and repeated again and again, in substance. But we have no disposition, nor have we the space, to take them up singly, in their numerical and repetitious order, for consideration. And, besides, the fallacy of nearly every one of them has been demonstrated in what we have already written. This being the case, we have determined to take the general scope of the criticism, and thus, as briefly as may be, make suggestions which, if carried out, will answer its assumptions, as well as its attempted efforts at deduction.

We remark, then, in the outset, that we are happy to meet the writer upon the common ground of a Sabbath having originated in Eden, and inserted in a law of perpetual obligation on both Jews and Gentiles.

Let the reader keep these mutual concessions continually before his eyes. They are of great significance in this debate. 1. They prove that the Sabbath is not Jewish in its origin, but was given to Adam, as their representative head, for the benefit of the whole race, more than two thousand years before there was a Jew in existence. 2. They also prove that the Sabbath institution was rendered obligatory upon all men by a divine precept, with the phraseology of which we are all acquainted. 3. That that precept is explicit in its declaration that the last and not the first day of the week was the Sabbath. 4. That before any other day can be substituted in the place of the one designated, the Power which originated it must authorize the change.

So much for the important results which necessarily flow from the principles which we hold in common, if indeed we are right in supposing that the writer *really* means what he *actually* says; namely, that he holds to the perpetuity of the fourth commandment of the decalogue. We shall see, hereafter, whether or not his statements are to be taken for all which they express.

We advance, now, in our examination of the criticism before us.

What direction, then, does the effort take in the main? It will be granted that the plan of defense adopted is that of attempting to prove that the early church did violate the seventh, and did honor the first, day of the week. But with what success has the effort been attended? We know that it is stated several times that the apostles disregarded what the author is pleased to call the *Jewish* Sabbath—after he had conceded the principle that that of the commandment was *Edenic* in its origin—but did he make out his case? So far from it, in every instance where he has found them connected in the record with the Sabbath day, it has ever been in the performance of duties *religious in their nature.* For should we concede that he is right in supposing that Paul went into the synagogues to teach on the Sabbath day, simply because he would find hearers there, this, assuredly, would not prove that Paul was a Sabbath-breaker.

Let me take the gentleman's favorite illustration of a missionary in a foreign land, at the present time. Now suppose that his lot were cast in a country where the first day of the week, or the day of the sun, was regarded as holy by the natives, and he should be found on that day regularly teaching them in their places of assembly, would *that* decide the question that he was necessarily a violator of the first-day Sabbath? You answer immediately in the negative. So, too, in the case of Paul. The fact that it can be shown that it was his custom to teach in the synagogues on the seventh day of the week, if it has no power to prove that he was a conscientious *observer* of that day, cannot at least be cited as furnishing evidence that he *disregarded* it. We ask, then, again, Has a scintilla of positive testimony been given that Paul ever broke a single Sabbath of the Lord, as contained in the divine precept? Once more it must be conceded that there has not. But is it not a little singular that in a history of thirty years, where the Sabbath is so often mentioned, not one single action has ever been discovered in the least incompatible with Paul's veneration of the seventh day? We let the reader answer.

Furthermore, we have from the pen of our opponent himself the frank admission that, in the historic territory over which he has been passing, it has been uniformly true that both Luke and Paul have ever, when speaking of the seventh day, called it "the Sabbath." Now let the reader remember that this confession is full and sweeping in its character. Then let him ask himself whether it is natural to suppose that men, having repudiated an old Sabbath, and zealous for the establishment of a new one, would be likely to make up the record in question in such a form that the old Sabbath, whenever spoken of, should always be styled "the Sabbath," and the new one be mentioned merely as the "first day of the week?" In order to impress the fallacy of such an idea, we have but to call attention to the fact that men, at the present time, possessing the same natures and dispositions as formerly, would avoid such a course with the most scrupulous care. Instance the fact that seventh-day observers never allude to the Sunday as *the Sabbath*, but avoid such a reference under all circumstances; while the devotees of the Sunday, when speaking of the last day of the week, almost uniformly speak of it as the *Jewish Sabbath*, if Sabbath they will allow themselves to call it at all.

But again. We are told, very candidly, that by the word Sabbath, in Acts 13:44, where it is said that the "next Sabbath day came almost the whole city together" to hear the word of God, is meant the next seventh day succeeding the first seventh day on which Paul addressed the Jews at Antioch. This being true, it is settled beyond dispute that, in the mind of Luke, there was no Sabbath day occurring between the one on which Paul spoke to the people, and the seventh day of the next week when he addressed them the second time; for, if there had been, then it would not have been proper to call the last Sabbath mentioned the "*next*" one, since another Sabbath would have intervened between the two in question. In other words, according to the view of our friend, the Sunday, which was the next day after the first discourse of Paul, was really the next Sabbath which followed it; whereas, the inspired penman ignores it altogether, and, passing over it with silence, calls the last day of that same week "the Sabbath."

Again, it is stated in Acts 15:21, that the "Scriptures are read in the synagogues *every* Sabbath day." Here, again, it is conceded that the reference is to the seventh day of the week. If this be true, however, then James, as well as Luke, had, in his lexicon of terms, the "Sabbath day" as the one which answered to the seventh day and not to the first; for no one will insist that the Scriptures were read in the synagogues of the Jews regularly on the first day of the week; but James says that they were read there *every* Sabbath day; therefore, in his mind—as we have already remarked—the first day was not the Sabbath.

Once more: It is stated of Paul that he reasoned in the synagogues *every* Sabbath, and persuaded the Jews and the Greeks. Here also it is urged—admitting that the reference is to the seventh day—that Paul went into the synagogue in order to get a hearing. But this he could not do on the first day, since he would have found the synagogue closed, and no audience. Nevertheless, the statement stands unqualified that Paul preached "*every Sabbath.*" Now if this be true, and the first as well as the seventh day might, according to the view of the historian, be called a Sabbath, then we have him stating that Paul preached in the place in question on both the first and seventh days. On the other hand, if he regarded the first day as alone the Sabbath, then he meant to teach that Paul preached in the synagogue on that day, and that day only. But my opponent will not insist upon either of these positions. The only conclusion that is left us, therefore, is that the Holy Ghost, who inspired Luke in the selection of terms, employed the appellation of Sabbath as applying only to the day which had been sanctified in Eden, and had always been known by that title.

Now let us give our attention for a moment to the objection so strongly urged that in the book of the Acts, and in the epistles, there is no well-authenticated instance in which the apostles held meetings, with Christians exclusively, on the seventh day. The point of the proposition might be thus stated: If the early Christians did hold meetings on the seventh day, the record would have shown it: this it fails to do; therefore, the presumption is that they did not regard it as holy.

This is a sword that cuts *both* ways, if it cuts at all. We do not wonder that, when our friend laid hold of its hilt, he said, tremblingly, This is a *negative weapon;* so that, when we should attempt to borrow it of him, we might find the edge, which was designed for his *own neck,* *dulled by his own concession.*

But let us proceed. Is it true, so far as the ancient Sabbath of the Lord is concerned, that, unless we can find historic accounts of its observance in the New Testament, we must therefore conclude that it was not regarded? We answer, No; simply because its observance is not alone taught by precedent. It rests upon a positive command of God, incorporated in a law which was brought over into this dispensation, as we have seen, and made obligatory upon Christians. It was not, therefore, necessary that a detailed account of its observance should be placed upon the record, in order to prove that it was regarded by the early church; since the very fact that they acknowledged the law of God, is in itself proof that they sanctified the Sabbath which it ordained. Until, therefore, the gentleman can shake the pillars of that law—as we shall show he has not yet succeeded in doing—it is of itself a guarantee that every seventh day was regarded with solemnity by those who were endeavoring to keep its precepts.

In proof of this, we have but to mention the fact that from Moses to David—a space covering five hundred years—the term Sabbath is not employed once in the sacred history; and yet the gentleman will agree with me that the good men of those ages hallowed it, simply because he agrees with me that they had a precept requiring them to do so.

But, again, we must be allowed to insist that the very silence of which the gentleman complains does indirectly prove, independent of the commandment, that the first generation of Christians were Sabbatarians. What we mean to be understood as saying is, that they at least did not violate the regulations concerning the strict observance of the Sabbath, as enforced among the Jews; for had they done so, a record of thirty years could not have failed to bring to light numerous collisions, which would have been inevitable between Jews and Christians, the one class despising and trampling down the Sabbath of the law, and the other following them with that vulture glance of inquisition, by which—as in the case of our Lord—they were in the habit of watching their antagonists, with a view to condemning them before the law. And, besides, with what show of consistency could Paul have stood up before them, announcing himself as one who had never violated the customs of the fathers (Acts 28:17), if he had been seen weekly transgressing the law of one of the dearest institutions handed down to them from the remotest antiquity?

Thus much for one side of the logic of our opponent. Now let us apply it to the Sunday. As we do so, it will be recollected that there has been no effort made, as yet, to place it upon a positive precept. Its existence, therefore, if such it has at all, must be attributable to precedent. Thus far, such precedent has not been cited, except by way of anticipation. When it comes up, we will consider it in order. In the meantime, let it be remembered that our friend has voluntarily taken a position which will compel him to admit that, unless he can find at least one clear and unquestionable case in which the Sunday was from beginning to end devoutly celebrated, his cause is a hopeless one. Nay, more, to make out his point, every candid mind will demand that, in the absence of positive command, he shall be able to show numerous instances in which the day, whose claims he seeks to vindicate, was intelligently honored; for, be it remembered, that, according to his own declaration, the apostle was traveling from point to point, writing and preaching, and Luke was keeping a diary of his labors, for the purpose of instructing that generation of Christians, as well as this, concerning duty and doctrine. If, therefore, Sunday sanctity came under the head of those doctrines, it was important, overwhelmingly so, that such a fact should be set forth clearly, since an habitual disregard on the part of any, of the new Sabbath, would bring upon them the condemnation of Heaven. Furthermore, the line of demarkation, which the new day would have drawn between the disciples and the Hebrews, would have been so broad, and the discussions upon those points would have been so numerous and so full, while the transition was taking place, that its existence could not have failed to become discernible in the writings of that period.

Here we must change our line of argument, and turn to the consideration of Col. 2: 14–17, and of Rom. 14: 5. Our opponent intimates that

Sabbatarians are in the habit of evading these texts. In this remark, he does us great injustice. The statement is so far from being true that I make no doubt that, within the last twenty years, Seventh-day Adventist preachers alone have, by voice and pen, commented upon them at least a thousand times. But the best method of showing the charge to be untrue will be found in an examination of the texts themselves. The first is as follows: "Blotting out the handwriting of ordinances that was against us, which was contrary to us, and took it out of the way, nailing it to his cross; * * * Let no man therefore judge you in meat, or in drink, or in respect of an holy day, or of the new moon, or of the sabbath days: which are a shadow of things to come; but the body is of Christ." Col. 2:14, 16, 17. Now be it remembered that he affirms that these scriptures teach the abolition of the creation Sabbath; also, that, while we concede the point that there are here mentioned sabbaths which were abolished at the crucifixion of Christ, we deny that the seventh-day Sabbath was among them, and insist that they were simply the ceremonial sabbaths of the Jews to which reference is made.

In proof of our position, we offer the following considerations: 1. That which was repealed is represented as having been "blotted out." Now the Scriptures are remarkable for the force and propriety of the illustrations which they employ. But who will say that the terms "blotting out" could properly be applied to writing engraved in stone, as was the Sabbath law in its original copy? 2. That which was blotted out was the "handwriting of ordinances;" but the commandments were the finger-writing of God. 3. That which was blotted out was found among ordinances that were "*against* us, and *contrary* to us." But Jesus says, "The Sabbath was made *for* man." Mark 2:27, 28. 4. That which was blotted out and taken out of the way "was nailed to his cross." But it is inconceivable that such language could be spoken of the tables of stone, since they are not of a nature such that the work spoken of could be readily accomplished, and therefore the figure will not apply to them except when forced. 5. It must be admitted that these things concerning which we are not to allow men to judge us were either all of them shadows of Christ, or that if the *others* were not, the *sabbath days* were. If they were all shadows, then the sabbaths undeniably were such; for the expression, "which were a shadow of things to come," stands immediately connected with the term "sabbath days."

But this decides the point in controversy; for our friend has already voluntarily declared that the seventh-day Sabbath originated in Eden. This being true, it cannot be regarded as a "shadow" or type of Christ, since it was in being before man had ever fallen, and, consequently, before a Saviour was either needed or promised. It is commemorative in its character, and was calculated to carry the mind back to the creation, to the rest of Jehovah, rather than forward to the crucifixion of his Son. Do you inquire, then, what sabbaths the apostle had in view? We answer: He locates them among "commandments written in ordinances." In other words, in the Mosaic ceremonies. Now take your Bible and turn to the twenty-third chapter of Leviticus, and you will find that the Jews had three annual feasts—the passover, the Pentecost, and the feast of tabernacles—besides the new moons, and the seven annual sabbaths. The sabbaths were as follows, to wit.: 1. The first day of unleavened bread. 2. The seventh day of that feast. 3. The day of Pentecost. 4. The first day of the seventh month. 5. The tenth day of that month. 6. The fifteenth day of that month. 7. The twenty-second day of the same. These are the ones, beyond all question, to which reference is here made.* 1. Because they were in the handwriting of Moses, and could be blotted out. 2. Because they were found in handwriting of ordinances. 3. They were among ceremonies that were against us, and contrary to us (Acts 15:10). 4. The law in which they originated might have been nailed to

---

*"It is not clear that the apostle refers at all to the *Sabbath* in this place [Col. 2:16], whether Jewish or Christian; his σαβ-βατων, *of sabbaths, or weeks,* most probably refers to their feasts of weeks."—*A. Clarke, in loco.*

the cross. 5. That law was also one which shadowed forth Christ (Heb. 10:1).

To the second text we shall give but little space. In the presentation of it, our friend attempts to be *facetious*. Nor are we disposed to find fault with him for this. It is sometimes admissible, even in the discussion of the *gravest* questions, to indulge in *harmless* humor. That the effort in question partakes of *this character*, *i. e.*, that it is *harmless*, we shall not dispute. At all events, when we read it, it amused rather than offended us. A second thought, however, suggests the possibility that if *we* were not damaged by the sally, it might have been *pernicious*, nevertheless, since it is possible for it to *react upon its author*. Certain it is, that it will damage either him or Paul, because he represents the great apostle as making a special effort, in his general labors, to teach men that they must under *all* circumstances keep *one* day holy, and that under *some* they might be allowed to regard a *second* also in the same light. But, unfortunately, if this exegesis is correct, and if the language of Rom. 14:5, applies to the weekly Sabbath at all, Paul blundered egregiously in communicating his intentions; since he virtually told those whom he was addressing that, of the days of which *he was speaking*, they *need not* keep them at all, or they *might*, at will. Here follows the text: "One man esteemeth one day above another: another esteemeth every day alike. Let every man be fully persuaded in his own mind."

Now we have heard men who believed in no Sabbath employ this text again and again to prove that there is now no holy time; we have also heard conscientious first-day observers argue forcibly and conclusively that this text proved no such thing, simply because it referred to days that were connected with meats and drinks, and not to the weekly Sabbath at all. But we confess that the position of our friend is somewhat novel. Nevertheless, we feel sure that the reputation of the great apostle for perspicuity will not suffer by this attempt, and we think that, so far as he is concerned himself, reflection will prevent him from ever seriously urging it. In conclusion on this point, we append a brief comment from the pen of Adam Clarke, whose reputation, and the fact that he was an observer of Sunday, will give him no little authority with our opponent. He says: "Reference is here made to the *Jewish* institutions, and especially their festivals; such as the passover, pentecost, feast of tabernacles, new moons, jubilee, &c. The converted *Jew* still thought these of moral obligation; the *Gentile* Christian, not having been bred up in this way, had no such prejudices."—*Com. in loco.*

The only remaining text cited is that of Gal. 4:10. After what has been said, no further comment from us will be required. The reader, desirous of satisfying himself that this text also has no reference to the weekly Sabbath, and of necessity refers either to heathen festivals or Jewish ceremonial days, can read the context, and consult standard authorities, such as Clarke or Barnes.*

Let us now survey the ground over which we have passed. So far as we have gone, what has been done toward proving a practice of first-day observance on the part of the early church? We answer, Nothing, absolutely nothing. The only texts which have been cited for this purpose are 1 Cor. 16:2, Rev. 1:10, and Acts 20:7. So far as they are concerned, we have previously shown that the first of them does not in any way affect the question of Sunday observance; that the second relates to the seventh day of the week and not to the first; and that the third proves that Paul traveled nineteen and one-half miles on the Sunday. When our reviewer shall attempt to stir a single stone in the structure of argument which we reared in our former articles on these points, we shall be by his side, to see that he does it fairly. Until then, the intelligent reader need not be told that it is vain for him to try to make capital by quoting them as above.

Thus much for the first day. We inquire next,

---

*"The days here referred to are doubtless the days of the Jewish festivals. * * * * It is not a fair interpretation of this to suppose that the apostle refers to the *Sabbath*, properly so called, for this was a part of the decalogue, and was observed by the Saviour himself, and by the apostles also. It *is* a fair interpretation to apply it to all those days which are not commanded to be kept holy in the Scriptures."— *A. Barnes, in loco.*

What has been conceded or proved, which is favorable to the seventh-day Sabbath? 1. That it originated in Eden. 2. That it was enforced by the fourth commandment. 3. That that commandment is still binding. 4. That the effort to show a change in its phraseology from Col. 2: 16, Rom. 14:5, and Gal. 4:10, was a complete failure; and therefore that it reads as it did formerly, that "the seventh day is the Sabbath of the Lord." 5. That there is a Sabbath in this dispensation. 6. That, being enforced by positive command, it stands in need of no precedent. 7. That, while the apostles did many times preach on that day, there is not one instance in which they violated it. 8. That had they desecrated it, the conflicts which would have been thus created, must have found a place in the history of those times. 9. That in the book of Acts it is always called "the Sabbath." 10. That it was the only Sabbath known to the apostles, since they speak of it not only as "*the* Sabbath," but as "the *next* Sabbath," and "*every* Sabbath."

In concluding, we suggest that we leave our reviewer in a situation which, to a man of his clearness of perception, must be a very unsatisfactory one. Having insisted upon the perpetuity of the fourth commandment, he is compelled to take one of two positions. Either, 1. That it reads the same as it did when it enforced the seventh day; or, 2. That its phraseology has been changed. We confess that we have been unable to decide which of these positions he prefers. Nor is it material here. If he adopts the first, the thoughtful reader will agree with me that it is simply absurd to argue that a statute, while reading the same, means differently from what it did formerly. On the other hand, should he adopt the latter, then we inquire why he has not given it to us as it reads since it has been changed, and thus ended the controversy by gratifying our most reasonable request.

STATESMAN'S REPLY.

ARTICLE THREE.

TESTIMONY FROM THE GOSPELS FOR THE FIRST-DAY SABBATH.

IN a previous article it was seen that from the resurrection of Christ there is no instance recorded in Scripture of the observance of the seventh day as the Sabbath of the Lord by any assembly of Christians. On the contrary, it was seen that the Judaizing spirit, which in some instances insisted on such observance by Christians, was rebuked by the inspired apostle. In connection with this was noted the fact that in the case of Jews converted to Christianity, yet inclined still to regard the seventh day with other Jewish celebrations, Christians were directed to bear with such observance as a weakness in their brethren. It was also seen that while the observance of the seventh day was not continued, another day of the week, the first, took its place as the stated day for religious assemblies and services. Let us now examine the testimony from the Gospels for this day, reserving the remainder of scriptural proof for another article.

The manner in which the first day of the week is pointed out in the Gospels as the day of the Lord's resurrection, is itself striking and significant. All four of the evangelists concur in making prominent the fact that it was on this day that Christ rose from the dead. This fact is stated by Matthew, 28:1-6; twice by Mark, 16:1-6, and again in verse 9; by Luke, 24:1-6; by John, 20:1, 2. This concurrent, particular mention of the first day of the week as the day of the resurrection, in four independent historical accounts, the earliest of which was written probably about twenty years after that event, has a significance readily overlooked, but well worth noting.

To appreciate this fully, we must distinguish between the words of the historians and the words of the persons whose sayings they record— a most important point in the study of any history. Observing this distinction, then, we note that the promise of Christ, as recorded by the historians, was, that he would rise from the dead on the third day, dating from and including the day of his crucifixion and burial. The chief priests and Pharisees, asking Pilate to have the sepulcher guarded; the angels at the sepulcher the morning of the resurrection; the two disciples, conversing with the risen Lord on the way to Emmaus, and the Lord himself, speak of it as the *third* day. In no other way does any one whose language is recorded by the historians refer to the day of the resurrection. Now, had the historians themselves, writing after an interval of from nearly twenty to over sixty years, simply desired to state the fact of the Lord's resurrection, it would have been sufficient for them to say that, according to His promise, he rose on the *third* day. But instead of this, they all concur in pointing out particularly the *first* day of the week as the resurrection day. On the supposition that, when the historians wrote, the first day was regarded precisely like the second and third days of the week, as it was at the time of the resurrection, this change of statement is singular and inexplicable. On the other hand, on the supposition that the first day had become an honored and noted day among Christians, this mention of it by all the evangelists, and that, too, in a uniform and somewhat formal phrase, and the difference between the language of the historians and that of the persons of whom they write, are naturally and satisfactorily explained. In this change of language, then, on the part of the inspired historians, and in their concurrent and prominent mention of the first day, we have strong presumptive evidence in favor of the marked character of that day at the time when the Gospel histories were written. Testimony of this kind, in the form of unstudied allusion or undesigned coincidence, though easily passed without notice, is acknowledged on all hands to be of great weight.

After showing himself probably four times to one or more of his disciples during the day of his resurrection, Christ appeared late in the evening to the disciples collectively, Thomas alone being absent. "Then the same day at evening (*opsia*, *late evening*, from *opse, late*), being the first day of the week, when the doors were shut where the disciples were assembled for fear of the Jews, came Jesus and stood in the midst, and saith unto them, Peace be unto you." (John 20:19.) Let the facts be noted. 1. It was the evening of the first day of the week. 2. The disciples were met together, manifestly, *not* to commemorate the resurrection, but for what purpose, or where, it does not matter. 3. The Lord came and blessed them, and, as we learn from the following verses, imparted to them spiritual instruction, and breathed on them the Holy Ghost. These facts should be borne in mind as we proceed.

We come now to the record of the first day of the following week: "And after eight days again his disciples were within, and Thomas with them. Then came Jesus, the doors being shut, and stood in the midst, and said, Peace be unto you." (John 20:26.) This interval of eight days, from and including the resurrection day, brings us, according to the common mode of reckoning, and as no one is disposed to dispute, to the first day of the next week. The preceding first day, the disciples were met collectively. Again, this first day, they are met, and Thomas with them. It has been said that very probably the disciples met every day during the interval, and, therefore, they put no special honor upon the first day. But the question is not just here whether the disciples meant to honor the first day or not. Did the Lord himself single it out from the days of the week and honor it? This is the question at present. It may be admitted that the disciples met every day during the interval. This is exceedingly probable. The fact remains clear that the Lord did not meet with them. And this very passing by of these supposed meetings of the disciples by the Lord, during six days, the last of which was the seventh-day Sabbath, renders his actual meeting with them, as recorded, on the first day again, all the more significant. The disciples may not have designed to honor the day, but the Lord himself, passing by the seventh day along with the other five intervening, selects and honors the first day by once more meeting on it with his disciples.

Nor is it to be admitted that the disciples were destitute of all regard to the returning first day of the week as the day of the Lord's resurrection. The very circumstances in which, by the ordering of the Master, they were placed, could not fail to teach them to look upon it with special regard. They had been assembled on the evening of the preceding first day. The Lord had met with them and blessed them, and breathed on them the Holy Ghost. Earnestly longing to enjoy his comforting and cheering presence again, we may suppose they met on the second day. But the Lord does not come. More deeply feeling their need, they assemble again the third day. Still the desired presence is withheld. So on, with ever-increasing desires, they meet, day after day. How natural would it be for them to think of the seventh day, on which they had so often enjoyed sweet counsel with the Master, going to the house of God. "Surely," their thought might well be, "He will meet with us in our assembly to-day." But no. The time for the special manifestation of himself to his worshiping disciples in their collective gathering had not come. Would not the disciples then remember, if they had ever forgotten it, that it was on the first day of the week the Lord rose from the dead, and on that day he had stood in the midst of them and said, Peace be unto you? And remembering this, they would meet on the return of the first day with earnest expectation of the return of the Master. Nor are they disappointed. Once more he comes, and stands in the midst, and grants his benediction.

Here then are the facts concerning sacred time, as recorded in the Gospel history, subsequent to the resurrection of Christ. The seventh day is not mentioned. If the disciples met on that day, as they probably did, the inspired penmen take no notice of the fact. There is no meeting of the risen Lord with his disciples. The seventh day is passed by. On the other hand, the first day is mentioned in a particular manner, in changed and special language, by all the evangelists, as a noted day would naturally be mentioned and marked out as the resurrection day. On it the Lord repeatedly met with his disciples, blessed them, taught them important spiritual lessons, and breathed on them the Holy Ghost, the earnest of the abundant outpouring of the Spirit. How full of meaning these facts! On the last seventh day on which the disciples rested according to the commandment, the Lord himself is lying in the tomb. The glory of the seventh day dies out with the fading light of that day throughout the whole of which the grave claimed the body of the Redeemer. But the glory of the Sabbath of the Lord survives. It receives fresh luster from the added glories of the Lord of the Sabbath. "The stone which the builders refused is become the head-stone of the corner." It is very early in the morning the first day of the week. Again God said, Let there be light, and there was light. The Sun of righteousness has risen with healing in his wings. This is the day which the Lord hath made; we will rejoice and be glad in it. The first day of the week has become the Lord's day.

A REJOINDER.

"TESTIMONY FROM THE GOSPELS FOR THE FIRST-DAY SABBATH."

WITHOUT prolonged preliminary remarks, we shall endeavor to consider the points of argument presented by our reviewer in the article entitled, "Testimony from the Gospels for the first-day Sabbath." In entering upon our task, we feel almost as if we were doing a work of supererogation, from the fact that what we are called upon to answer is so far from being a refutation of what we had said in our positive argument, that it appears to be little more than a re-statement of positions which we believe we have once fairly met and conclusively answered. Nevertheless, we express our satisfaction at the concessions apparently made by the writer. The common plea that the disciples were assembled on the day of the resurrection in order to honor the resuscitation of the body of Christ, is seemingly ignored. The points now urged seem to be those of a disposition on the part of the Lord himself to honor the first day of the week, and of such a use of language on the part of the historians as it would be natural for them to make, provided it had become a settled thing with them to regard the Sunday as a day which Christ had set apart for holy uses.

So far as it regards the position assumed, that there is peculiar significance in the manner in which the first day is pointed out, with it we are ready most heartily to agree. But so far as the assertion is concerned, that, in the *manner* of the pointing out, there is found strong presumptive evidence that they design to teach succeeding generations that they looked upon the first day of the week as *holy time,* we can by no means admit that it is correct. On the contrary, we believe that their language establishes, beyond controversy, the opposite position. Matthew, Mark, Luke, and John, were blunt, straightforward, direct men in all that they said. They had nothing to disguise, nor could anything be gained by indirection in statement.

Furthermore, every motive of esteem for Christ, as well as that which would actuate them in their desire to instruct subsequent generations in regard to the estimation in which they should hold the day of Christ's resurrection, demanded that their language should be full and explicit, and that it should state, in so many words, that it was sacred to holy uses. But have they done this? No; the gentleman does not so much as urge that they have. All his emphasis is placed upon the fact that, in speaking of it, they call it the "first day of the week," instead of the "third after his crucifixion." He may well say that the distinction between these two forms of expression would be readily "passed over." Has it come to this, then, that the Holy Spirit, in enforcing important duties upon Christians, is compelled to depart from the natural, clear, and positive statement of facts, and to employ polemical niceties which, we believe, if they have any force at all, can only be discerned by minds whose susceptibilities for refinement are infinitely superior to those of common men and women, and the poor and ignorant to whom the gospel was preached.

If the *Sunday* had become the "*Christian Sabbath*," why not *say so?* If, indeed, it was on the " Lord's day " that Jesus arose, why was not this asserted ? Or, if the first day of the week was regarded as the Christian Sabbath, why such a studied avoidance of the application of this term to that day? Will the gentleman insist that if the evangelists had stated, in so many words, that the Lord appeared among them after his resurrection on the first "*Lord's day,*" or the first "*Christian Sabbath,*" that it would not have been just what the facts would have warranted, if his theory be correct, and that thereby all dispute, as to which day is the Lord's day, or Christian Sabbath, would have been forever terminated? Then why endeavor to impress the reader with the thought that there is really any peculiar significance in the form of expression employed, or that it furnishes a strong presumptive argument in favor of first-day sanctity?

The language of the historians is just that which men would use when speaking of a secular day, and not that which they would naturally employ when alluding to a consecrated one. The expression, "first day of the week," was not only the briefer —as compared to the other, that is, the "third day after the crucifixion"—but was definite in every particular. Once more, therefore, we insist that the fact that the inspired evangelists persisted, twenty years after the occurrence of the events recorded, in calling the Sunday "the first day of the week"—as they have done in the six times in which they have mentioned it—if guided at all in the selection of this term by the usage and opinions of the times in which they wrote, have furnished us with a commentary which, if it proves anything at all, proves that the day now regarded as holy was not so esteemed at that time by the disciples generally, else those among them who, as historians, would have been glad to have conferred upon it this honor, would have referred to it in the use of its sacred title, "Sabbath," or the "Lord's day."

As it regards the *design of Christ*, we take is-

sue with our friend, and offer the following reasons for our confident assertion that he is wrong:
1. His conclusion is not one which is either necessary or obvious. God has shown us his method of making a holy day. That method he has set forth in clear and positive statement, and the observance of such a day he has enforced by explicit command. This being the case, we must infer that he chose that manner because it was the best. Hence we should naturally conclude that when he wished to change the day of his choice, once enforced by a law still binding, he would make known his mind in a manner so clear and impressive that there could be no room for doubt. This, however, in the action of Christ alluded to, is far from being the case, because the meeting of the Lord with the apostles did not necessarily affect the nature of the time on which it occurred. Instance the fact heretofore cited, that he met with them on a fishing day (John chap. 21), and again on Thursday, the day of the ascension, without in any way changing the character of those days, as all will admit. Now, if this could be true of those two days, might it not also be true of the first day of the week?
2. Because, as we have seen, there is not the slightest evidence that the *apostles inferred* that it was the intention of Christ to produce the impression claimed. For, had this been the case, their convictions must have found expression for our benefit. 3. Because, manifestly, the conver-

sation of Christ is given, so far as it inculcated any duty not elsewhere expressed; and in his words there is no allusion to any design on his part to teach them that the time on which they were assembled was holy. 4. Because there is a sufficient reason found for the meeting of Christ with the apostles on these two occasions, in his desire to establish them in the conviction of his resurrection, and to instruct them in regard to future action.

Before passing from this branch of the subject, we must be allowed to express our surprise that, in the anxiety of our friend to make out his case, he has made a declaration which we think he would not have done had he been more deliberate in his selection of facts. He says, in speaking of John 20 : 26—the second and only additional instance in which, after the first, he claims that Christ met with the apostles on the first day of the week—as follows : "This interval of eight days, from and including the resurrection day, brings us, according to the common mode of reckoning, and as no one is disposed to dispute, to the first day of the next week." To this we reply that, if he means to be understood, by this statement, that there is no dispute as to whether the second gathering under consideration did occur just one week after the first, he mistakes greatly. It is by no means true that this is a matter about which there is no difference of opinion. In order to show the reader that we are right in this, we quote the following from many testimonies which might be introduced: "'After eight days' from this meeting, if made to signify only one week, necessarily carries us to the second day of the week. But a different expression is used by the Spirit of inspiration when simply one week is intended. 'After seven days,' is the chosen term of the Holy Spirit when designating just one week. 'After eight days,' most naturally implies the ninth or tenth day; but allowing it to mean the eighth day, it fails to prove that this appearance of the Saviour was upon the first day of the week." In a note on the above remarks, the same author says: "Those who were to come before God from Sabbath to Sabbath to minister in his temple, were said to come 'after seven days.' 1 Chron. 9 : 25; 2 Kings 11 : 5."—*Hist. of Sabbath, by J. N. Andrews*, p. 148.

Right here, also, is the proper place to give attention to the elaborate argument which is made to produce upon the mind of the reader the impression that the presence of Christ, in the two instances mentioned, was expressly designed for the purpose of distinguishing the two first-days (?) upon which he manifested himself to his disciples. We should not do justice to our opponent, should we refuse to grant him credit for making a doubtful circumstance go as far in his favor as it were possible for any man to do. What he has said is both poetic and pathetic. Poetic, because it is purely a figment of his own imagination. Pathetic, because the spectacle here brought to view is one which appeals most forcibly to the sympathies of the generous reader. Who would not commiserate the condition of men who, for six weary days, sat in public assembly, waiting the momentary expected advent of their Lord? Who would not rejoice when finally he appeared in their midst, even if it were on the first day of the week? How natural, too, it would be for the reader, having his sympathies thus aroused, to follow him who has shown an art, at least dramatic, in playing upon their feelings, to the conclusion to which he springs—not by the route of logical deduction—but by that of a more fascinating sentimentalism.

But before he does this, let us descend for a moment from the hights of fancy to the lower grounds of prosaic fact. It strikes us that the gentleman will discover that he has paid too high a price for what he has obtained. Where did he learn that they assembled on the six days in question? Assuredly not from the record, for that is silent upon this point. Nay, more; he does not himself claim that he has any written authority for it, but simply says that he "believes" so and so, and then proceeds to his deductions. Well, with this understanding of the matter, and knowing that it is merely an inference of the writer, let us follow his conclusions to their legitimate consequences. Having done this, we perceive, 1. That at last we have reached a whole week, every day of which was one of religious meetings, and yet not one word recorded in regard to the gatherings which occurred on six out of the seven days of the week. This being true by his own concession, what has become of that argument in which he indulged so largely in his effort to prove that because there was no account of a meeting of Christians on the Sabbath, they were consequently not in the habit of meeting on that day? Does it not fall to the ground, utterly emptied of all its force, if it ever had any? 2. Where, now, is his oft-repeated declaration that there is no account of the meeting of any of the apostles with a Christian church on the Sabbath, and the conclusion therefrom, that they therefore held none? Here is the admission of the writer himself, that the apostles and the church at Jerusalem did meet on at least one seventh day after the resurrection of Christ. 3. What has become of the instructive lesson which Christ imparted to his followers on the evening of the day of his resurrection? Has it not been insisted that that visit was made for the *especial purpose* of teaching them, by example, and by meeting with them, that the day on which it occurred was *holy time?* If we have rightly apprehended the logic of our opponent, this was the precise moral which our Lord designed to convey by his manifestation on that occasion. How clear it is that such a conviction has rested upon the mind of the writer, and how often he has repeated it.

But how was it with the apostles? Now, certainly, they were not *more obtuse* than *we* are. Assuredly, they knew as much about the will and purpose of Christ in meeting with them the first time, as we do now. Did *they* then infer that Christ met with them expressly for the purpose, not of honoring by positive precept, but by the fact of his assembling with them, the day on which that assembly occurred? If so, why should they, according to the view we are considering, have gathered themselves together every day for the whole subsequent week, expecting his presence? Would they not have discovered that *such presence*, under *such circumstances*, would have utterly *nullified* the moral lesson of the *first visit*, since it would not afterwards be true that the first day of the week was the *only one* which he had thus distinguished, thereby marking it out from the rest of the week?

So much for the consequences which would necessarily follow, had that occurred which the writer says he "believes" took place. But, fortunately, or unfortunately for him, the whole thing is a myth from beginning to end. The only force which it posseses lies in the assumed fact that it brings together eight meetings on consecutive days, on two of which, and two only, the

Lord met with his followers, those two being first days of the weeks to which they belonged. Therefore, before the statement can possess any argumentative power, we must first grant him the privilege of, assuming that six of these meetings occurred when there is not a scintilla of evidence in the sacred narrative to favor his view.

That must be a desperate cause indeed which compels its advocates to such a resort to make out their case. Nevertheless, if the conception has accomplished nothing more, it has furnished us a key by which we have been able to unlock the secret conviction of the writer, and by that means, we learn that he does not himself believe either that Christ *told* his disciples on the day of the resurrection that that was holy time; or that they had decided *in their own minds* that his visit necessarily pointed out this fact; or that the meeting of a Christian church on a secular day proves that they regarded that day as sacred; or that it is necessary to suppose that any church *disregarded the Sabbath*, simply because there is no *historic mention* of their observance of it. This being true, we hope from this time forward that we shall see a line of argument pursued which will be consistent with the admissions inadvertently made above.

Finally—as we have the concession of the writer, that the mention of the term, "first day of the week," in the texts under consideration, accorded with the use of language as employed twenty years after the crucifixion—let us glance at his proof-texts for ourselves. In doing so, the reader will bear in mind that these texts furnish all the gospel testimony in reference to the supposed repudiation of God's ancient Sabbath and the substitution of a new one in its place, and also that the terms employed, as stated above, were used with reference to their meaning at the time they were penned.

The first is found in Matt. 28 : 1-6. In Matt. 28 : 1, the apostle says : " In the end of the Sabbath, as it began to dawn toward the first day of the week, came Mary Magdalene and the other Mary to see the sepulcher." Now which day, in the parlance of the disciples of our Lord, twenty years after his death, was styled the Sabbath ? Which was mentioned by the use of a secular title, whereas, custom, reason, and religion, all warranted and would have seemed to demand the application to it of a religious title, such as Sabbath, or Lord's day ? We leave the reader to answer.

The next scripture is found in Mark 16 : 1, 2. Here, again, the same distinction is preserved between the holy and the profane. "When the Sabbath was past," the women who had bought sweet spices came to the sepulcher very early in the morning, the first day of the week. The next passage is in verse 9 of the same chapter, where it is barely stated that Jesus, having risen on the first day of the week, appeared first to Mary

Magdalene. Did the historian, Mark, ruthlessly wound the feelings of his Christian brethren, by neglecting two splendid opportunities for settling the matter of a change of days for all future generations, or did he not believe in such a change? Which view is the more consistent, under the circumstances, with the manner in which he speaks?

The next text in order, with the context, will be found in Luke 23 : 54–56, and 24 : 1. Let the reader turn to these passages in his Bible and examine them carefully. In Luke 23 : 56, it is stated that the women "rested the Sabbath day, according to the commandment;" and in the first verse of the following chapter, it is said that "upon the first day of the week, very early in the morning, they came unto the sepulcher." Here, again, Luke—than whom there is no sacred writer who uses terms more frequently with reference to their technical meaning—furnishes us a comment in perfect harmony with that of the others. Mark him; he is very specific. He says the women "rested the Sabbath day, according to the commandment." Observe, it is not the "*old* commandment," but "*the* commandment." But again, What day was it upon which they rested? It was the Sabbath day. How did it stand related in the order of the week to the first day? It was the day before it. Did the women, according to his statement, observe the first day? No; for they came to do that upon it which they would not do on the Sabbath, *i. e.*, to embalm the body of Christ. But were they deceived, and was the day on which they came to the tomb, after all, sacred to the Lord, because of the resurrection of Christ, which had occurred early in the morning? Was this indeed the Lord's day, the Christian Sabbath? And had the old Sabbath expired at the cross (Col. 2:16) before the deluded women rested upon it? Then we inquire again, Why should an inspired apostle pass by unimproved this magnificent opportunity for recognizing the new order of things by dropping that plain, unpretending "first day of the week," and stating for the benefit of posterity that the day on which they repaired to the sepulcher was the Sabbath of the commandment, as changed by the authority of Christ?

The remaining passages are those of John 20: 1, 19. Here, once more, it is stated that "the first day of the week cometh Mary Magdalene early to the sepulcher;" and also in the 19th verse, that Jesus met with his disciples in the evening of the first day of the week. In these words, John, the beloved disciple, like all before him, alludes to the day as though it were a common one.

Thus we have seen that the four gospel historians all unite in ignoring the sacred title of Sunday, if it had any, and merely designate it by its proper numeral; while three of them call the seventh day the Sabbath, and locate it in the week as the day which precedes the first.

Now we appeal to the candid reader in view of these facts, and ask him to decide which day of the week was looked upon as peculiarly sacred at the time the gospels were written, provided the gentleman is *right* in supposing that the historians used language with reference to its acceptance when they wrote, instead of what it meant when the events, which they record, transpired. We believe the verdict will not be long delayed. They call the seventh day "the Sabbath of the commandment." That commandment, it is conceded, is still binding. If it reads the same now that it did then, the day which was the Sabbath at that time, according to that commandment, is still the Sabbath according to the same commandment. But if that commandment has been changed, we once more challenge the religious world to furnish us a copy of it as it now reads. Until they do so, we shall continue to observe the Sabbath upon which the devout women rested; on which our Lord himself rested in the tomb from his labors; and which four inspired men, twenty years later, more or less, still persisted in calling "*the* Sabbath."

STATESMAN'S REPLY.

ARTICLE FOUR.

ARGUMENT FOR THE FIRST-DAY SABBATH FROM THE GIFT OF THE HOLY SPIRIT ON THE DAY OF PENTECOST.

THE testimony brought forward in our last number from the Gospels for the first-day Sabbath finds abundant confirmation in other portions of the New-Testament Scriptures. We shall confine ourselves in this article to the argument drawn from the beginning of the second chapter of the Acts: "And when the day of Pentecost was fully come, they were all with one accord in one place." There has been so much discussion of this passage that a somewhat careful consideration of it may be of interest in itself, as well as from its important connection with the subject now specially in hand. In regard to it, we note:

1. The day of the outpouring of the Spirit was the day of Pentecost—not some day preceding or following. The correct rendering of the original words is not, as Lightfoot gives it, "when the day of Pentecost had passed," nor as Hitzig would have it, "as the day of Pentecost was approaching its fulfillment;" but, "while the day of Pentecost was being fulfilled;" that is, during the progress of that particular day, or, as our authorized English version has it, "when the day of Pentecost was fully come."

2. This day of Pentecost, on which the Holy

Spirit was given, was the first day of the week. A number of eminent authorities, chief among whom is the chronologist Wieseler, compute it to have been the seventh. This question hinges upon that of the day of the Lord's death. It is almost universally admitted that Christ was crucified on Friday. But it is disputed whether that Friday was the fourteenth or the fifteenth of Nisan. From Leviticus 23:15, 16, we learn that Pentecost, signifying literally the fiftieth, was counted from the second day of unleavened bread. The paschal lamb was killed at the close of the fourteenth day of the month Abib or Nisan, and the next day, the fifteenth, was the first day of unleavened bread. This day was regarded as a holy Sabbath; and from the morrow following, that is, from the sixteenth of Nisan, fifty days were to be reckoned to determine the day of Pentecost.

Wieseler contends that the Lord was crucified on the fifteenth of Nisan—the first day of unleavened bread. The sixteenth of the month would therefore fall on the seventh day of the week, and fifty days, reckoned from and including this, according to the manner of the Jews, would fix the day of Pentecost on the Jewish Sabbath. It is interesting to observe that many who agree with Wieseler in regarding the Friday of Christ's crucifixion as the fifteenth of Nisan, still reckon the fifty days so as to make Pentecost fall on the first day of the week. Prominent among these chronologists is Canon Wordsworth.

In all frankness, we would admit that Wordsworth's reckoning will not hold. If the Friday on which the Lord was crucified was the fifteenth of Nisan, and if that day was observed as the first day of unleavened bread so that the specified fifty days would be reckoned from the following day, then Pentecost must have occurred on the seventh day of the week.

Others of our ablest scholars, such as Greswell, Elliott, and Schaff, maintain that the day on which our Lord was crucified was the fourteenth of Nisan. An exhaustive discussion of this whole question would be out of place in these columns. We give a brief, and we think conclusive, argument in favor of the view that the Friday of our Lord's death was the fourteenth of Nisan, and that therefore the fifteenth Nisan, or first day of unleavened bread, coincided with the Jewish Sabbath. The reasons in favor of this view are the following:—

(1.) The language of John, chap. 18 : 28, intimates clearly that the Jews had not, on the morning of Friday, yet partaken of the passover. Friday could not therefore have been the fifteenth of Nisan.

(2.) The same day, Friday, John states that "it was the preparation of the passover." (Chap. 19 : 14.) It seems next to impossible to understand this expression in any other way than as referring to that day, Friday, as the day of preparation for Passover observance, or, in other words, as the day preceding the fifteenth Nisan.

(3.) John's statement, in chap. 19 : 31, that the Sabbath following the day of crucifixion was "a high day," admits of no easy or natural explanation except that of the coincidence of the first day of unleavened bread, or the fifteenth Nisan, with the seventh-day Sabbath.

(4.) The anti-typical character of Christ, as the Paschal Lamb of God and the true Passover

Sacrifice (John 1:29, 36; 1 Cor. 5:7), would lead us to expect that the very day and hour of his death would correspond with the time of the killing of the typical Passover lamb. If it be urged that Christ himself, with his disciples, in obeying the requirements of the law, killed the Passover on the evening of the fourteenth, and that the Synoptical Gospels intimate this, it may be replied that such an interpretation of Matthew, Mark, and Luke, is not required, and that the exceeding difficulty, not to say impossibility, of harmonizing it with the statements already quoted from John, is quite decisive against it. It is much easier to interpret the Synoptists in the light of John's Gospel. In this chapter, 13:1, we are informed of a supper *before* the passover. That this was the same supper spoken of by the Synoptists, though one day before the usual time, in order that the true Passover lamb might be put to death at the time appointed, appears from the peculiar nature of the message sent by chosen apostles to the "good man of the house"—a message of special direction, pointing out something of an unusual character. (See Matthew 26:18; Mark 14:14; and Luke 22:11.) There are also in the Synoptical Gospels a number of statements showing that the Friday on which our Lord was crucified was not marked by the Sabbatic sacredness belonging to the first day of unleavened bread. (See Matthew 27:59; Mark 15:42, 46; Luke 23:56.) This seems to be the easiest and most natural way of harmonizing the apparent discrepancies between the Synoptists and John.

(5.) Wieseler's own chronological tables may be used against him to show that the Friday of our Lord's crucifixion was the fourteenth of Nisan. We would speak with becoming diffidence, in any attempt to make out a system of chronology for the events recorded in Scripture. There are, however, in Wieseler's elaborate book, tables independently proved to be accurate. By them, admitting the year of our Lord's crucifixion to have been A. D. 30, which is regarded by most chronologists as highly probable, and admitting also that the day was Friday, which will not be disputed, it is shown, beyond all doubt, that Christ died on the fourteenth of Nisan, and must have eaten the passover with his disciples on the first hours of that day, the preceding evening. The tables referred to show, by the most minute and accurate calculations, that in the year A. D. 30, the new moon for the month Nisan appeared on Wednesday, the next to the last day of the preceding month, corresponding to March 22, at eight minutes past eight o'clock in the evening. Hence, it would follow that the first day of Nisan commenced on Friday evening, March 24, corresponding, as to daylight, with Saturday, March 25; of course, the Friday of the next week, would be the seventh Nisan, and the same day, the following week, the fourteenth. Thus, according to Wieseler's own tables, Friday of the week of our Lord's passion is made out to be the fourteenth of Nisan. The fifteenth of Nisan, then, or the first day of unleavened bread, coincided at that time with the seventh day of the week, or the Jewish Sabbath; and reckoning fifty days from the morrow, that day included, we find Pentecost falling on the first day of the eighth week following our Lord's crucifixion.

So clear and emphatic is the testimony of the

primitive church to this fact that many who hold that the Friday of Christ's death was the fifteenth Nisan still do so in cordial indorsement of that fact. They reconcile the apparent difference between John and the Synoptists by supposing that the Jewish authorities, probably because of the crucifixion, or for some other reason, did not observe the Passover at the usual time, but, passing by the fifteenth Nisan, in reality kept the sixteenth in its place; and thus counting the fifty days from the seventeenth of the month, instead of the sixteenth, Pentecost would fall on the first day of the week.

It is worth mentioning, before we pass on, that the Karaite Jews, like the Sadducees before them, understand the word "Sabbath" in Leviticus 23: 11, 15, 16, to mean, not the first day of unleavened bread, which was kept as a Sabbath, on whatever day of the week it might fall, but the seventh day of the week, the regular weekly Sabbath of the Jews. According to this understanding, the fifty days would always be reckoned from the morrow after the seventh day, and Pentecost would always fall on the first day of the week.

Having thus been at some pains to establish the fundamental position in this argument, a position to which scholars generally are coming with constantly increasing unanimity, we need not dwell long upon the manifest application of what has been proven. The facts here, after Christ's ascension, are full of significance, as we have seen the facts to be concerning the days just succeeding his resurrection. After the Lord's ascension, his disciples abode in Jerusalem, awaiting the promised gift of the

Spirit. Many days passed by, including two seventh days, and still no fulfillment of the promise. On the first day of the second week after the ascension, the disciples were all with one accord in one place. Once more, the day which the Lord had singled out and honored is specially honored by the plentiful effusion of the Spirit of God. And thus the day which Christ taught his disciples to regard with special sacredness, by repeatedly appearing to them in their collective gatherings, and blessing them, is even more clearly and significantly marked out from the other days of the week by this most marvelous outpouring of the Holy Spirit.

If it be objected that it was the Jewish festival, and not the first day of the week, that was honored, it is readily replied that there is no trace of the services of the Jewish festival on that blessed day. The Holy Ghost was given, not to persons observing Jewish ordinances and keeping the Pentecost of the old dispensation with a new meat-offering and first-fruits. He was given to Christian disciples met on the Christian's honored day; and the disciples who on that day had received important spiritual instructions from the Lord just after his resurrection, and who now, on the same day, received the promised Spirit, begin the true work of the Christian Sabbath by preaching the gospel of salvation, and three thousand souls are added to the church of Christ.

The objection, on the score that Pentecost only happened to fall on the first day that year, is unworthy of any one who believes that "not a sparrow falls to the ground, without our Heavenly Father's notice." It has been admitted that if the view of the Karaite Jews were true, and Pentecost occurred every year on the first day of the week, then would there be a strong argument for the first-day Sabbath in the pre-arrangements of God's providence. But to our mind, the argument from the pre-arrangement of providence is stronger on the other and better interpretation of Leviticus 23:11, 15, 16. He who in infinite wisdom arranged everything from the beginning, so ordered all events connected with Christ's death, as to make the day of Pentecost coincide with the Christian Sabbath, and then gathered to himself, not the first-fruits of the fields of grain, but three thousand immortal souls, the first-fruits of the ingathering of the spiritual fields white to the harvest—the harvest of all the Gentile nations yet to be brought into the church of Christ, with the restoration of the covenant people of old. This is a Pentecost worthy of the church of Him who died for sinners of every race, and of the honored day which commemorates his rising from the dead.

A REJOINDER.

"ARGUMENT FOR THE FIRST-DAY SABBATH FROM THE GIFT OF THE HOLY SPIRIT ON THE DAY OF PENTECOST."

It is always a source of satisfaction to one, in examining opinions from which he is compelled to differ, to feel that the presentation of them which he is considering is the best which could be made under the circumstances. With pleasure, therefore, we recognize the manifest tokens of research and erudition on the part of the author of the views presented in the columns of the *Statesman*, in the communication entitled, "Argument for the first-day Sabbath from the gift of the Holy Spirit on the day of Pentecost." We do not flatter ourselves, however, that all which has been said in that article was for our benefit. It is not a little remarkable that three-fourths of its contents are devoted to the settlement of a point, which—while indeed it affects the question at issue—is not one upon which we bestowed many words, having preferred to consider, for the sake of argument, that the Pentecost did, on the year of our Lord's crucifixion, fall upon the first day of the week; and then, having done this, to prove that this coincidence in no way affected, necessarily, the nature of that day.

Nevertheless, we must beg leave here to express our gratitude that, notwithstanding the concession in question, the readers of the *Statesman* are at last instructed by an abler pen than our own in reference to the diversity of opinion which exists among the learned as to whether, indeed, it is safe to conclude that the Sunday, to the exclusion of the Sabbath, was the day upon which the Holy Spirit descended upon the apostles. Be it remembered, also, that the learned men who stand as the advocates of the seventh day as the one which God thus honored were not observers of that day as the Sabbath. All the authorities quoted are men who, if they regarded any Sabbath at all, gave their preference to the first, and not to the last, day of the week. This being the case, they certainly cannot be charged with any bias in favor of the creation Sabbath. Not only so, but all their predilections were doubtless against that day, and favorable to its rival. Hence we see that when, under these circumstances, it is admitted that such distinguished men as Lightfoot, Weiseler, and Hitzig, have agreed that the last day of the week was the one on which the Pentecost occurred at the time in question, they did so—not in the interest of preconceived notions, nor for the purpose of bolstering up a theory which was in desperate need of help—but because there was, to their minds, at least, much which compelled a conclusion they would gladly have avoided.

Right here, also, in order to widen the breach in the wall of evidence, we beg leave to act in harmony with the plan pursued by the writer, and to present a note from the pen of one no less distinguished than Professor Hackett, which will make it manifest beyond dispute that the scholars who at the present time sympathize with those cited above, who regard the seventh day of the week and not the first as having been the day of the Pentecost, are both numerous and celebrated: "It is generally supposed that this Pentecost, signalized by the outpouring of the Spirit, fell on the Jewish Sabbath, our Saturday." Quoted in "Hist. of Sab.," by J. N. A., page 150. Let the reader bear in mind that we are not assuming to decide between these long lines of doctors who differ so widely upon a very important point, as regarded by some ; but that our purpose is simply to call attention to the fact of this discrepancy, and to show its bearing upon the subject under discussion.

The first query which should be propounded, therefore, is this : Has God ever declared that the day of the Pentecost, which we are trying to locate, was identical with the first day of the week ? The answer is in the negative. There is not one word in the text (Acts 2 : 1, 2), or in the Testament, in regard to the day of the week on which these events occurred. It is simply stated that they took place "when the day of Pentecost was fully come." How remarkable, if the object was not to honor a feast which occurred annually, but especially for the purpose of distinguishing the first day of the week ! Before, however, that day could be illustrated by the outpouring of the Holy Spirit upon it, it must first be decided—and that, too, from Bible evidence—that such outpouring did occur on the day specified. Can this be done ? We appeal for a response to the average Christian men and women of this time. Tell me, after having read the three-column argument of the gentleman, has not the effect of what he has said been to unsettle, rather than to establish, your convictions upon the point before our minds? If .never before, is it not now true that you feel somewhat shaken in regard to the identity of the Sunday with the Pentecost, on the year of the crucifixion? In view of what has been written, would you undertake to establish your faith from any deduction which you yourself could make from plain Scripture declarations? Is it not true that your opinion in the premises depends entirely upon the faith of the one or the other class of scholars who have ranged themselves on both sides of this subject? Has the religion of Jesus Christ then changed? Is it no longer true that its great and important practical truths are withheld "from the wise and prudent, and revealed unto babes"? Has God left the important question of first-day sanctity, not upon the solid basis of explicit command, but upon the doubtful inference which is to be derived from certain transactions which occurred on a certain day, and then left the day of their occurrence to occupy a position in the week so doubtful that the most learned of those who had a desire to keep it should be honestly divided in opinion as to which day it was? We believe not. To our mind, it is simple presumption to intimate that God—who is not willing that any should perish, and who has said that he will do nothing but he will reveal it to his servants the prophets—should deal with his creatures in a manner at once so indirect and so obscure.

Having seen that there is a wide divergence of views among the very men who are the observers of the modern Sunday, in regard to its claims to distinction on the score of its having been first honored by the outpouring of the Spirit on the fiftieth day after the resurrection, let us look for a moment at the situation with reference to the possible effect upon the seventh day, of the logic employed. Taking it for granted that our friends would not fly from their favorite deduction provided it should prove to be true that they are mistaken in regard to the time of the Pentecost, let us concede, for the time being, that the long line of celebrities, headed by such men as Lightfoot, Weiseler, and Hitzig, were right in arguing that Saturday, and not Sunday, was the day on which the great Jewish festival occurred; then, beyond all dispute, it must be conceded by our opponents that this was but another effort on the part of Jehovah to illustrate, for the benefit of succeeding generations, the day which he had previously made memorable by his resting, his blessing, and his sanctification. In other words, with this view of the design of the outpouring of the Spirit, the effect upon the ancient Sabbath would be the same as it is now claimed to have been upon the first day of the week. The point, therefore, of the identity of the days is to *them* a *vital* one.

If they are wrong in this, they are wrong in all. We appeal to them, therefore, in view of the infinite consequences which hang upon the proper celebration of the right Sabbath, to at least make their logic so plain that it will be accepted by men of their own faith, before they speak of its strength with great assumption of confidence. Before any person has a right to employ the events which transpired at the time of the Pentecostal outpouring of the Spirit in the interest of Sunday sanctity, he must be able to solve, at least to the satisfaction of his own mind, all the difficulties which complicate this question. As God has never seen fit to say that the Jewish feast, at the time under consideration, transpired on the first day of the week, he must be able to establish that proposition independently of an explicit *thus saith the Lord*.

There are two ways by which this may be attempted. (1.) By proving that the Pentecost always took place on the first day of the week; or, (2.) By demonstrating that Christ was crucified on Friday, the fourteenth day of Nisan, and that consequently the Pentecost must have fallen upon a Sunday following, and separated from that day by about fifty days. But, so far as the first proposition is concerned, which would be by far the easier of demonstration, if it were true— should the reader be inclined to favor it—he must convince himself that he could establish it against the conviction and the learning of the writer in question; for he rejects it as being untenable. Should he therefore turn to the second, then, as remarked above, he must be able to prove, not merely that Christ died on the fourteenth day of the Jewish month Nisan, but that likewise that fourteenth day of the month was also the sixth day of the week. When we say that this will be a task which few minds are capable of performing, and from which those who are best informed will the most readily turn away, we but assert what the writer in question has very distinctly shadowed forth in the facile manner in which he disposes of the obscurity of the statements in the three Synoptical Gospels by arbitrarily deciding that they must be interpreted by that of John.

What the real object of the writer was in making the statement that the Karaites and the Sadducees held to the first theory stated above, we are at a loss to decide, since he himself concludes that they were wrong in their hypothesis. But let us suppose for a moment that they were right, and that the Pentecost always followed the weekly Sabbath; would that prove that it occurred on Sunday? We answer, Yes. But would it prove that Sunday was therefore holy time? We answer, No; it would not so much as touch this independent question. Or rather, it should be said, if it affected it at all, it would increase the strength of the seventh-day Sabbath argument. Do you ask, How? We answer that, according to their theory, you must first have a weekly Sabbath before you could decide when you had reached the Pentecost Sunday. The direction in Leviticus was, that they should count to themselves seven Sabbaths from the day that they brought the sheaf of the wave-offering, which would bring them to the feast in question.

Now let it be supposed that the crucifixion answered to the ancient Passover, and that the apostles proceeded to the determination of the time when the Pentecost would be reached, according to the theory of the Karaites. The first thing which would have been necessary was, the weekly Sabbath, which immediately followed the crucifixion of Christ. Having found it, they would have numbered seven Sabbaths, and have decided that the day immediately following the last of these answered to the feast. But unfortunately for them they would have discovered— had they believed in the modern doctrine that the law of the Sabbath was nailed to the cross, Col. 2 : 16 (?)—that they were deprived of a starting point; for the Sabbath institution is a thing of commandment. Take away the commandment, and the institution is gone. Therefore, as the cross had accomplished its work, and had been taken down on Friday, God had removed the landmark from which they were commanded to measure the time which should bring them to the Pentecost at the very period when they needed it most. In reality, there was left them no Sabbath which answered to the one in Leviticus.

Should it be replied, however, that the Sabbath, though gone in fact, existed nevertheless in name, it might be responded that this would indeed be an anomalous condition of things. Mark it: it is not the incidental mention, by its proper name, of an institution which had ceased to be, which we are considering; but it is the deliberate action of that God who knows the end from the beginning, in compelling the disciples to treat the seventh day of the week as the Sabbath, in order to the decision of an important fact; for eight weeks after, as is claimed, it had lost its Sabbatic character.

Again; should it be urged, as a means of escape from the embarrassments of the situation, that God did not actually require them to count the seventh day as the Sabbath, since there was really no day of Pentecost which they were obliged to keep on the year of our Lord's crucifixion, we answer, Very good. Then, of course, we shall hear nothing hereafter from the argument for Sunday sanctity which is based upon the hypothesis that the day of Pentecost fell on the first day of the week in the year in question, since it will have been admitted that there was no Pentecost that year, and consequently that it could not properly be said to have fallen upon any day.

Once more; should it be insisted that though

the Pentecostal feast was not binding in the year of our Lord 30, or thereabout, but that the antitype of the feast was the thing of importance, then, in reply, it may be said that God rendered it necessary for them, in order to locate that antitype according to the Karaite view, to count the Sabbath which followed the crucifixion as the Sabbath of creation, a thing which certainly will be very difficult of explanation by those who can speak as becomingly of the providence of God as did the gentleman in the article which is passing under review.

Finally, we repeat, therefore, that, if indeed there were a legal Pentecost this side of the death of our Lord, and if the Karaite system for locating it were the right one, then the seventh day which followed the death of Christ was distinguished by three very significant facts. 1. It was honored by the women (and therefore by the disciples) by their resting upon it. 2. Luke, in speaking of it thirty years subsequent to its occurrence, mentions it as the Sabbath, "according to the commandment." 3. God made it necessary that the whole Jewish nation should keep the Pentecostal feast fifty days after the crucifixion of the Lord; and, in doing so, that they should count the seventh day of the week as still continuing to be the Sabbath.

In passing to the last branch of the subject, which will be treated in this article, we invite the reader to note the following facts, as we shall have occasion to employ them hereafter: 1. That the writer proceeds with his reasoning upon the hypothesis that the months at the time of the crucifixion were Jewish months, commencing with the new moon. 2. That the days were Jewish days, commencing and ending with the setting of the sun. These points we have previously urged, and are happy to see that they are conceded as being correct.

In conclusion, we turn our attention to the remaining feature of the communication in the *Statesman*, *i. e.*, that portion of the article which relates to the real matter in dispute, namely—granting, for the sake of argument, that the first day of the week was the one on which the Pentecost fell in the year under consideration—whether that fact necessarily affected the character of that day so as to mark it out as one which God had chosen as peculiarly his own. For, be it remembered, that—though the whole argument which has been made respecting the identity of those two days should be conceded—we should then simply be prepared to decide whether the facts agreed upon would prove what is claimed, or not.

We ask, therefore, the candid attention of all to the use which has been made of the elaborate argument which we have been carefully considering, point by point. We would naturally have expected—if the gentleman felt that he had proved what he desired to, namely, that the Pentecost fell upon the first day of the week—that the real sinews of a masterly logic would have been discovered in an effort to show that it followed of necessity that it must therefore have been holy time. But has he done this? Or, in other words, if he has, in what manner has he brought it about? Has it been by fair logical deduction? We believe that there are very few who will insist that he has attempted such a deduction, with any measure of success, at the very point where it should have been expected most.

What he has said in the connection is very *pretty*. Yes, pretty is the word which precisely expresses it. How handsomely he alludes to the analogy between the natural harvest and the ingathering of souls. But who does not know that such analogies are cheap things, and that one gifted with a prolific fancy can multiply them indefinitely? What was expected, and what we had a right to demand, was something which partook of the nature of certainty. How great was our disappointment at learning that the writer did not even *pretend to have any authority from the Lord*, so far as written statements are concerned. The whole thing he thought was fairly *deducible* from the coincidence of days, since nothing ever merely "happens" to occur in the providence of God.

What has been gained, then? Manifestly, simply the point that God had some object in view in having the Pentecost fall on the first day of the week in the year of our Lord 30, or thereabout. The next question to be decided is, What was that object? Right here is where we *need help*. God could have given it to us, had he *seen fit* so to do. He has not done so, therefore it is safe to conclude that it was not important that we should know what his purpose was.

But if any gentleman can be found who is *wise above what is written*, and who is able to decide with unerring certainty as to the motives of God at all times, and under all circumstances, we should like to propound a few questions to him. First, what did God mean when, in his providence, he allowed the Pentecost to fall upon Monday, Tuesday, Wednesday, Thursday, Friday, or Saturday? It is said that God *had a purpose* in it; but can any one tell us *what* that purpose was? When he has answered this, then we have a list of similar interrogatories, to the solution of which his wisdom will be invited. In the meantime, we shall adopt the suggestions of men in regard to plans of Deity with great caution, for, if it should fall out in the day of Judgment that we had followed their fallacious inferences, to the disregard of a positive, written law of God, we know not what defense could be made for our course of conduct, since we had been previously informed that "his judgments are *unsearchable*," "and his ways *past finding out*."

Now let us look at the proposition concerning the outpouring of the Spirit. It is agreed on all hands that the manifestation occurred as written. It is inferred by the writer in question that it was done with reference especially to the honoring as sacred of the day of the resurrection. Here, again, is the assumption of knowledge which has never been imparted by divine authority. God has never *said* that he meant any such thing. Not only so, but it cannot even be fairly inferred that such was his purpose. First. Because he does not so much as mention, in the record, the first day of the week by name, an omission which can never be explained satisfactorily by those who insist that the events which occurred on the day of Pentecost transpired with especial reference to the honoring above all others, on the part of Jehovah, of the first day of the week. Secondly. Because, were we to judge at all in the matter, as he passed over six first-days, waiting for the arrival of the Pentecost, we must conclude that there was something in connection with that feast which induced him to act when he did, and as he did. Thirdly. Because the Pentecost furnished an opportunity for the display of the power of the ascended Christ before thousands of Jews and proselytes from all parts of the habitable globe, more advantageously than could be done at any other time; thus rendering it unnecessary that any other reason should be sought in explanation of its selection from among the other days of the year for the great outpouring of the Spirit. Fourthly. Because, in apostolic times, it was not an uncommon thing for the Holy Ghost to fall upon men on all days of the week; thus proving that God is not restricted in the outpouring of his Spirit to holy times and places, and that it is not safe to conclude that any display of his power in this direction was made at any one time because of a special regard for the particular hours on which it took place.

In conclusion, as the fabric of Sunday sanctity, in so far as it is based upon the transactions of the day of Pentecost, is seen to rest, purely upon the opinions of men, and since those who observe the day are divided in sentiment as to whether the Pentecost did indeed really fall upon it at all, we close this article, as we did the last, by stating that we have a *positive commandment* which is admitted to be binding, and which, as given in the Bible, says that the "seventh day is the Sabbath of the Lord thy God; in it thou shalt not do any work." Also, that our advice to those who are weary with threading the interminable labyrinth of conjecture and hypothesis is, Place your feet upon the rock of the written word; there, and there only, you are safe. Should any one seek to lure you from this position by the assertion that the law upon which you have planted yourself has been amended, it will be safe to follow them only when they are able to tell you when and where the commandment, as given in Exodus, was changed, and exactly how it reads since the change has occurred.

STATESMAN'S REPLY.

ARTICLE FIVE.

THE FIRST-DAY SABBATH AT TROAS.

THE day on which the Saviour rose from the dead, the day which the risen Saviour singled out and blessed repeatedly with his presence, the day on which the Holy Ghost was given to the church,—this honored day certainly could not pass without stated observance by the disciples of the risen and ascended Lord. It is but reasonable to expect that the day which Christ and the Holy Spirit honored would be honored by the early church.

Passing on in the sacred narrative, we come to the account of first-day Sabbath observance some twenty-six or twenty-eight years after the Pentecostal gift of the Spirit. In just such a matter-of-course way as that in which a well-known and established custom would be noted, is the observance of the first day at Troas mentioned in Acts 20 : 6, 7 : " We sailed away from Philippi after the days of unleavened bread, and came . . . to Troas in five days, where we abode seven days. And upon the first day of the week, when the disciples came together to break bread, Paul preached unto them, ready to depart on the morrow, and continued his speech until midnight." Several important points should here be noted :—

1. Paul and his companions remained at Troas

seven days—from the third day of one week until the second day of the next week.

2. At this time, there was at Troas a company or church of Christian disciples, who would, of course, hold regular religious services.

3. Besides the Trojan Christians, there were at Troas, during these "seven days," at least nine others, including Paul and Luke (see verse 4), who would not let a week pass without observing a stated day of worship. And yet,

4. Neither the disciples resident at Troas, nor Paul and his companions, pay any regard to the seventh day. The whole narrative plainly intimates that Paul held himself in readiness to depart, waiting only for the stated weekly day of public service. And the seventh day has no more sacredness assigned to it than the fifth or sixth. Had it been the customary day of meeting, the disciples would have assembled on it, and Paul would have been ready to depart *on the morrow*, the first day of the week. On the other hand,

5. The first day of the week was observed as the stated, customary weekly day of divine service by the Christians at Troas. The word, rendered "came together," indicates this. It is most intimately related to the word in Hebrews 10:25, rendered "assembling together." The latter is the noun, with an added preposition from the former word, the verb. These two terms, and another kindred word, are the common terms for regular church meetings in the New Testament. (See Hebrews 10:25; 1 Cor. 11:17, 18; 14:23, 26.) Again, it will be noticed that the meeting of the disciples on this first day was for regular public services of the Christian

church. They came together to "break bread," or observe the Lord's supper, and to hear the preaching of the gospel. Besides, let it be noticed, it is not said that Paul summoned the disciples together; but it is said that they "came together." Or, if we follow the reading of the oldest manuscripts, the customary character of this Christian first-day assemblage will be made even more manifest. This reading is as follows: "And upon the first day of the week, when *we* came together." Whether this is the correct reading or not, it expresses undoubtedly the fact. Paul, Luke, and their companions, as well as the Trojan Christians, met for divine service, according to the usual practice of Christians generally, on the first day of the week.

It remains for us to consider the mode of reckoning time which would fix Paul's departure from Troas on the morning of the first day of the week. Frankness and justice require us to state that even so authoritative a writer as Mr. Howson, in that able and scholarly work, "The Life and Epistles of St. Paul," adopts this mode of reckoning, and, in accordance with it, pictures out Paul's solitary journey from Troas to Assos on the hallowed hours of the Christian Sabbath.

No one will dispute for a moment that, according to the Jewish mode of reckoning, the day would begin at sundown, and in this way the evening of the meeting at Troas would be the evening succeeding the seventh day, and Paul's journey of nearly twenty miles would be on the first day of the week. But it is perfectly clear from the Scriptures that the Roman method of reckoning the commencement of the day had already, to some extent, supplanted the Jewish mode. Nor is it any wonder that the method of the Romans, who were at the time in authority in Palestine, should have obtained some recognition, even among the Jews.

John, in a passage quoted in a former article, uses the following language: "The same day at evening, being the first day of the week." (John 20:19.) The meeting at Troas, in the evening of the first day, may not have been without reference to the meeting of the Lord with his disciples late in the evening of the same day he arose from the dead. But whether there is any reference in the meeting at Troas to the meeting recorded by John or not, the passage above quoted clearly proves that the late evening succeeding the first day of the week was reckoned a part of the first day, and not a part of the day following—"The *same* day at evening [*opsia*, late evening, after dark, it would appear], being the first day of the week."

Matthew, writing particularly for Jewish Christians, adopts the Roman method in chap. 28:1, in the expression: "In the end of the Sabbath [literally, late of the Sabbath, *opse*, late, away on after dark], as it began to dawn toward the first day of the week." Here, manifestly, the seventh day is reckoned as continuing during a number of hours, which, according to the Jewish mode, belonged to the following day. If Matthew, writing for Jewish Christians, employs the Roman mode of reckoning, is it not altogether probable that Luke, writing especially for Gentiles, would adopt the same mode?

But we need only look carefully at Luke's own language to settle this point. His statement is that Paul preached, "ready to depart *on the morrow.*" It is agreed on all hands that the Christian disciples at Troas came together on the first day of the week, and that Paul preached to them on that day. Now, if the time of meeting was the evening succeeding the seventh day, according to the Jewish mode of reckoning, could it be said that Paul, taking his leave at a later hour that same day, departed *on the morrow?* The original term, *epaurion*, is an adverb, literally signifying "upon the morrow." But connected with it is the feminine article, agreeing with the word, "day," understood. This makes the expression, if possible, still more explicit— "the day which is the morrow," the next day. Can there remain the slightest doubt as to Luke's meaning? The Christian congregation at Troas met on one day of the week. Paul preached to them on that day. It was the first day. *On the morrow*, not the same day, but another, the following, the second day of the week, Paul departed, as he had held himself for some days in readiness to do, on his way to Assos. Thus, as we have a right to expect, there is no violation by the apostle and his fellow-Christians of the law of the Sabbath.

We have not dwelt upon this question of different modes of reckoning because of any importance which may be claimed for it in connection with the main inquiry before us. It is entirely immaterial to the point at issue in this discussion whether Luke employs the Jewish or the Roman mode. Even if it could be made to appear that he makes use of the former, there could be found nothing in his narrative in favor of the seventh-day Sabbath. The argument for the first-day Sabbath would still remain in its integrity, leaving for consideration simply the question as to the consistency of certain acts, in a certain case, with the law of a holy day of rest and worship. For the sake of giving a pretty full exposition of a passage important in itself, and because a wrong interpretation has been given by high authority in countenance of a mischievous theory of the Sabbath, we have occupied much of our space for this issue in showing that the evening or night of the first day of the week was the end of the Christian Sabbath, and that Paul and his companions, like good, Sabbath-keeping Christians, waited, though ready to depart, until Monday morning, before starting on their journey to Assos.

We propose to conclude the argument from Scripture in our next number. After this, we shall give the testimony of the standard authorities of the first three centuries of the Christian era. And then, with the facts concerning sacred time before us, we shall inquire what theory of the Sabbath harmonizes all the authenticated facts into one consistent whole.

A REJOINDER.

"THE FIRST-DAY SABBATH AT TROAS."

IN entering upon an examination of the propositions laid down in the article entitled, "The First-day Sabbath at Troas," it will be well for us first to inquire into the object which the writer had in view in presenting them for our consideration. In doing so, we shall find that he does not claim that the text or context of Acts 20:7, furnishes any positive precept for Sunday observance. His effort is merely to establish a custom. Suppose, therefore, that we should grant all that he asks, so far as the church of Troas is concerned, would that prove that Christians universally are under obligation to follow a like custom? We think not, unless it can be shown that God has adopted this mode of inculcating religious duty. But this he has never done. If the writer had first established a positive law, then he might, with some show of reason, appeal to custom to show that that law was interpreted as he understands it; but when he reverses the order, and endeavors to prove the law by the custom, then he has reversed God's great plan, which is that of teaching by explicit statute.

Furthermore, even should a custom be established, the writer must be able to show that such a custom was kept up, not as a matter of convenience or taste, but because of a conviction of religious duty. In other words, it is possible, to say the least, that the church at Troas were in the habit of meeting on the first day of the week, not because they looked upon it as holy time, but for certain utilitarian purposes, best known to themselves. Let us furnish an illustration precisely in point:—

Should some person, eighteen hundred years hence—provided time should last so long—write a history of the present period, as he cast his eye over the literature of our day, he would find that, in all parts of this country, Christians were in the habit of assembling on Wednesday evening, for the purposes of worship. Would he, therefore, be justified in concluding that Wednesday is regarded by us as peculiarly sacred to the Lord? You answer, No, and most properly, for you know that our motives are entirely different from what he would understand them to be. So, too, with Troas. Granted, for the sake of the argument, that, as the writer claims, they were in the habit of assembling on the late Sunday evening; it by no means follows that they did so because they regarded it as devoted to the Lord. Does he say that they partook of the sacrament on that day? Grant that, for the sake of the argument. But does not every student of the Bible know, and is it not the conviction of the world to-day, that the Lord's supper can be partaken of with as much propriety at one time as at another? Is it not a fact that the time of its institution did not coincide with Sunday? Is it not true that originally they partook of it on all days of the week? (Acts 2:42, 46.) If so, it would manifestly be unsafe to attach any special significance to the fact that, at this time, it was celebrated on the Sunday, So much for the hypothesis of the *custom* in question.

Now that we have said what we have with reference to a custom made out, it will be well to inquire in the next place, Has the writer established the usage which he sought to prove? If so, we have failed to discover the process by which it has been done. Has he found an explicit statement that the church at Troas was in the habit of meeting on the first day of the week? Very far from it. Having traced the sacred narrative for twenty-six years—mark it, reader, over one-fourth of a century—he has found a solitary assembly of Christians convened on the first day of the week. But what were the facts in the case? Was this an ordinary occasion? Were they by themselves alone? No; it was a time of unusual interest. The great apostle to the Gentiles was there, paying them a flying visit. He was about to depart on the morrow. It was perhaps the last time they would ever see him. They wanted to partake of the emblems of the Lord's body from his venerated hand. They wanted to shake that hand in a final farewell, and to plant the kiss of love upon his careworn face. The circumstances, then, were unusual. The same combination of facts might never exist again. There is, therefore, so far as the general view is concerned, nothing which would justify the decision that they had ever convened for like reasons, previously, at the same time of the week, or that they ever would thereafter. The writer evidently felt this, and, with an acuteness of intellectual perception which to the common mind is almost incredible, he has discovered overwhelming support for his theory, where the ordinary reader would have discerned none.

How strange it is that, again and again, we find that the strongholds of Sunday sanctity are located just beyond the boundary where the man of average ability and learning is permitted to go. The Greek, he is told, has a significance which, if rightly expressed, would establish a custom beyond all doubt. Well, we have seen above what the value of a custom is, unless explained. But we ask—and we ask it in the behalf of the millions who have never so much as seen even the Greek alphabet, and yet to whom eternal life is as precious as to the man of letters—can it be possible that God has suspended the terrible realities of Heaven and hell upon the discharge of a duty vailed from their eyes by the obscurity of a language whose mysteries they can never hope to penetrate? For, mark it, this is not one of those points which can be settled without difficulty, even by those familiar with the tongue in question. Were our learning equal to that of the gentleman who has penned the criticism under consideration, we might flatly contradict the statements which he makes; but this would simply serve to produce a dead-lock in the mind of the reader, while he remained as far from a satisfactory solution of the difficulty as ever. The only reply which we shall make, therefore, is as follows:—

The distinction drawn between the present

text and the original is either obscure, or it is obvious. If it is obscure, it is unimportant; if obvious, then it could be seen by scholars, and is so important that it would have attracted universal attention and comment by first-day writers and translators. What, therefore, are the facts in the case? Certain it is that, if it exists at all, it escaped the notice of the translators of our common version. That they would have given a rendering as favorable to the first day as the facts would warrant, no man will dispute. The suggestion that the text would bear the translation, "*we* having come together to break bread," &c.,* while it does not materially alter the sense, so far as the practice of the church at Troas is concerned, if admissible, renders it highly probable that Luke and his associates were there until the breaking of the bread; a point which we shall use hereafter. In the meantime, we give the following translations in order to show the conviction of their authors, respecting the meaning of the original:—

"And on the first day of the week, when we assembled," &c.—*Syriac.*

"On the first day of the week, when we were met together."—*Wesley, N. T., with Notes.*

"And upon the first day of the week, when the disciples were got together."—*Wakefield.*

---

* As it is not insisted that this translation is a correct one, I shall not turn aside for the purpose of showing, as might easily be done, from the original, that it is not admissible where the rule of strict construction is followed.

"And on the first day of the week, the disciples being assembled."—*Whiting.*

"And on the first day of the week, we, having come together to break bread."—*Am. Bible Union.*

"And on the first day of the week, we being assembled to break bread."—*Sawyer.*

"And on the first day of the week, when the disciples met together."—*Doddridge in Campbell and Macknight's Trans.*

"And on the first day of the week, we having assembled."—*Emphatic Diaglott.*

We think the reader is now ready to admit that the traces of a custom which relies for its existence upon an original text, rendered as given above by so many different persons, none of whom can be charged with favoring the seventh-day Sabbath, are, to say the least, too faint to be of practical argumentative utility. To our mind, the inference is simply this: Paul, about to depart on his journey to Jerusalem, appointed, for himself and his companions and the disciples at Troas, a final meeting, at which it was announced that the Eucharist would be celebrated. At this meeting, all the parties came together, agreeably to the announcement previously made, and partook of the Lord's supper. A fitting close of a week of apostolic labor in an Asiatic city.

The next item worthy of our attention is found in the hypothesis, that, during the time Paul was at Troas, the seventh day of the week was passed by without any religious meeting occurring thereupon; and that Paul waited until the arrival of the first day, because that was the one on which the meetings of the church were regularly held. How a writer so intimately acquainted with the character and labors of St. Paul, as the individual in question undoubtedly is, could draw the inference which he has, is more than we can fathom. Who, that has read the history of a man whose nervous activity drove him to dispute daily in the school of Tyrannus (Acts 19 : 9), and to seek every opportunity for the presentatian of his gospel to the Jews in their synagogues, and the Greeks in their places of public gathering, could be induced to believe that he could remain for seven long days in the city of Troas without a solitary religious assembly, until the expiration of that time? And yet this is the very decision which we are called upon to indorse. Before we can do this, however, we ask for the proof. The answer is, it must be so, because the record contains no account of the holding of such meetings until the first day of the week.

But is this satisfactory? Do not all the circumstances of the case, as well as the temperament and character of Paul, render certain the fact that such meetings were held, even though it is not stated in so many words? Paul with a Christian church at Troas for one week, and not preach to them! Impossible. To show the writer that the mention of religious meetings in a brief history is not necessary in order to prove that they occurred on a given day, or on stated days, let me call his attention to the fact, that, between the day of Pentecost and the meeting at Troas, according to his own showing, there were at least twenty-six intervening years; that during those years, agreeably to his view, there were thirteen hundred and fifty-two first-days, all of which were holy time, and nearly all of which must have been honored by stated meetings on the part of the apostles; and yet, out of that whole number, he only claims to produce the record of one solitary day on which such meeting occurred. What are the facts, then? Paul probably preached every day of the seven, while he was at Troas. Do you ask why the account is not given of such meetings in the book of the Acts? I answer that the Holy Spirit was giving, through Luke, a succinct history of the more striking occurrences which transpired in their travels. The story of the first-day meeting at Troas found its way into the sacred narrative, because its importance to after generations was enhanced by the accidental fall, and the miraculous restoration to life of Eutychus, and perhaps by other facts connected with that event, of equal interest. I think that one of them was a disposition on the part of God to provide his commandment-keeping servants in succeeding generations with a passage in the life of Paul, which should forever silence the cavils of men who should undertake to belittle his ancient Sabbath, and to foist into its place a day which He never commanded. This we will further consider in our next point.

Having endeavored to establish the point that the seventh-day Sabbath was not observed at Troas, an effort is made to show that a change of time had occurred, so that Luke, in giving his account of the transactions mentioned above, treated the day as commencing and ending, not according to the Jewish method, with the setting of the sun, but after the Roman fashion, with midnight. The reader will readily discover the object to be gained by this maneuver, if such I may be allowed to call it. We had insisted that the first day of the week commenced at sunset; that Paul met with the disciples in the dark portion of that day (verse 8), preached to them during that night, and on the next morning commenced a journey of nineteen and a half miles on foot, on that which answered to the daylight portion of our Sunday. This, if true, with the majority of readers, would have forever settled the question that Paul did not believe in first-day sanctity. A remedy, therefore, must be had. The gentleman thinks he has found one. That he has made a desperate effort to obtain it, we are compelled to admit. No man, it seems to us, would ever resort to an experiment so hazardous, who did not find himself in the stress of a situation which otherwise would be utterly insupportable. With the most deliberate calculation, and in the face of authority which he himself highly honors, he has decided that the journey in question occurred on the second day of the week, instead of the first, which ended at twelve o'clock the previous night. Well, suppose we admit, for a moment, that this was true; what then? The Sunday is thereby rescued from profanation by Paul; but it is also true that the second day of the week is thereby honored with the meeting of a Christian church, and that it was it, and not the first, after all, which was honored by the breaking of bread during its hours.* So much for some of the consequences of the position, if well taken.

But now let us turn to the argument for the change. Is it really true that Roman, and not Jewish, time, is employed in a portion of the New Testament? If so, the perplexities of the situation are very great. How shall we know when to apply the one, and when the other? How can we tell precisely where the dividing line should be drawn? We hope, in all conscience, independently of the question at issue, that the writer is not correct. He seems to find the first intimation of a change in the gospels. Matt. 28:1, and John 20:19, are referred to in

---

* The honoring of the second day here alluded to rests upon the hypothesis that the breaking of bread spoken of in Acts 20 : 11, answers to the Lord's supper. It is, however, by no means certain that this was the case, since scholars differ widely in opinion respecting the matter; some holding to the opinion that reference was made to the Lord's supper, and others to the view that the breaking of bread referred merely to a common meal.

support of his view. Now suppose we concede for a time the point which he desires, and admit that these passages prove the use in them of Roman time; also that, as he claims, the meeting spoken of in John 20:19, occurred in the evening (Roman time), and after the coming on of darkness. This done, we inquire, Was it a Jewish day or a Roman day that was sanctified by the resurrection of Christ, and his appearance to his assembled disciples? We think that few will dispute that it was a Jewish day.

But when did the Jewish day commence? The undeniable answer is, At sunset. But when did Christ appear to the disciples, according to Roman time, as argued? We answer, In the darkness of the evening, and, therefore, after the ending of the Jewish first day. What is the necessary conclusion? We reply, One of two things. 1. Either that the visit of Christ had no reference to the sanctity of the day on which it occurred; or 2. That it was designed to honor the second day of the Jewish week. We leave the writer in question to take whichever horn of this dilemma he pleases. If he should insist that John employed Roman time, then all which he has said in reference to the effect of the visit of Christ upon the first day of the Jewish week is emptied of all force. Never was self-stultification more complete. In his effort to escape from the paws of the Trojan bear (secular travel on

Sunday), the writer has thrown himself into the jaws of the lion (no Scripture precedent for Sunday-keeping). For, if he is right in supposing that the meeting in John 20:19, occurred on the Roman evening of that day—that is, after sunset, and the coming on of darkness—then, of course, it did not transpire on the Jewish first day of the week, which had previously ended, according to his own admission, at the going down of the sun; but it actually took place after the commencement of the second day of the Jewish week.

Not only so, but the second meeting of Christ with his disciples (after eight days), according to his own reasoning, must have fallen on the second Jewish day of the next week. And, finally, accepting his logic that the meeting of Acts 20:7, also fell on the Roman evening of the first day of the week, that precedent, so long cherished, and so often cited, is now forever disposed of, since it, too, illustrates the second Jewish day of the week, and not the first, if, indeed, it adds luster to any. But, reader, it would be neither Christian nor manly to adopt an exegesis of Scripture presented by an opponent, simply because such an exegesis would prove his overthrow. Truth is worth more than mere victory. The gentleman has made a mistake in deciding that Roman time is employed in the Bible, and that mistake has brought him to confusion. But now we propose to show that Roman time is not employed, even though in so doing we shall assist him out of his trouble for the time being. Let no one suppose, however, that the relief which we shall afford him will be permanent, for, unfortunately for him, we shall rescue him from one death simply to deliver him to another.

The whole question turns upon the commencement and end of the Bible day. If it can be shown that it began and terminated with the setting of the sun, then, beyond all dispute, the meeting in Troas occurred at the commencement of the first day of the week, at the coming on of darkness, the only period in that day when lights could be employed to advantage (verse 8). We proceed, therefore, to our task. We have heretofore quoted from the Tract Society's Bible Dictionary, under the article, day, to prove a general agreement that the Hebrews commenced and ended their day with the setting of the sun. In addition to this, we might refer the reader to Smith's Comprehensive Dictionary of the Bible on the same subject. In fact, we might multiply authorities without end; but this is not necessary here. By turning to Genesis, chapter 1, the reader will find that God measured the day by "the evening and the morning" (darkness and light). He will here observe that with the ancient Hebrews the whole night preceded the day to which it belonged. Advancing to Leviticus 23:32, he will there read the command of God, that the people should keep their Sabbaths "from even to even." But as the Sabbath was the last day of the week, and was to commence and end with the evening, he will discover that it will be necessary that all the other days should commence and end in the same manner.

Passing now to the New Testament, he will find the same custom prevailing in the days of our Lord. Nay, more; he will there obtain the authority of Luke himself, who wrote the book of Acts, for believing that Christ and the Jews followed that system of beginning and ending the day which God had inaugurated in the outset. We read in Luke 4 : 40 : "Now when the sun was setting, all they that had any sick with divers diseases, brought them unto him; and he laid his hands on every one of them, and healed them." By tracing back the event, as given by Luke, in its parallel, as found in Mark 1, we find that Christ was healing in the synagogue on the Sabbath day, and that he subsequently repaired to the house of Peter, and healed his wife's mother; and that, "at even, when the sun did set," the Jews brought to him all those that were diseased, and possessed with devils, for the purpose of having him heal them. This, however, they could not have done on the Sabbath day, according to their views; therefore they prove that the custom was still prevalent among them of ending the days with the setting of the sun. But, furthermore, has it not been argued by the writer himself, that the day of Pentecost was coincident with the first day of the week? We think this will hardly be disputed. If it be true, however, and if the logic be sound, that the Spirit which was poured out on the day of Pentecost was designed to indicate that it corresponded with the Christian Sabbath, then we need not argue further, for no man will deny that that day was emphatically Jewish in its beginning and ending.

This array of Scripture testimony, gleaned from a history of 4000 years, if met at all, it will be necessary that it should be done by clear and emphatic statements emanating from the same source from which the authorities in question are drawn. Has the gentleman furnished any such evidence? The reader will readily discover that he has not. The only texts brought forward in support of the change upon which he insists are John 20:19, and Matt. 28:1. In reference to the first of these, it will only be required that attention should be called to the fact that, with the Hebrews, each day had two evenings. (Exodus 12:6, margin; and Numbers 9:3, and 28:4, margin.) On this point, the Bible Dictionary says: "The Hebrews reckoned two evenings in each day. * * * According to the Karaites, this time between the evenings is the interval from sunset to complete darkness, that is, the evening twilight. According to the Pharisees and the Rabbins, the first evening began when the sun inclined to descend more rapidly; that is, at the ninth hour; while the second or real evening commenced at sunset." (Art. Evening.) Now let it be supposed that Christ met with his disciples somewhere between three o'clock and sunset, on the day of the resurrection, and the statement that he met with them the "same day at evening," is at once verified, and the necessity for the supposition of a change of time disappears.

In explanation of Matt. 28:1, we cannot do better, perhaps, than to append the following comment from Albert Barnes: "The word *end*, here means the same as *after* the Sabbath; *i. e.*, after the Sabbath was fully completed, or finished, and may be expressed in the following manner: 'In the night following the Sabbath; for the Sabbath closed at sunset, as it began to dawn toward the first day of the week.'" That Mr. Barnes is right in his criticism, will become apparent when we compare Matt. 28:1, with the parallel passage in Mark 16:1, 2, where the same historic fact is introduced with these words: "When the Sabbath was past." A complete harmony is thus preserved between the two evangelists, and all requisition for the extreme resort to the hypothesis of a sudden and unprecedented employment of the Roman system for the computation of time is dispensed with.

As it regards the objection, which is based upon the use made in Acts 20:7, of the words, "on the morrow," we reply that it is not well taken. That it was perfectly compatible with a Jewish custom, when speaking of the daylight portion of any day from the stand-point of the previous evening, to allude to it as "the morrow," we cite the following passages: " Then the soldiers, as it was commanded them, took Paul, and brought him by night to Antipatris. *On the morrow* they left the horsemen to go with him, and returned to the castle." Acts 23 : 31, 32. "Saul also sent messengers unto David's house, to watch him, and to slay him in the morning; and Michal, David's wife, told him, saying, If thou save not thy life to-night, *to-morrow* thou shalt be slain." 1 Samuel 19 : 11.

In addition to the above texts, we might quote the authority of Mr. Howson, who is so justly complimented for his scholarship by the writer. He cannot be charged with leaning toward our views of the Sabbath, and, therefore, if he had any bias in the case, it would be against, and not in favor of, the position which we are trying to maintain. If there was really any force in the criticism which is offered respecting the use of the preposition and the term with which it is connected, assuredly the discriminating eye of this gentleman would not have allowed it to escape detection. Nevertheless, he, as the writer admits, deliberately decides, while examining at length the very passages now before us, that the events there spoken of, journey and all, did transpire on the Sunday. In doing so, it follows, as a matter of course, that he did not regard the difficulty which is urged concerning the words, " on the morrow," as one at all formidable.

Thus much by way of a brief refutation of the diversity theory for the commencing of the days of the Bible. We have seen heretofore, that, if the advocate of this theory were right and we wrong, he has lost to his cause the three precedental meetings of John 20 : 19, John 20 : 26, and Acts 20 : 7, since they occurred on the second, and not the first, Jewish day of the week. Let us now view the situation from the stand-point of one who believes that the sacred, instead of the heathen, method is followed consistently throughout the Scriptures. In Acts 20 : 7, the text which is passing under review, it is said that there was a meeting held upon the first day of the week, and that Paul preached until midnight. It now becomes important to know on what portion of the first day of the week this meeting fell. By examining the record, we find the statement that there were many lights employed in the chamber where they were gathered. We know, therefore, that the meeting must have taken place during the dark portion of the first day of the week. But as we have seen that the Jewish day commenced with sunset, the only hours of darkness which belong to it were to be found between that time and the next morning. Advancing, we learn that, having spent the night in preaching, breaking of bread, &c., the apostle devoted the daylight portion of the first day of the week to the accomplishment of a journey of nineteen and a half miles, while his companions sailed the vessel a greater distance round the headland to Assos. Here, then, is apostolic example for travel upon the first day of the week. The writer endeavored to escape this conclusion, by asserting that the meeting in question and the travel took place on the second day of the week. This view, we have met, and successfully answered. The record states that it was upon the first day of the week when they came together. It then proceeds to give a connected account of what transpired on that day, and among other things, is found the story of Paul and his companions starting for Jerusalem. Now, if the events related did really transpire on two days, instead of on one merely, as would naturally be inferred from the context, the burden of the proof is with our opponent. We rest the matter, therefore, right here. The only attempt which he has made has been a complete failure. That he thought it was the best he could do under the circumstances, we doubt not.

There remains now no item of difference between ourselves and the writer in the *Statesman* which should occupy us longer. For, between him and myself there is no room for dispute respecting the morality of traveling on the Sabbath, since, according to his own confession, the object which Paul had in remaining at Troas was that of a good "*Sabbath-keeping Christian,*" who was unwilling to violate the sacredness of holy time by the performance of secular labor. Here, then, we pause. As we do so, we appeal to the judgment of the candid men and women who have read the criticism of our friend and our reply thereto. Did Paul conscientiously regard the first day of the week, while traveling on foot nineteen and a half miles upon it, and did Luke and his six companions, in sailing a much greater distance on the same hours, transgress the law of God, and ignore the example of Christ; or, did they look upon the first day of the week as one which God had given to man for the purposes of labor and travel? If you still decide that it was holy time, you must be able to reconcile their action with this theory. This, however, you can never do. If, on the contrary, you shall determine that they treated it as a secular day, then it remains so still, for its character has not changed from that day to this.

STATESMAN'S REPLY.

ARTICLE SIX.

TESTIMONY OF PAUL AND JOHN TO THE FIRST-DAY SABBATH.

Two important portions of the inspired records remain to be considered. The first of these reads as follows: "Now concerning the collection for the saints, as I have given order to the churches of Galatia, even so do ye. Upon the first day of the week let every one of you lay by him in store, as God hath prospered him, that there be no gatherings when I come." (1 Cor. 16:1, 2.)

From this passage it is clear that the churches of Galatia, as well as the church at Corinth, or that Christians generally, were required to set apart a proportion of their worldly goods, as God prospered them, for benevolent purposes. It is also clear that the act of setting apart the required proportion of means was to be performed statedly, every week, on the first day of the week.

Whatever may be the correct interpretation of the words, "lay by him in store," enough is beyond all doubt and agreed upon by all, to show that the first day of the week was regarded by the apostle and the Christian churches as a special day, and one more fitting than others for the benevolent and religious duty enjoined.

The phrase rendered in our version "by him," is unquestionably an idiomatic Greek expression for "at home." (Compare Luke 24:12, and John 20:10.) And even if we understand this phrase to be connected with the word rendered, "in store," which is a participle signifying "treasuring up," the proof of first-day sacred observance is still clear and strong. But the true connection of the words, "at home," is with what precedes. "Let every one place or devote at home." Place what? The answer is not hard to find—a proportion of the weekly earnings; a suitable part of what God in his bounty had given. When this proportion was separated by each Christian at home, from the rest of his weekly earnings, it was to be treasured up. But where? This is the important question. Where was the money each Christian set apart at home on the first day of the week, from his weekly receipts, to be kept in store ? It appears that this treasuring up was not at each Christian's home:

1. Because the phrase, "at home," grammatically connects, not with the word "treasuring," but with the preceding verb. This verb does not mean "lay by," but "lay," or "place." The preposition rendered "by" is part of the phrase, "at home." If it is insisted that the idea of treasuring in store is in the word rendered "lay," then we have this tautology: "Let every one place in store or lay by at home, placing in store." Paul did not write in this way.

2. The first day of the week must have offered a special facility for doing what was required. True, if nothing more is meant than laying by at home, even that marks the first day with distinguishing honor. But the placing or putting of God's portion by itself, separated from the remainder of the receipts of the past week, on each first-day, in each Christian's home, was in order to something else, for which the first day alone gave opportunity. On that day, as we have learned from Acts 20: 7, and other portions of Scripture, Christians were accustomed to meet for public religious services, and at these public gatherings, each Christian put into the treasury of the church what he had set apart at home from the rest of the gains of the week.

3. The most conclusive argument, however, is drawn from the end that Paul desired to accomplish. He states expressly that his aim in giving his directions was to avoid the necessity of gatherings or collections when he should come. The force of this consideration is evaded by ex-

plaining the apostle's words as meaning "small collections." But if every Christian had his money laid by at home, whether it were much or little, the "collections" would still have to be made. Each Christian, it is true, would have his sum already made up, and would need to make no personal gathering. But the apostle's word is much more naturally and fittingly applied to collections on a larger and wider scale. And to effect the apostle's end, and avoid such collections at his coming, the Corinthians, like the Galatians, were to make a collection every Lord's day, of what each one at home had set apart or placed aside from the proceeds of his business during the preceding week. In no other way would the moneys needed be in perfect readiness for the apostle. If left in the hands of individuals scattered around, there would be uncertainty about the apostle's receipt of them, and there would still be trouble in connection with collections on his arrival. But with the moneys already gathered, at the regular weekly meetings, into the common treasury of the church, and there waiting his coming, his aim is satisfactorily accomplished.

The only remaining passage is Rev. 1:10: "I was in the Spirit on the Lord's day." It has been admitted by opponents of the first-day Sabbath, that if, by the Lord's day in this passage, the first day of the week is meant, their cause is lost. And lost it is; for no other day can be meant. Three interpretations have been given of John's words:—

1. By the Lord's day is meant the day of Judgment. Wetstein, in his elaborate edition of the Greek New Testament, in the year 1752, first

advanced this view. His comment is; "Hunc diem judicii vidit in spiritu; *i. e.,* prævidit representatum." "John saw in Spirit the day of Judgment; that is, he foresaw it represented." The phrase, "the day of the Lord," does mean in the Scriptures the day of Judgment. But that phrase is different from the one here employed. The literal rendering of the former is, "the day of the Lord." The literal rendering of the other is, "the dominical day." This was not a day foreseen, but a day on which John was in the Spirit—a day of weekly recurrence which the Lord claims as his own, as he claims the dominical supper.

2. By the Lord's day, it is maintained again, is meant the seventh-day Sabbath. In support of this view it is said that the phrase employed by John corresponds with such Old-Testament expressions as "a Sabbath to the Lord," and with the Saviour's language: "The Son of man is Lord even of the Sabbath." But the very fact that the seventh day had a well-known and distinctive name by which it was always designated, is strong presumptive proof that this new and unusual phrase used by John cannot apply to it. It would be most natural to suppose that some other day is meant, and this is clearly proved to be the fact.

3. The phrase, the Lord's day, was the common expression for designating the first-day Sabbath from John's time onward. As the meal which the Lord hallowed as his own was called the Lord's supper, so the day hallowed by the Lord's resurrection, by his repeated meeting with his disciples after rising from the dead, by the descent of his Spirit, by the weekly religious

assemblies of his people with their communions, preaching and hearing the word, prayers and almsgiving, was properly termed the Lord's day. It has been argued on the other side of the question that the Lord had a day, and but one in the week, called specially his own. But as has been shown, Jesus himself, after his resurrection, paid no regard to the seventh day. His disciples did not observe it. It could not, therefore, have been the Lord's day. On the other hand, Jesus did honor the first day, and the Christian churches everywhere did the same; and thus this honored day is the only one of which John could speak when he said he was "in the Spirit on the Lord's day." By this name, as will be seen in our next article, the first day of the week was known in the early church.

A REJOINDER.

"TESTIMONY OF PAUL AND JOHN TO THE FIRST-DAY SABBATH."

WITH no small degree of interest we have perused the article entitled, "Testimony of Paul and John to the First-day Sabbath." The two texts which it brings forward in defense of the theory of a changed Sabbath, are regarded by the friends of that theory, generally, as among the strongest of its supports. The first of them (1 Cor. 16.: 1, 2), we had assailed, and adduced a criticism, from the pen of Mr. J. W. Morton, which was of great importance. In it, the very stronghold of the Sunday argument had been fearlessly attacked, and, to our mind, carried beyond all question. The writer whom we quoted presented twelve versions and translations, all of which clearly sustained the position that the expression, "by him," was equivalent to the term, "at home." If this were true, then beyond all dispute the Sunday argument had been denuded of all its strength, provided it ever had any; for the support of its logic was the assumption that the transaction brought to view in this text was to take place in the respective assemblies of the saints.

It is, therefore, with the most profound satisfaction that—if we rightly apprehend the remarks of our reviewer—we accept his concession of the point that the words, "by him," do indeed answer to a Greek idiom, of which the original terms are equivalent to the expression, "at home." This being true, we are agreed that at least a *portion* of the duty which Paul commanded was to be performed, not at the house of assembly, but at the *dwelling of the individual Christian*. In other words, he admits that the money which they were to "place or devote" to charitable purposes, was first to be estimated and separated while yet they were in their own houses. Having conceded thus much, he reasons that the money was to be carried to the place of worship, and laid up in store, or deposited among the collections regularly made on the first day of the week. In order to sustain this view, he offers a grammatical criticism to which it cannot be objected that it is not drawn finely enough to meet the taste of the most fastidious. But the writer does not seem to plant himself so squarely upon it as we would naturally expect one would who feels that he is standing upon solid ground.

The *force of his logic* seems to be drawn from the *object* which Paul had in view, in ordering beforehand this weekly laying aside of money for the poor saints at Jerusalem. The writer thinks that the evident reference of Paul, in the words, "that there be no gatherings when I come," is to contributions to be taken up in the congregation when he should have reached the place. If he is wrong in this, he is wrong in all; for no one will dispute that money *could** be

---

* This point is an important one; and as we are anxious to satisfy the reader that it is well taken, we append the following remarks of Albert Barnes, who—though agreeing with the writer in the *Statesman* that this passage furnishes proof for Sunday observance—nevertheless frankly concedes, as will be seen, that the construction of the original phrase for "treasuring up," is such as to admit of the idea that the work was to be done at home. He says: "The phrase in Greek, 'treasuring up,' may mean that each one was to put the part which he had designated into the common *treasury*. This interpretation seems to be demanded by the latter part of the verse. They were to lay it by, and to put it into the common treasury, that there might be no trouble of collecting when he should come. Or, it may, perhaps, mean that they were individually to *treasure it up*, having designated in their own minds the sum which they could give, and have it in readiness when he should come."

"laid by in store" *at home*, as well as in the church, since to lay by in store, is to put in some safe and accessible place.

Right here, then, we inquire, What were the "gatherings" which Paul sought to avoid on his arrival? They could refer to but one of two things; either, first, the collection of moneys in the church; or, secondly, the collecting of them by individuals from those who were indebted to them. That the first was not the sense in which Paul employed the word, we submit is apparent, from the fact that the end to be gained by writing months beforehand, in order to prevent the taking up of a collection in the church, was not commensurate with the dignity which is given to it by so prominent a place in the sacred epistle. So far as the collection itself was concerned, it could have been brought about, unquestionably, within the space of fifteen minutes. The amount of time, therefore, which it would consume, is too insignificant to be worthy of mention.

Again, as it regards the moral complexion of the act, it will not be objected by our reviewer that it was to be avoided from any scruples in that direction, since he believes that such collections were taken up on every first day of the week. On the other hand, taking the second view as being the one which properly expresses the facts, we find that it is in perfect harmony with the circumstances of the case, and consistent with the notion that Paul had a sufficient motive for writing before hand, as he did, concerning the collections. He was about to make a brief visit to Corinth. How long he should remain, he could not tell. While there, he wanted the undivided attention of the people to be given to religious purposes, and also that the money which he expected, should be in readiness, so that no delay might be necessary.

This, however, could not be, since, not knowing the exact time of his arrival, they would not be likely to have it on hand when he should come, unless they laid it by, weekly, at their homes. Should he, therefore, drop in upon them suddenly, they would be thrown into a confusion of mind illy compatible with the purposes of daily worship during his visit, since they would be annoyed and distracted by the necessity of gathering from this direction and that, the amounts of the weekly contribution which they had agreed to make for the benefit of the suffering saints at Jerusalem.

But once more: Having settled the point that the explanation claimed does not satisfactorily account for the mention of the subject in an epistle, while the one which we present meets the requirements of the case in every particular—since it both supplies the money, and furnishes the apostle with a body of Christians ready to listen to the preaching of the word—let us look at the matter from another stand-point.

The plan proposed by Paul could have been

arrived at in but one of two ways. Every Christian was expected, either, first, to give a fixed sum, every week, of an amount equal to that which the general valuation of his property would require; or, secondly, he was, as the writer supposes, to pay in a fluctuating amount weekly, that amount to be determined by the gains or losses of the week.

We will suppose, for a moment, that the first theory is correct, and will test the plan in question thereby. While doing so, for convenience' sake, we will employ the currency of our own time. Here is a Corinthian Christian who is worth, say $10,000. He decides that he will give, for the purposes mentioned, ten dollars per week. He has money in his purse, and nothing to prevent his doing it at any time. Being anxious to obey the injunction of Paul, he proceeds as the writer suggests. On Sunday morning he is at home, knowing just what he must contribute on that day, when he goes to church, having previously decided this point. The amount, as we have seen, is precisely ten dollars. But Paul says he must do something with it "at home," before going to church. What was he to do with it? The writer says, "to place or devote it." Well, he takes out his purse; from it he extracts just ten dollars. He holds it in his fingers. Now, what shall he do with it? The writer says he must "*place* or *devote* it." Yes, but we inquire, What does *place* or *devote mean*, in such a connection as this? In other words, What shall he do with the money at home? Shall he take it out, and turn it over, and look at it, and put it back into his purse again, and then go to church and place it in the contribution box? We answer that this would be a solemn farce. To say, also, that having taken it out of his purse he must not put it back again, but must place it in some other pocket, and then carry it to church, is simply ridiculous. So far, therefore, as the men were concerned whose property was fixed, and whose contributions were the same, weekly, all that was said by Paul about "devoting or placing" at home was pure nonsense, in the light of the exposition offered.*

Now for the other class, or the men of fluctuating resources. How shall they proceed? Were they to estimate the amount of their weekly gains, and to collect in the sum, on the last day, which they were to give on the first day of the week? If so, then in their cases, as well as in those of the first order, the whole process was a mere sham, an empty and meaningless form. For they also, at their homes, would simply have to take out their

---

*Instead of selecting a wealthy person, able to contribute ten dollars per week, as has been done above, let an individual be chosen from the poorer classes of Corinthians—say from among those who would be able to donate only twenty-five cents per week—and the reader will be more forcibly impressed with the unreasonableness of that construction which makes it necessary that so small a pittance should first be placed or devoted at home, and then carried to the church, and there deposited in the general collection.

money and look at it, and then put it back and go to the church for the purpose of donating it.

But again; as we have seen, that unless the work of deciding how much they ought to give, and separating the amount for that purpose while at home on the first day of the week, was a part of the plan of the apostle, the whole suggestion had in it neither rhyme nor reason, we now turn to the only alternative left our opponent; which is the conclusion that the work indicated by the term, "place or devote at home," was that of *deciding upon* and *separating* the sum which they could spare to the weekly contribution.

What are the consequences of such a position? We reply, It overturns and utterly uproots the whole theory of Sunday sanctity; for the lesson taught by 1 Cor. 16:1, 2, instead of being favorable to the conception that Paul held to such a theory, shows that he regarded the first day of the week as secular time. Do you ask, How do you reach such a conclusion? I answer, It is inevitable, since the men who were acting under the instruction of Paul could not carry out the work prescribed by him without devoting at least the morning of the first day of the week to worldly business, such as that of figuring up and deciding upon the losses and profits of the preceding week, and, perhaps, collecting from outstanding matters the pro-rata amount necessary for the stated collection at the church.

Should it be objected that our suggestion is

open to the criticism that the well-to-do class of Christians could have furnished their means at any time, we answer, Very true; but that, should week after week elapse without the separation, on the part of the wealthy, of the stipulated sum, it might, before the arrival of the apostle, reach figures which it would be difficult even for them to meet without perplexity. And besides, the better, easier, more natural, and we think, spiritually, the more profitable method, even for them, would be found in doing it weekly. We might offer many reasons for this conviction, had we space. Paul was giving a general rule to meet the condition of all classes. The poor comprised the larger portion of these classes, and a principle was laid down, therefore, which, while it was better for the rich than any other, was indispensable, for the purposes in question, to the men of moderate circumstances.

Our interpretation, stated in brief, is simply this: The apostle instructed them on the first day of the week to lay by in store, at home, what they proposed to give to the saints at Jerusalem, hoarding it up until he should visit them, so that at his arrival they might put it into the common treasury; thus avoiding the possibility of being unable, on the one hand, to meet their pledges, and on the other, of being necessitated to have their minds occupied with temporal affairs, during his stay. This conception is free from embarrassments. Even were the gentleman's translation of the passage correct, it cannot be shown to be unsound. He would read the scripture substantially as follows: "Let every one of you devote at home, treasuring up, that there be no gatherings when I come." To our mind, there is no tautology, even in the declaration of the apostle thus expressed, which is worthy of mention; for should the term, " treasuring up," be interpreted to mean the same as placing or devoting at home, it is explanatory, not of the command, but of the purpose of the command. A paraphrase, which is often employed with profit in the writings of Paul, will make it all clear: "Upon the first day of the week, let every one of you lay aside, or devote to the Lord, an amount commensurate with the prosperity which he has bestowed upon you, treasuring it up, so that there need be no gatherings when I come."

The only difference between the gentleman and myself, therefore, would be as to the *place where* it was to be treasured up; he insisting that it was at the church, and we, at the house of the individual Christian. We have shown that his opinion is not only unnecessary, but that it is also absurd, since it divides a transaction which Paul does not divide; and, after admitting that a part of it transpired at the home of the individual, it represents the other part as having taken place at the church; whereas, neither the *church*, the *contribution box*, nor the *assembly*, are so much as mentioned. And besides, it presents Paul in an attitude which certainly does not compliment his sagacity. Mark you, it is "every one of you" that he instructs to "lay by at home." It must therefore be, not the church collectively, but its individual members who are called upon to treasure up, or lay by in store. Just here we submit that the language employed is literal, and not figurative, and that, this being true, the moment that the saints at Corinth placed their funds in the common treasury, they violated the injunction of the apostle, which was that they should treasure it up, or lay it by in store, individually. By way of enforcing our logic, we inquire of the reader, who has doubtless contributed many times to church collections, Can you look upon money thus bestowed as in any proper sense of the term belonging to you individually? or as still treasured up or laid by in store? We think that your answer will not be equivocal. To lay by in store, as before stated, is to put in some safe and accessible place; but money once donated is not accessible to the individual contributor, since he has no longer any individual property in it.

Here we must terminate our remarks on 1 Cor. 16:1, 2. As we do so, we have disposed of the last Bible text which will be cited in the support of a supposed practice of Sunday-keeping on the part of the early church. Error begets error. Having rejected the obvious teaching of Acts 20:

7, that Paul, after holding a meeting on the first day of the week, traveled nineteen and a half miles on foot, and having endeavored to explain away this journey by inferring that it took place on the second day of the week, which is not mentioned in the connection, our opponent comes to the consideration of 1 Cor. 16:1, 2, lugging along in his arms a precedent which God had clearly taught him was not designed to teach the lesson which he sought to extract from it. With this precedent, thus illegitimately obtained, he seeks to explain the language of Paul which we have been considering. By this means, he has been led to indorse error. But we need not recapitulate.

In conclusion on this point, we remark: How admirable is the providence of God! He has instructed us in his word, in regard to duty, by clear precepts, and has never told us to study its requirements simply in the light of human example. How remarkable, therefore, that he should have condescended to so order, by his Spirit, the record which has been made in the case of every precedent brought forward, that the text and context would utterly overthrow every effort of him who should attempt to employ them in the interest of a false doctrine. On the day of the resurrection, as if to show that it was not holy time, two disciples are brought to view as traveling fifteen miles; a portion of the distance in company with their approving Lord, and the remainder of it after he had appeared to, walked and conversed with, them. In Acts 20:7, apparently perceiving the use which might be made of it, he places, in the foreground of the sacred record, the apostle, threading a weary journey on foot from Troas to Assos; and lastly, in 1 Cor. 16:1, 2, he framed the language so that it should inculcate, not the idea that the first day of the week was holy time, but, on the contrary, that it might be devoted to the secular work of casting up accounts and collecting funds.

With the exposition offered of the words, "I was in the Spirit on the Lord's day," Rev. 1:10, we shall make short work. What we have previously said on that passage is not sufficiently disturbed to warrant extended remark. Be it remembered, then, that, as said above, the passage proves that God has a day in this dispensation. At this point commences our divergence. We say that the term, "Lord's day," refers to the seventh-day Sabbath. The writer says that it refers to the first day of the week. The declaration that Christ paid no attention to the seventh-day Sabbath after his resurrection, needs no reply here, except that he was under no obligation to do so, and there was no good reason why he should, since he regarded it strictly in his lifetime, and enjoined it upon his followers. Perhaps, however, it would be well to add that he at least never did anything after his resurrection which might be construed into a desecration of it; whereas, in the case of the only first-day on which it can be *proved* that he ever met with his disciples, after his death, he devoted a portion of its hours to travel on the highway.

To the objection of the writer that, if the term, "Lord's day," in the case before us, does apply to the seventh-day Sabbath, it is strange that it should have been called in every case but this "the Sabbath," we reply that, were this true, this would simply prove a choice in titles, and implies no disrespect to the day itself, since the term "Sabbath," equally with that of "Lord's day," was a sacred denomination. Not so, however, if he be right in the supposition that the term, "Lord's day," applies to the Sunday; for, if he be correct in this, then indeed we have something which is *passing strange*. For, in all the New Testament, that which he is pleased to style the "Christian Sabbath," and to which, according to his theory, belonged the honorable name of "Lord's day," is not only so called but once; but, being spoken of nine times by inspired men, it is mentioned eight times out of the nine by them in an utter disregard of its hallowed nature, in the terms employed, since it is referred to by its secular name, first day of the week, in all these instances. The reader will recollect that, in our positive argument, we showed that the term, "Lord's day," was a fitting one for the last day of the week, provided the term translated "Lord" was applicable to God, the Father, as well as to Christ, the Son. 1. Because it was the day which he blessed and sanctified in Eden, thus claiming it as his own (Gen. 2:3). 2. Because, in the commandment, he calls it "the Sabbath of the Lord." 3. Because, in Isa. 58:13, 14, he makes mention of it in the use of the terms, "Sabbath," "my holy day," "the holy of the Lord," &c.

In addition, we might cite other honorable and distinguishing terms by which it is pointed out in the Bible as a day which belongs peculiarly to the Lord our God, but these are sufficient.

If it be replied that the word translated "Lord" in Rev. 1:10, is necessarily limited to Christ, we answer: 1. As we have argued formerly, that he said he was Lord of the Sabbath. Mark 2:27, 28. 2. That the following texts show conclusively that the divine Son of God was engaged, equally with the Father, in the creation of this world; and, therefore, that he undoubtedly shared in the rest which furnished the foundation for the Edenic Sabbath, as well as in the act of blessing and sanctifying it, or setting it apart for religious purposes. "All things were made by him [Christ]: and without him was not anything made that was made." John 1:3. "He was in the world, and the world was made by him, and the world knew him not." John 1:10. ". . . Who [God] created all things by Jesus Christ." Eph. 3:9. "For by him were all things created, that are in heaven, and that are in earth; . . . all things were created by him, and for him." Col. 1 : 16. "God . . . hath in these last days spoken unto us by his Son, whom he hath appointed heir of all things, by whom also he made the worlds." Heb. 1 : 1, 2. Even though we should grant, therefore, which we do not, that the term translated "Lord," as above, applies exclusively to the Son of God, we cannot see why the seventh day might not, with all propriety, be called after him, the Lord's day.

In the concluding remarks on this branch of the subject, it will not be considered out of place for us to remind the reader of the protest which we offered, in the rejoinder to the second article of the gentleman of the *Statesman*, against his effort to obtain all the benefit which could be derived from his interpretation of Rev. 1 : 10, before he had struck a single blow, either in the direction of overturning our construction, or establishing, by fair argument, his own. The reason why this protest was offered is now apparent. The gentleman there, by anticipation, *assumed* that John meant by the term, "Lord's day," the first day of the week. He *promised* that in due time he would make good his assertion. But how has it proved, now that he has reached the very point where he should have fulfilled this engagement?. Every one must see that he has utterly failed. *Proof* was the very thing which was *promised*, and which was *needed*, right here. It is the very thing, also, which he has neglected to adduce. All that is said in reference to the theory of Wetstein, may have served to give respectability, in point of length, to the treatment of that which he has regarded a most important scripture in his line of evidence; but it was utterly irrelevant to anything which we had said; for the reader will remember that we emphatically planted ourselves on the position that it was the weekly Sabbath to which allusion is made.

To the restatement of the scriptures employed in vindication of this last opinion, there can be no objection, but we inquire again, Where are the passages, where the deductions from Scripture teachings, by which the gentleman has proved that the Lord's day is the first day of the week? He has not so much as cited one. He has not made even a respectable effort at argument; but, with a haste which is irreverent, if not indecent, he rushes away from the book of God, as if impelled by the conviction that his view will find no support there, and plunges headlong into the regions of patristic myth and moonshine. At this we are not surprised. It is just what we expected. Sabbatarians are as well acquainted with this device as they are with the emptiness of the so-called Bible argument for the Sunday. It simply serves to strengthen their conviction, so often expressed in these articles, that the stronghold of first-day observance will ever be found in writings which have been manipulated, retrenched, and interpolated, by the church of

Rome. For, be it remembered, it is from the authorities to which the gentleman now appeals, that the papacy brings its stoutest testimonials for apostolic succession, papistic supremacy, and the other heresies which blacken the record of its apostasy.

All it is necessary to say to the reader here is, therefore, that he should bear in mind that Sabbatarians are willing to leave the arbitrament of this whole question where it can be determined from the stand-point of Bible evidence. It is the opposition, and not we, who make it necessary, in the investigation of this subject, to go upon forbidden ground. "All Scripture is given by inspiration of God, and is profitable for doctrine, for reproof, for correction, for instruction in righteousness; that the man of God may be perfect, thoroughly furnished unto all good works." 2 Tim. 3:16, 17. If, therefore, first-day sanctity has no warrant in the Bible, which we have seen to be the case, then it is not among those things which are *profitable*, or which, as Christian doctrines, are *necessary to furnish the man of God unto all good works.*

STATESMAN'S REPLY.

ARTICLE SEVEN.

TESTIMONY OF THE EARLY FATHERS TO THE FIRST-DAY SABBATH.

BESIDES the inspired records of the Scriptures, there have come down to us the writings of men who were contemporaneous with some of the apostles, and the writings of others who lived in the immediately succeeding generations. We shall quote from the writings of those who lived during the two centuries following the close of the canon of inspiration. These writers give evidence enough that they were not inspired, as were the penmen of the Divine Word. But it will be borne in mind that we appeal to them here simply as witnesses to a matter of fact. Many of their opinions and interpretations of Scripture may not be worthy of acceptance; but their testimony to the existence of the Lord's day, as an admitted fact, cannot be disputed. As there has been a great deal of loose citation from the early fathers on this question, we have been at considerable pains to translate carefully from the original in every case, and accompany each quotation with minute and accurate reference.

The first writer from whom we shall quote is Ignatius. This father stood at the head of the church at Antioch at the close of the first century and the beginning of the second. After occupying that position for many years, he was condemned to death, as a Christian, by Trajan, transported in chains to Rome, and there thrown to lions in the Coliseum for the amusement of the populace, probably in the year 107. On his way to Rome, he wrote seven epistles to various churches. Eusebius and Jerome arrange these writings as follows: (1) To the Ephesians; (2) to the Magnesians; (3) to the Trallians; (4) to the Romans; (5) to the Philadelphians; (6) to the Smyrneans; (7) to Polycarp, bishop, or presbyter, of Smyrna. These seven epistles, in connection with a number of others confessedly spurious, have come down to us in two Greek copies, a longer and a shorter. A Syriac version of three epistles has recently been found. Without entering into the controversy concerning these Ignatian Epistles, we give the conclusion reached by Dr. Schaff, which is very generally accepted : "The question lies between the shorter Greek copy and the Syriac version. The preponderance of testimony is for the former, in which the letters are no loose patch-work, but were produced, each under its one impulse, were well known to Eusebius, probably even to Polycarp, and agree also with the Armenian version of the fifth century." (History of the Christian Church, vol. i. p. 466.) It is admitted, even by those who do not accept the Greek copy as genuine, that it is the work of the close of the second century, or a little later. In any event, then, it is important testimony. In the epistles to the Magnesians occurs the following language : "Be not deceived with false doctrines, nor old, unprofitable fables. For, if we still live in accordance with Judaism, we confess that we have not re-

ceived grace. For even the most holy prophets lived according to Jesus Christ. . . . If, then, they who were brought up in ancient things arrived at a newness of hope, no longer keeping the Sabbath, but living according to the Lord's life, . . . how can we live without him? . . . Since we have been made his disciples, let us learn to live according to Christianity."*
—*Ad Magnes.* capp. 8, 9 ; Coteler's Edition, vol. ii. pp. 19, 20. Amsterdam, 1724.

In this passage, it will be observed, the writer draws a contrast between Judaism and Christianity. To keep the seventh-day Sabbath was to live according to Judaism. To live according to the dominical life, or, as the thought is otherwise

---

*Not a few eminent writers, such as Dwight, and Wilson, of Calcutta, who are followed by many lesser authors, quote Ignatius as saying: "Let us no more Sabbatize, but keep the Lord's day." From the literal rendering of the original above given, it will be seen that these writers take an unwarrantable liberty with their author. The words of Ignatius are, ἀλλὰ κατὰ τὴν κυριακὴν ζωὴν ζῶντες. To separate the noun ζωὴν from the preceding adjective, and connect it with the following participle, so as to read, "Living a life according to the Lord's day," is an unnatural separation of the words of the original. To drop out the word ζωὴν is unwarranted. If this word were spurious, then the rendering would be, "Living according to the Lord's day," the adjective κυριακη, without the noun for "day" being expressed, occurring frequently for "the Lord's day." But there is no ground for rejecting the word "life." To color the language of an author for the sake of giving it point in favor of one side of a question is unworthy of a seeker after truth. In the present case, there is really nothing gained by departing from the precise language of the writer. Another passage, often quoted as from Ignatius, is part of the spurious epistle to the Galatians. It is as follows : "During the Sabbath, Christ continued under the earth, in the tomb in which Joseph of Arimathea had laid him. At the dawning of the Lord's day, he arose from the dead. The day of the preparation, then, comprises the passion ; the Lord's day contains the resurrection." This certainly has some weight as the testimony of a comparatively early writer, but it must not be ascribed to Ignatius.

expressed, to live according to Christianity, was opposed to the keeping of the seventh-day Sabbath. The argument of Ignatius tells strongly in favor of the first-day Sabbath. If Jews, he argues, brought up in the old order of things, on turning Christians, no longer keep the seventh-day Sabbath, but live according to the dominical life, observing as part of that life, the dominical day, the day on which the Lord rose from the dead, surely those who never had been Jews should live according to Christianity, and not give heed to Judaizing teachers.

Passing on, we come to a document called "The Epistle of Barnabas." This letter, though not the composition of the Barnabas of the New Testament, was written in the early part of the second century. It cannot be determined who was the author, but *the early date* of the letter is fully established; and that is the main point. Its language is: "We celebrate the eighth day with joy, on which Jesus rose from the dead." —*Coteler's Edition of the Apostolic Fathers*, vol. i. p. 47.

The testimony of Justin Martyr is full and explicit. As an itinerant evangelist for many years during the first half of the second century, just after the time of the apostle John, he enjoyed an excellent opportunity of becoming acquainted with the customs of the whole church. Writing in the year 139 to the Emperor Antoninus Pius, in vindication of his Christian brethren, he gives the following account of their stated religious services: "On the day called the day of the sun is an assembly of all who live either in cities or in the rural districts, and the memoirs of the apostles and the writings of the prophets are read ;" *i. e.*, the Old and New Testaments. Then he goes on to specify the various parts of their first-day services. Just as at the present day, in Christian congregations, there were preaching, prayer, the celebration of the Lord's supper, and the contribution of alms. As reasons why Christians should observe the first day, he assigns the following: "Because it was the first day on which God dispelled the darkness and chaos, and formed the world, and because Jesus Christ, our Saviour, rose from the dead on it."—*Robert Stephens' edition of the works of Justin Martyr*, p. 162. Lutetiæ, 1551.

In another of his works, the Dialogue with Trypho the Jew, written about the same time as the Apology, from which we have quoted, occurs this passage: "The command to circumcise infants on the eighth day was a type of the true circumcision by which we were circumcised from error and evil through our Lord Jesus Christ, who rose from the dead on the first day of the week; for the first day of the week remains the chief of all the days." (Stephens' Edition, p. 59. See also Trollope's edition of the Dialogue with Trypho, pp. 85, 86.) The careful reader of Justin Martyr will observe that, in addressing Trypho the Jew, he uses different terms for the days of the week from those which he employs in addressing the Emperor Antoninus. Addressing a heathen emperor, he employs the heathen names for both the seventh and the first day of the week.

Two important notices of the Lord's day, all the more important because of their incidental character, are found in the History of Eusebius. Dionysius, bishop or presbyter of Corinth, A. D.

170, in a letter to the church at Rome, a fragment of which is preserved by Eusebius, says: "To-day we kept the Lord's holy day, in which we read your letter." (Hist. Eccles. iv. 23, Paris Ed. 1678, pp. 117, 118.) The other of these notices is in regard to a treatise on the Lord's day, by Melito, bishop of Sardis, A. D. 170. This treatise, Eusebius remarks, along with others by the same writer, had come to the historian's knowledge.—*Hist. Eccles.* iv. 26, Paris Ed. 1678, p. 119.

Although the letter of Pliny to Trajan is so well known as hardly to need quotation, we shall close this article with its interesting testimony in confirmation, from a pagan quarter, of what has already been adduced from Christian writers: " They [the Christians] affirmed that the sum of their fault, or error, was that they were accustomed to assemble on a stated day—*Stato die*—before it was light, and sing praise alternately among themselves to Christ as God—*carmenque Christo, quasi Deo, dicere secum invicem."* (Plin. Epist. x., 97.) Here we have the fact that Christians in the early part of the second century met regularly on a stated day, and this stated day, as all the Christian authorities of the same date prove, was the first day of the week, the Lord's day.

Additional patristic evidence will be given in the next article.

A REJOINDER.

"TESTIMONY OF THE EARLY FATHERS TO THE FIRST-DAY SABBATH."

THERE is one feature which has characterized this debate, hitherto, which has been a source of considerable satisfaction. The controversy, up to this point, has been urged purely with reference to the teaching of the Bible, as drawn from its sacred pages. Henceforth, however, this is not to be the case. We are now to have, not the "sure word of prophecy," with the clear and forcible lines of textual evidence, drawn from its inspired utterances, but that "word of prophecy," supplemented and explained by the apostolic fathers.

It has been said, and well said, that history repeats itself. If there was one thing which marked the religious impulse that Protestantism gave to the world, it was an utter rejection, in the decision of religious opinions, of everything but Bible authority. The voice of Martin Luther even now seems to reverberate in our ears, as —when fighting the very battles which Sabbatarians are being called upon to fight over again —he retorted in sharp and stinging words upon his cowled and priestly opponents, who were ever citing patristic evidence, The Bible, and the Bible alone, is our rule of faith. Again, as we read the words addressed by him to those friends who were hopefully waiting the expected reply from the Romanists of his time, to a courageous assault which he had made upon them from the stand-point of the Bible, it seems as if they were designed to be prophetic of our time, rather than descriptive of his own. He said: "You are waiting for your adversaries' answer; it is already written, and here it is: 'The fathers, the fathers, the fathers; the church, the church, the church; usage, custom; but of the Scriptures—nothing!'"—*D'Aubigné's Hist. Ref.*, vol. viii., p. 717.

Wearisome as these repeated conflicts may be to the child of God, there is a satisfaction in the thought that we hold in our hands the same weapons, and bear aloft the same banners by which, under the blessing of God, victory, complete and universal, has been attained in the past. The opponents of Bible truth have never yet been able to stand before the thunder of its power, or to balance the ponderous weight of its influence, in the decision of religious questions. The homely phrase of the great reformer is just as potent and irresistible in the present contest as it was in that for which it was framed: "When God's word is by the fathers expounded, construed, and glossed, then, in my judgment, it is even like unto one that straineth milk through a coal-sack, which must needs spoil the milk, and make it black; even so, likewise, God's word of itself is sufficiently pure, clean, bright, and clear; but through the doctrines, books, and writings, of the fathers, it is very surely darkened, falsified, and spoiled."

The elegant and convincing logic of Philip Melancthon, the greatest theologian of the sixteenth century—who, in the following brief lines, discussed and summed up the whole question—is just as sound and unanswerable now as it was when, under the blessing of God, it carried confusion and defeat into the ranks of the papacy, three hundred years ago. He says: "How often has not Jerome been mistaken! how often Augustine! how often Ambrose! How often do we not find them differing in judgment—how often do we not hear them retracting their errors! There is but one Scripture divinely inspired, and without mixture of error." (*Idem.*, p. 219.) In fine, we might prove from history that nearly every Protestant writer, for the last three centuries, has forged for us weapons which could be employed with the most telling effect in the controversy in which we are now engaged.

This, however, we have not space to do, but must content ourselves with several brief citations, by which we will show that the authorities of our own times—equally with those of the past—are uniform in their expressions of contempt for testimony which is so largely relied upon by our reviewer in the present discussion. "To avoid being imposed upon, we ought to treat tradition as we do a notorious and known liar, to whom we give no credit, unless what he says is confirmed to us by some person of undoubted veracity. . . . False and lying traditions are of an early date, and the greatest men have, out of a pious credulity, suffered themselves to be imposed upon by them."—*Archibald Bower*.

"But of these, we may safely state that there is not a *truth* of the most orthodox creed that cannot be proved by their authority; nor a *heresy* that has disgraced the Romish church, that may not challenge them as it abettors. In point of *doctrine*, their authority is, *with me, nothing*. The WORD of God alone contains my creed. On a number of points, I can go to the Greek and Latin fathers of the church, to know what *they believed*, and what the people of their respective communions believed; but after all this, I must return to God's word to know what he would have me to believe." (A. Clark, Com. on Prov. 8.) "We should take heed how we quote the fathers in proof of the doctrines of the gospel; because he who knows them best, knows that on many of those subjects they blow hot and cold." (Quoted in Hist. of Sab. from Autobiography of Adam Clarke.)

"Most of the writings, bearing the name of the apostolic fathers, are regarded as spurious by various modern critics. The genuineness of all has been disputed; but the fragments that remain are curious as relics of an early age, and valuable as indicating the character of primitive Christianity." (Am. Cyc., Art. Apostolic Fathers.) Thus much for the estimate which Protestants place upon the authorities which are brought forward by the gentleman in the *Statesman*. Assuredly, he would never have appealed to them, had he not felt that his cause was a hopeless one, when left to the arbitrament of Scripture.

Should it be pleaded in extenuation of his cause that they have not been advanced with a view to influencing the judgment of the reader in reference to the continuity of the old Sabbath, but were introduced simply to furnish, as suggested in the outset, a criticism showing the use of the term, "Lord's day," in the first three centuries, then, we inquire, why cite Ignatius at all? It will be perceived at a glance that, according to the rendering which he has given us—and for which, and his note thereon, he will receive our thanks, since it will save us much labor—there is not in it a single mention of the term, "Lord's day." If the passage conveys any meaning at all, it is either that the Sabbath should be observed in a manner differing from that in which it was kept by the Jews, or else that it should not be observed at all.

But the last of these propositions, the writer will not admit to be sound, since he has fairly repudiated such a conception, and has, in so many words, stated that he heartily agrees with us in the perpetuity of the Edenic Sabbath. He has also stated that the fourth commandment—which it will be admitted commences with the words, "Remember the *Sabbath day*, to keep it holy"—is a Sabbath law which is still binding, and which, the words of Ignatius to the contrary notwithstanding, forever settles the question that this is not a Sabbathless dispensation.

What shall be done, then, with the language of the venerable father? We are well acquainted with the office which it has performed hitherto, and are anxious to know where it is to throw its baleful shadow hereafter. In the past, hundreds of individuals whose consciences have been aroused by appeals to the Bible on the subject of the perpetuity of God's holy day, have had their fears quieted, and have been lulled into security by the very extract with which we are here favored. Why, they have said, was not Ignatius a disciple of John, and did he not therefore know what John believed? Did he not also prove his integrity by becoming a martyr to the faith? Since, therefore, he was possessed of both knowledge and piety, and since he has called the first day of the week the Lord's day, are we not justified in keeping the day which he kept, and rejecting the day which he rejected? Supported and encouraged in this position, as they have been by the brethren of the writer who—having either less candor, or less scholarship, than he—have insisted again and again that Ignatius did call the first day of the week the Lord's day, it has been in many cases utterly impossible for Sabbatarians to disabuse their minds of this impression. With gratitude, therefore, we shall add the name of the gentleman to the rapidly increasing list of scholars who, headed by Kitto, and others of equal distinction, frankly concede that Sabbatarians have been in the right, and that Ignatius did not speak of the Lord's day at all, but simply alluded to the Lord's life.

But what shall we say for those who have been deluded upon this point, and have thus been prevented from doing what they felt that duty required? There is a terrible responsibility somewhere. For the scholars who have abetted this deception, there can be no defense. For the unfortunate victims of the fraud, it may be said that their situation would be more hopeful had they not brought themselves into the difficulty by going upon forbidden ground. Should one be led astray by an incorrect translation of the Scriptures, God would undoubtedly pardon the mistake; for the person had done the best he could under the circumstances, and had sought for light where God had instructed him so to do. But to those who, having left the only true source of trustworthy knowledge, have allowed any class of persons, ancient or modern, to shape their belief differently from what it would have been had they relied wholly upon the Bible, we fear that Christ will say—as he did to those in like circumstances in his day, who, having followed the traditions of their ancestors, were found violating the law of God—"In vain do ye worship me, teaching for doctrines the commandments of men."

Before closing on this point, and in order that the citation may not be employed in the interest of no-Sabbath views, let the reader consider, for a moment, another feature, and a very important one in this argument. Having seen that Ignatius —if he wrote the above—did not mention the Lord's day, it is proper now to inquire whether it is certain that he ever penned the language in question, at all? To this it may be replied, that it is very far from being so. Nay, it is in the highest degree probable, as the following extracts will prove, that the venerable man either never wrote a word of those which are cited, or, if he did, what he said has been so manipulated that it is very far from conveying the impression which he intended. "From Smyrna, he (Ignatius) wrote to the churches at Ephesus, Magnesia, Trallia, Rome, and Philadelphia, and on his voyage, to Polycarp, and the church at Smyrna. These letters are still extant, though the genuineness of the first three is doubted by some learned men." (*Cyc. Relig. Knowl. Art. Ignatius.*)

The distinguished historian and scholar, Kitto, speaks on this point in his Cyclopedia, Art. Lord's Day, as follows: "We must notice one other passage as bearing on the subject of the Lord's day, though it certainly contains no mention of it. It occurs in the epistle of Ignatius to the Magnesians (about A. D. 100). The whole passage is evidently obscure, and the text may be corrupt." Originally, there were fifteen letters attributed to Ignatius. Centuries ago, however, eight of them were rejected as hopelessly spurious. The remaining seven have been also denounced as forgeries, by many writers, with John Calvin at their head. Others, while holding on to four of the seven, have condemned three, and among them the letter to the Magnesians, from which the citation which we are considering was taken. A poor stone, this, which purports to come from Antioch, for the headstone of the corner of the temple of patristic testimonials to the Sunday.

The way is now prepared for the consideration of the second extract, namely, that of Barnabas. Here, again, the confession of the gentleman is of service to us, by way of saving labor, since he unequivocally admits that the Barnabas who wrote the letter from which he quotes, was not the Barnabas of New-Testament fame. It becomes important, however, that we should know just who he was who wrote this epistle, before it should be received as authority in a grave religious discussion. Few persons would have the temerity to commit their spiritual interests to the hands of nameless individuals who lived 1700 years ago, unless they could feel some assurance that the men in whom they were thus confiding were persons whose judgment should have weight in the decision of matters of faith.

It is not enough that it should be established, even beyond doubt, that the writer in question lived in the second century. For no one will insist that *all the men* who lived at that time were proper exponents of the views held by Christians in that period. It is, therefore, but reasonable that, before any man is brought forward to testify in so important a matter, he should have either a name which will show that he was qualified, both morally and intellectually, to act the part of a public teacher of the opinions held in his time, or, at least, that what he has written must be of a nature to commend his utterances to our judgments. Neither of these requisitions, however, is met in the case of the Barnabas (if his name was really Barnabas) quoted above.*

That his epistle has been employed in a gigantic fraud, no one will dispute. It is headed, "The general Epistle of Barnabas." At its close, as given in the apocryphal New Testament,

---

* Did it not appear to be indispensable to the enlightening of the reader, as to the consummate folly of the author of the epistle of Barnabas, we should not append, as we do, his language in the following note, since it is hardly worthy of a place in a chaste and dignified discussion. For its citation, we hold those responsible who have made this action necessary, and who value the testimony of a man so utterly devoid of common-sense: "Neither shalt thou eat of the hyena; that is, again, be not an adulterer; nor a corrupter of others; neither be like to such. And wherefore so? Because that creature every year changes its kind, and is sometimes male and sometimes female." Chap. 9: 8.

is the subscription, "Barnabas, the apostle, and companion of Paul." Now, if he wrote these words himself, the gentleman will admit that he is unworthy of the slightest confidence, since he has told a deliberate falsehood. If, on the other hand, it be insisted that this was the work of subsequent generations, then we must move with extreme caution. In the region where this epistle lies, are the unmistakable footprints of men base enough to pervert the facts, and to employ its contents for an unworthy purpose.

The only alternative left us, therefore, since the author of the document is unknown to history, is that of examining what he has said, with reference to its character. Before doing this, however, it will be well to state—by way of putting the reader on his guard—that the history of this epistle is of a nature to awaken the most serious suspicion. By consulting the Am. Cyc., Art. Epistle of Barnabas, he will find it there stated that this epistle was lost to the world for eight hundred years, namely, from the ninth to the seventeenth century, and that, when it came to the surface after its long disappearance, it was found in the hands of one Sigismond, a Jesuit of that age. The desperate character of the order to which this man belonged, and the recklessness with which its members treat documents of the most sacred character, when they can thereby serve a favorite purpose, need no comment here.

Prof. Stowe, while arguing favorably to the epistle, in some respects, employs the following words, which have in them great significance, in view of what has been said above: "We admit that the epistle of Barnabas is strongly interpolated."—*Hist. of Books of the Bible*, p. 423.

It is now time to ponder, for a moment, the words of the nondescript writer quoted above. They are as follows: "We celebrate the eighth day with joy, on which Jesus rose from the dead." In them is found not a single fact which, granting their authenticity, is at all decisive in the matter at issue. For, be it remembered, the controversy is not as to whether the ancients were in the habit of holding convocations for any purpose whatsoever, on the first day of the week, but, whether they called it the Lord's day. It will, therefore, be admitted that the term, Lord's day, is not so much as mentioned; whereas, the day which it is supposed was entitled to the honor of being thus designated, is termed the "eighth day, the one on which Jesus rose from the dead." Nor is it so much as intimated that the day in question was observed as a Sabbath, or esteemed as holy. The statement employed is that "they celebrated it with joy." But this could be said with perfect propriety of any day of the week on which there regularly occurred a religious festival.

As an illustration of this, it might be mentioned here that a historian of the present time, while mentioning the usages of this period, could not be charged with inaccuracy should he declare that the 25th of December, which is supposed by some to be the day of the Lord's nativity, is regularly celebrated. Should he do so, and should coming generations infer therefrom that it is now regarded as holy, you will readily perceive the mistake into which they would fall. What we want, if we must have recourse to such *miserable material* as that which we are handling over, is something positive and definite. This the text undeniably fails to give. We leave it, therefore, as worthless; 1st. Because we do not know *who* wrote it. 2d. Because we do not know *when* it was written. 3d. Because it is found in an epistle so corrupted by interpolations that it is not at all reliable as authority. 4th. Because it has no direct bearing upon the subject. 5th. Because its author—by the absurd and ridiculous sentiments to which he gave expression—manifestly had a judgment too weak to allow us to suppose that, in the providence of God, in which nothing falls out by mistake, he should constitute a pillar in any way necessary to the establishment of sound religious doctrine.

The third authority brought forward is Justin Martyr. From him we learn that, on the day of the sun, the church at Rome were in the habit of convening, partaking of the Lord's supper, listening to preaching, engaging in prayer, and in the contribution of alms,

It will be at once perceived that here is the nearest approach yet made to the accomplishment of the task which our reviewer assigned himself, and for which he has led the reader away from the oracles of God to the opinions and practices of men liable to error and mistake. Let it not be forgotten that the *prominent* object to be gained by this departure, was the production of patristic authority for the use of the term, Lord's day, in the first three centuries. That this purpose has not been accomplished, hitherto, all must admit. The next inquiry, therefore, is, should all points of dispute respecting the reliability of what has been quoted above, be waived, and should it be granted that Justin Martyr said what is attributed to him, Has the desired object been reached ? The answer is emphatically in the negative. Justin Martyr avoids the application of Lord's day to the day of the sun, as if prevented from using it by the same fatality which has withheld all the others from doing so, who have thus far been cited.

Here we might pause, and insist that the gentleman has utterly failed, in the citation before us, to prove anything which is really relevant to the subject. It is in vain that he urges, in extenuation of the fact that Justin calls the first day of the week, the " day of the sun," that he is addressing a heathen emperor. He was not afraid to speak to that emperor of the Old and New Testaments, of the preaching of the word, of the Lord's supper, and of the resurrection of Christ; and why should he thus carefully avoid mention of the Lord's day? Surely, he did not wish to convey the impression that Christians observed the day of the sun because of its heathen character, since he gives the reasons for their doing so.

But, again, it is claimed that at this period the chosen and peculiar appellation which had been given by the Holy Spirit, was that of Lord's day, and that the Lord's day, or the Sunday, had become the holy Sabbath which God commanded. This being true, assuredly we might expect that, in the work of Justin entitled, "A Dialogue with Trypho, the Jew," he would set forth, in the use of its peculiar title, the claims of that day which had been elevated, by divine command, to the position of the ancient Sabbath. But does he do this? The gentleman does not urge it. He does say that, in writing to the Jew, he drops the heathen titles of Sunday and Saturday, and speaks of the first, and the seventh, day of the week. But mark again; it is not urged that he anywhere calls the first day the Lord's day. Once more, therefore, he has failed on this branch of the subject.

Now it will be well to regard the matter from the other side of the question. It must be conceded, as remarked above, that what Justin Martyr says furnishes stronger support for the idea of worship on the Sunday than anything else which has been adduced. But here again, we protest that the Bible, alone and unexplained, is sufficient for the settlement of this point. Others, if they like, may form their religious faith upon the practice of uninspired men, handed down to us through the perilous transit of the ages, protected and shielded from corruption and innovation by no denunciation of divine wrath against those who change its phraseology; but we much prefer to stand under the covering ægis of these words: "If any man shall add unto these things, God shall add unto him the plagues which are written in this book." (Rev. 22:18.) Nor do we think that the gentleman himself would seriously urge that this position is unsound. Let us test it. Justin Martyr is assumed to be a fair exponent of the religious sentiment of his time. Now, therefore, what he believed they believed; and what they believed, we ought to believe, if our position, taken above, is not correct. Proceeding a step farther, we inquire, what was the faith of Justin Martyr and his contemporaries, allowing his writings to be the criterion of judgment? To this it may replied:

1st. That they believed in no Sabbath in this dispensation. Proof: "For if before Abraham there was no need of circumcision, nor of Sabbaths, nor of feasts, nor of offerings before Moses; so now in like manner there is no need of them, since Jesus Christ, the Son of God, was, by the determinate counsel of God, born of a virgin of the seed of Abraham, without sin." (Dial. of Trypho.) Does the writer believe this? The reader well knows that he does not, for he has nobly repudiated it, again and again.

2d. They believed that the Sabbath was imposed upon the Jews for their sins. Proof: "It was because of your (*i. e.*, Jews) iniquities, and the iniquities of your fathers, that God appointed you to observe the Sabbath." (*Idem.*) But our reviewer holds—as must all who accept the words of Christ (Mark 2:27, 28)—that it was given to Adam in the garden of Eden, as their representative head, for the benefit of the whole race, more than two thousand years before there was a Jew in the world.

3d. They believed that, in the administration of the Lord's supper, water should be employed. Proof: "At the conclusion of this discourse, *i. e.*, that of the Bishop on Sunday, we all rise up together and pray; and prayers being over, there is bread, and wine, and water offered." (First Apol. Trans. by Reeves.) But modern Christendom look upon this as an innovation of popery.

4th. They believed that the reasons why Christians should observe the first day of the week were found in the facts that God dispelled the darkness and chaos on the first day of the week, and that on that day, Christ rose from the dead. Proof: Extract given above by the writer in his article. But the first of these opinions, modern Christians will not admit at all, and the latter furnishes only one-half of the obligation, since it ignores all positive law upon the subject.

So we might proceed, but enough has been said to show that Justin Martyr, as quoted above, is no criterion for the faith of those who have the Bible in their hands, from which they can learn, contrary to his views: 1st. That we have a Sabbath. 2d. That it was given to all mankind as a blessing, and not to the Jews for their sins. 3d. That both the bread and the wine belong to the laity, as well as to the priests. 4th. That the reasons for the observance of the Lord's day do not rest upon the circumstance that God dispelled the darkness on the first day, but upon an explicit command of Heaven.

If the reader would satisfy himself from other sources that the statements of Justin Martyr are to be taken with extreme caution, and that his judgment was so easily imposed upon as to render him an unsafe guide in the plainest matters of fact, he will read the following extract from a publication of the Am. Tract Society: "Justin Martyr appears indeed peculiarly unfitted to lay claim to authority. It is notorious that he supposed a pillar erected on the island of the Tiber to Semo Sanchus, an old Sabine Deity, to be a monument erected by the Roman people in honor of the imposter, Simon Magus. Were so gross a mistake to be made by a modern writer, in relating a historical fact, exposure would immediately take place, and his testimony would thenceforward be suspected. And, assuredly, the same measure should be meted to Justin Martyr, who so egregiously errs in reference to a fact alluded to by Livy, the historian."—*Spirit of Popery*, pp. 44, 45.

In concluding the remarks which will be offered here—in reference to those productions which are attributed to Justin Martyr, and which have been brought forward for the purpose of influencing the mind of the reader in favor of a cause which has found no support in the Scriptures—it is proper to state that their authenticity is by no means above suspicion; or, to speak more accurately, that some of them have been tampered with, is a matter which is settled beyond dispute. Already the reader has seen that by some means they have been made to contribute to the interests of the Romish doctrine of the use of water in the sacrament, as early as the first part of the second century. If it be granted that the statement in question is historically true, then the leaven of the papacy had begun to work so manifestly in the lifetime of Justin, that the opinions of his associates, as well as of himself, ought to have no weight with us who have repudiated the great apostasy.

On the other hand, should it be denied that water was then employed, as stated by the venerable father, there remain but two conclusions between which the reader can take his choice; either, 1st. Justin did not correctly represent the faith of his time; or, 2d. What he did say originally has been molded and fashioned by the plastic hand of the man of sin, until it is made to support the heresies of the hierarchy. To our mind, the latter conclusion is undoubtedly the true one. Below will be found an extract from a distinguished historian of the church, which proves that what is said above respecting the treatment which the writings of Justin Martyr have received is correct: " Like many of the ancient fathers, he [Justin] appears to us under the greatest disadvantage. Works really his have been lost, and others have been ascribed to him, part of which are not his; and the rest, at least, of ambiguous authority."—*Milner's History of Church*, Book 2, Chap. 3.*

The fourth historic mention of the Lord's day, as brought forward, is in the following words of Dionysius: "To-day we kept the Lord's holy day, in which we read your letter." By turning to Eusebius, the curious reader will discover that the citation incidentally given occupies but little

---

*Since writing the above, the following interesting item in the *Christian Union*, for Feb. 19, has been brought to my notice, and will serve to show that continued investigation on the part of scholars is rendering the authenticity of the writings of Justin Martyr more and more doubtful:—"Dr. Franz Overbeck has lately examined, with great care, the 'epistle to Diognetus,' which has been regarded as one of the most precious relics of the age succeeding that of the apostles. He urges several reasons for coming to the conclusion that the work was written later than the era of Constantine, and was intended by its author to pass as a work of Justin Martyr's. Critics had already proved it no genuine work of Justin, and if Dr. Overbeck is right, it can no longer be assigned to the age of Justin."

more space than is required for the words as quoted. Their importance in this discussion does not demand for them any more room than was assigned them by the historian from whom they are extracted. The dispute is not whether there is indeed a Lord's day, for both parties are agreed respecting this question. What we wish to ascertain is, Which day of the week is entitled to this appellation? The reference before us in no way helps in the settlement of this point. It simply states that the letter was read on the Lord's day. Whether that was the first or the seventh in the cycle of the week is not stated, so we pass the language as unworthy of further consideration.

The allusion to the fifth authority is even more unsatisfactory than that of the fourth. It seems that Melito, bishop of Sardis, had written a discourse on the Lord's day, which had been seen by Eusebius. As to its contents, the letter says not one word, neither shall we; for, as it is not now in existence, it is impossible that any person should be able to decide which view it would favor, provided it were in being.

The sixth proof is brought from the writings of Pliny. It is couched in these words: "They [the Christians] affirmed that the sum of their fault, or error, was, that they were accustomed to assemble on a stated day, before it was light, and sing praise alternately among themselves, to Christ, as God." Without debating the propriety of bringing forward a heathen writer to prove the practice of a Christian church, we proceed to examine the testimony itself. Its utter inability to fill the place assigned to it will be discerned by every intelligent person who examines its phraseology. In it is the declaration that Christians were in the habit of assembling on a stated day, at which time they sang praises alternately among themselves, to Christ, as God.

Now that the statement of the facts is not incompatible with the idea that they were observers of the seventh day, all must admit. For surely, there is no incongruity in the notion that it would be in the highest degree proper for the observers of the ancient Sabbath of the Lord to devote its sacred hours to the delightful task of singing hymns of praise, and worshiping Christ, as God. That the language itself as completely harmonizes with this view, as with any other, will be felt when we remember that the writer does not say that they assembled on the first day of the week, or the Lord's day, at all; but, simply, that it was on a stated day that they gathered themselves together for the purposes of worship. A stated day is one which recurs at fixed intervals. The Sabbath might have been the stated day; or, so far as anything to the contrary in the passage is concerned, the Sunday might have been the one. Pliny does not decide the point for us. His declarations, therefore, have not the slightest force in proving anything favorable to the opinions of the gentleman.

Furthermore, if inference is to be taken at all, the preponderance would rather be in favor of the last day of the week, since, in devoting it to the worship of Christ, they would not only bring upon themselves the wrath of the heathen, because of their acknowledgment of our Lord's divinity; but, also, in the sum of their fault would be found the fact, that they ignored the sacredness of the day of the sun, and celebrated another, as holy, by divine command.

Thus much for the uninspired witnesses, brought forward from the first, and the early part of the second, century of the Christian era. Had they flatly contradicted what we have seen the teachings of the Bible to be, they would not have moved us one hair; for we remember that the great apostle has said, that, though "an angel from Heaven preach any other gospel unto you, let him be accursed." But, strangely enough, their testimony is utterly worthless for the purpose for which it has been introduced. Not one of them has styled the Sunday the Lord's day; not one of them has called it the Sabbath; not one of them has stated that it was regarded as holy, or that its hours might not, without sin, be devoted to secular pursuits. Here, then, we leave them, and wait for a fresh inundation of such as will answer the purpose for which they are called in a more satisfactory manner than the foregoing.

STATESMAN'S REPLY.

ARTICLE EIGHT.

PATRISTIC TESTIMONY TO THE FIRST-DAY SABBATH.

THE testimony already adduced from the early fathers in our last issue will be regarded by most of our readers as sufficient in itself. But for the sake of giving a complete view of the patristic testimony to the first-day Sabbath up to the close of the third century, we shall occupy some additional space with extracts, on the accuracy of which our readers may confidently rely.

First among the witnesses now cited is Irenæus, bishop or presbyter of Lyons, A. D. 178. Let it be remembered that in the case of this witness we have the testimony of one who was brought up at the feet of Polycarp, the disciple and companion of the Apostle John. The first point to be noted in the testimony of Irenæus is the abrogation of the seventh-day Sabbath. As the rite of circumcision was no longer required, so the observance of the seventh-day Sabbath had ceased. Each was a sign or shadow of the substance to come. This thought is dwelt upon at great length. (See *Contra Hæreses*, book iv. ch. 30, Grabe's Edition, Oxford, 1702, pp. 318, 319; also Benedictine Edit., Paris, 1710, p. 246.)

Lest his statements might be understood to be opposed to the authority of the ten commandments, Irenæus adds the following sentences: "The Lord spoke the words of the decalogue in like manner to all. They remain, therefore, permanently with us, receiving, through the Lord's advent in the flesh, extension and increase, not abrogation." (Book iv. ch. 31, p. 320.) Thus the law of the Sabbath remains, though not binding to the observance of the seventh day.

We now come to this writer's clear and distinct testimony, in its more positive aspect, to the Lord's day. Irenæus took a prominent part in what has been called the Quarta-Deciman controversy. The question at issue was—Should the anniversary of the Lord's resurrection be in connection with the Jewish passover, on whatever day of the week that might occur, or on the Lord's day invariably? This question first arose on a visit of Polycarp, bishop or presbyter of Smyrna, to Aniest, bishop of Rome, about 160, and was discussed for many years. Irenæus, acting as the representative of the Christians in Gaul, wrote to Victor, then bishop of Rome, in these terms: "The mystery of the Lord's resurrection should be celebrated only on the Lord's day." (*Euseb. Hist. Eccles.* book v. chap. 23, 24; Paris ed., 1678, pp. 155, 156.) It will be remarked here that while there was diversity of view in regard to the *yearly* celebration of the Lord's resurrection —a celebration of which we have no account whatever until the year 160, there was no question concerning the sacred observance of the first day as the *weekly* commemoration of the Lord's rising from the dead.

We simply add a reference to one of the best known of the fragments of Irenæus in which there is further explicit testimony to the Lord's day—testimony all the more important, because it occurs incidentally in a treatise concerning the passover, and in connection with a statement in regard to Pentecost." (*Fragmentum lib. de Pascha,* Bened. ed., Paris, 1742, p. 490.*)

For the sake of presenting a complete view of the testimony of the fathers for the first three centuries, we had thought of quoting from Clement of Alexandria, A. D. 194; Minucius Felix, 210; Commodian, about 270; Victorinus, 290; and Peter, bishop of Alexandria, 300. But as the testimony will be perfectly conclusive without these witnessess, and as space is valuable, we shall cite only three more authorities—three

---

* The culpable carelessness of Dwight, Wilson, and other authors, in citing from the early fathers, is nowhere more noticeable than in the case of Irenæus. These writers quote him as saying : "On the Lord's day, every one of us Christians, keeps the Sabbath, meditating on the law, and rejoicing in the works of God." There is no reference given to the writings of Irenæus. And for good reason. After a most careful examination, we are persuaded no such passage is to be found in his writings. The mistake was probably first made by President Dwight, whose weakness of sight compelled him to depend upon an amanuensis. "For twenty years of his presidency," we are informed by his biographer, "he was rarely able to read so much as a single chapter in the Bible in the twenty-four hours." (*Dwight's Theology,* London, 1821, vol. i. pp. 94, 95.) Others followed this high authority.

In order to guard our readers against injuring the cause they would advance, we must mention another important instance of censurable negligence. In a number of works on the Sabbath, Dr. Justin Edwards' "Sabbath Manual," for example, we find not only the blunders already noticed, but another quite as bad. The language—"Both custom and reason challenge from us that we should honor the Lord's day, seeing on that day it was that our Lord Jesus completed his resurrection from the dead," is ascribed to Theophilus, bishop of Antioch, about A. D. 162. The words quoted are in reality those of another Theophilus, who was bishop of Alexandria, at the close of the fourth century. We hand over these criticisms upon advocates of the first-day Sabbath to our seventh-day Sabbatarian friends, trusting to their honor and fairness not to separate them from the rest of this discussion. For our own part, whether it may be pleasant to the advocates of the seventh-day Sabbath, we desire to have for ourselves, and to aid others to have, the whole truth. It was in this spirit that we gave room in our columns for a full presentation of the arguments on the other side of this question.

well-known fathers, Tertullian, Origen, and Cyprian.

At the close of the second century, Carthage, the metropolis of Northern Africa, was the center of numerous flourishing Christian congregations. Living in Carthage for many years, Tertullian knew well the practice of the African churches. And although he became, about 202, one of the errorists known as Montanists, his testimony, however unreliable as to doctrines, is still indisputable as to facts. From the frequent references to the Lord's day in this author we select the following: "By us, to whom the [Jewish] Sabbaths are strange, and the new moons and festivals once pleasing to God, the Saturnalia, January, and mid-winter feasts, and Matronalia [of the heathen] are frequented. O better fidelity of the heathen to their own religion! They would not share with us the Lord's day, nor Pentecost, even if they knew them, for they would fear lest they should seem to be Christians." (*De Idolatria*, cap. xiv, Semler's edit., Halæ Magdeburg, vol. iv., pp., 167, 168.) The testimony of this passage is decisive in three points: (1.) The Jewish, or seventh-day, Sabbath was not observed by Christians. (2.) They were enjoined not to observe heathen festivals. (3.) To the Lord's day, as the proper day for Christian service, belonged the honor to which Jewish and heathen days had no claim.

The exercises of the Lord's day, when Christians assembled for public service, are described by Tertullian in a manner very similar to that of Justin Martyr, whose account has already been quoted. Prayer, reading the Scriptures, exhortations, and collections for benevolent purposes are all mentioned. (*Apol.*, cap. xxxix, vol. v., pp. 92-94.) It is to be noted that Tertullian, like Justin Martyr, in addressing the heathen, calls the first day of the week "the day of the Sun," as he also designates the Jewish Sabbath by its heathen name. (See *Apol.*, cap. xvi.)

We close these citations from Tertullian, with one which is of the greatest importance in proving that the early Christians observed the first day of the week, not as a mere holiday, but as a day of rest and worship—a holy Sabbath to the Lord: "On the Lord's day, the day of the Resurrection, we should not only abstain from that,* [bending the knee,] but also from all anxiety of feeling, and from employments, setting aside all business, lest we should give place to the devil." (*De Oratione*, cap. xxiii., vol. iv., p. 22.)

Contemporary with Tertullian at the beginning of the third century was Origen of Alexandria, one of the most scholarly and learned of all the early fathers. This writer contrasts the Lord's day with the Jewish Sabbath, and shows the superiority of the former. We may not agree with him when he maintains that the superiority was indicated by the giving of manna to the Israelites on the first day of the week, while it was withheld on the seventh. His test-

---

* As a matter of independent interest and importance, we would ask all who are interested in the question of the posture in prayer of worshipers in the early church, to compare with Tertullian's statement, that of Peter, bishop of Alexandria, A. D. 300, who says: "We keep the Lord's day as a day of joy, because of Him who rose on that day, on which we have learned not to bow the knee." (*Bibl. Patrum, apud Galland*, vol. iv., p. 107.) To the same effect is the decision of the Council of Nice, A. D. 325, requiring, as there were certain ones who bent the knee on the Lord's day, that it should be the uniform practice to give thanks to God, standing. (*Canon*, xx.)

imony to the fact of the sacred observance of the Lord's day instead of the seventh-day Sabbath is valid, though his reasons for the admitted superiority may not all be satisfactory. In the same connection he remarks: "On our Lord's day the Lord always rains manna from heaven." (*Comment on Exodus*, Delarue's ed. of Works of Origen, Paris, 1733, vol. ii., p. 154.) In another of his works he contends that it is one of the evidences of a true Christian "always to keep the Lord's day." (*Contra Celsum*, lib. viii., vol. i., pp. 758, 759.)

The most important passage in the writings of Origen is found in his Homilies on the Book of Numbers. Here we first meet with the name "Christian Sabbath" for the first day of the week, or the Lord's day: "Leaving, then, the Jewish observance of the Sabbath, let us see what the observance of the Sabbath by the Christian ought to be. On the Sabbath should be performed no worldly acts. If, therefore, you desist from all secular works, and do nothing of a worldly nature, but occupy yourselves with spiritual duties, assembling at the church, listening to the sacred readings and instructions, thinking of celestial things, concerned for the hopes of another life, keeping before your eyes the Judgment to come, and looking not at the things which are present and visible, but at those which are invisible and future—this is the observance of the Christian Sabbath." (*Hom. xxiii in Numeros*, vol. ii., p. 358.)

Cyprian, bishop of Carthage, about the third century, gives this explicit testimony to the Lord's day: "Since in the Jewish circumcision of the flesh the eighth day was celebrated, the ordinance was foreshadowed in the future, but completed in truth at the coming of Christ. For inasmuch as the eighth day, that is, the first day after the Sabbath, was the day on which the Lord rose and gave us life and spiritual circumcision, this eighth day, that is, the first after the Sabbath and the Lord's day, preceded in an image, which image ceased when the truth afterwards came, and spiritual circumcision was given to us." (*Epistle* lxiv., Works of Cyprian, Bremæ, 1690, vol. ii., p. 161.) The weight of this testimony is not a little augmented by the fact that the epistle in which it is found is a synodical epistle, which was sent forth in the name and with the authority of the Third Council of Carthage, A. D. 253. The epistle bears this inscription at its head: "Cyprianus et ceteri Collegæ qui in concilio affuerant numero LXIV. Fido patri Salutem."

With this authoritative statement of Cyprian and his sixty-six colleagues, or co-presbyters, we close our citations from the fathers. The testimony of succeeding writers is equally clear, but it simply confirms what has already been fully proved. And now, with the facts of history in view, as we have learned them from inspired writers and their immediate successors, it remains for us to examine opposing theories of the institution of the Sabbath. We shall endeavor to dispose of this concluding, and perhaps most interesting part of our subject, in two or three articles.

A REJOINDER.

"PATRISTIC EVIDENCE TO THE FIRST-DAY SABBATH."

In the rejoinder to the previous article on patristic testimony, the attention of the reader was called to the fact that our opponent had utterly failed to find a single instance in which the first day of the week was called the Lord's day, by the authorities which he cited, or in which it was stated by them that it was observed by divine command. Had we possessed the space necessary for the purpose, the significance of this failure would have been enlarged upon; for it must be borne in mind that in the one hundred and thirty-nine years which intervened between the death of Christ and the writing of the latest citation produced in his seventh article, lies the most important, and the most promising, field for such testimonials as would be of the highest value to the opposition. This is so, not only from the fact that the period in question was the one in which it is alleged that the transition from the old to the new Sabbath occurred; but, also, because it was one, which, from their premises, was the most likely to yield reliable evidence in regard to apostolic faith, since it lay the nearest to apostolic times. It is true that even then apostasy had begun its career; for Paul states that, in his time, "the mystery of iniquity had begun to work."

But all will agree that the farther we come this side of the fountain-head, the more natural it would be to find that the pure waters of the original stream should become steadily darker and more turbid, until they lost themselves in the sloughs of those corrupt teachings, which were so far to excel all others, that they were thought to be of a nature to demand especial attention in the prophecies. But here we are, as already remarked, seventy-five to eighty years this side of the cross, and the case of our reviewer in nowise helped by his effort. In fact, not only has he failed to place his Sabbath upon the foundation of the successors of the apostles, but he has also greatly weakened his probabilities for the future, since in the territory over which we have passed, we have seen not only the utter unreliability of the fathers themselves, as teachers, but, also, that their sayings have been tampered with by the "man of sin," who, reaching backward as well as forward, is reckless in his efforts to make everything contribute to the power and authority of the hierarchy.

But we must proceed in the examination of those individuals who are now introduced as additional witnesses for the Christian Sabbath. The first in order is Irenæus, Bishop of Lyons, A. D. 178. It will not be necessary to consider the language of the gentleman, in which he states that Irenæus taught the abrogation of the seventh-day Sabbath, since we have not quoted that father in the defense of an institution which *God has commanded.* Nor shall we enlarge upon the fact that Irenæus inculcates the binding obligation of the ten commandments, since it is enough for us to know that this doctrine is plainly set forth in the Bible.

The witness is the gentleman's. He has brought him forward to prove that, in his time, the year of our Lord 178, the term, Lord's day, was applied to the Sunday. Has he succeeded, at last, in the achievement of his purpose? If so, it is the first instance in which he has accomplished the desired object. Apparently, he has triumphed here. But let us proceed with caution. Has he produced the writings of Irenæus himself? No, he has not. The words quoted are these: "The mystery of the Lord's resurrection should be celebrated only on the Lord's day." By turning to the Hist. of Eusebius, book v., chap. 23, the reader will find that the language employed does not purport to be that of Irenæus, as penned by himself, but that of Eusebius, who is giving an account of a decree passed by certain bishops, which decree was in harmony with a letter from Irenæus. We quote enough in the 23d chapter to verify our statement:—

"Hence there were synods and convocations of the bishops, on this question; and all unanimously drew up an ecclesiastical decree, which they communicated to all the churches, in all places, that the mystery of our Lord's resurrection should be celebrated on no other day than the Lord's day; and that on this day alone we should observe the close of the paschal fasts. There is an epistle extant, even now, of those who were assembled at the time. . . . There is an epistle extant, on the same question, bearing the name of Victor. An epistle, also, of the bishops of Pontus, among whom Palmas, as the most ancient, presided; also of the churches of Gaul, over whom Irenæus presided, . . . and epistles from many others, who, advancing one and the same doctrine, also passed the same vote, and this their unanimous determination was the one already mentioned."

It will be observed here that the historian does not quote the language of the decree as being the exact language of the bishops; also that he does not pretend to give the precise words of Irenæus, but that he simply recounts the fact that the epistle of Irenæus was in harmony with the decree which he had previously given. This it was legitimate for a historian to do. Eusebius died one hundred and fifty years after Irenæus, and in his time, we frankly admit that the term, Lord's day, was frequently applied to the first day of the week. The historian, therefore, using the nomenclature of his own period, represents the bishop of Lyons as favoring the celebration of the passover on the Lord's day, simply because he had said it ought to be observed on the first day of the week. If we are right in this, then, of course, our opponents will throw up the whole passage as irrelevant to their present purpose—since they have not assumed to employ Eusebius, who lived in the fourth century, as a witness—but have cited his statement because it was supposed to contain the declaration of Irenæus, who lived at a much earlier period.

For the purpose of clinching the argument, and showing that the historic fact is in harmony with what we have said, we quote the following on the point from Eld. J. N. Andrews, in which it will be seen that in the original, the term, first day of the week, and not the Lord's day, as supposed, might have been employed:—

"Observe . . . Eusebius does not quote the words of any of these bishops, but simply gives their decisions in his own language. There is, therefore, no proof that they used the term, Lord's day, instead of first day of the week; for the introduction to the fiftieth fragment of his lost writings, already quoted, gives an ancient statement of his words in this decision, as plain first day of the week. It is Eusebius who gives us the term, Lord's day, in recording what was said by these bishops concerning the first day of the week."

That which has been said above in reference to the testimony found in book v., chap. 23, of Eusebius, will largely apply, in principle, to the citation found in chap. 24, of the same book. In the latter, as in the former, case, the historian is not giving the exact utterance of Irenæus, but simply declares, in substance, his decision in regard to the proper time for the celebration of the passover festival.

Before passing from Irenæus to the consideration of another case of the fathers, it would be proper to commend the candor of our opponent, as manifested in his hearty condemnation of the looseness of Dwight and others in their statements of historic facts. In making the concession which the gentleman has, he will doubtless bring upon himself the condemnation of those who exalt success above truth. He has taken from such one of their most potent weapons. The language of Irenæus, which is here admitted to be of spurious origin, has figured largely in the discussion of this question, in the past. It was pointed and decisive, and seemed to furnish just the material necessary to the satisfactory making out of a case, otherwise sadly deficient in the proofs which it needed. It will, therefore, be yielded up with reluctance. Nevertheless, we hope that the acknowledgment, made by our opponent in this article, will lead clergymen, for the future, to desist from the use of it, until they are able to refute what the writer in the *Statesman* here asserts.

In the meanwhile, the reader must not allow himself to suppose that the gentleman, by saying what he has, has really brought Sabbatarians under obligation to him for new light, since what he here asserts is but a fact with which they have been familiar for years, and which they have iterated and re-iterated until they have almost despaired of bringing their opponents to an acknowledgment of the real state of things. Occasionally, others outside of their ranks have, as does the gentleman, borne testimony to the accuracy of their statements. If the reader would have an illustration of this, taken from the writings of an anti-Sabbatarian author, he will find it in the works of Domville, in which, substantially, the same conclusions are reached, Mr. Domville not only tracing the mistake to Dr. Dwight, but also showing that the language cited was probably taken from the interpolated epistle of Ignatius to the Magnesians.

Up to this point, we have carefully examined, one by one, the historic quotations from ancient writers, which have been presented for our consideration; henceforth, we shall pursue a different course. As we have now reached, in the person of Tertullian, the close of the second, and the opening of the third, century of the Christian era, we find ourselves in a period when it is so generally acknowledged that the work of apostasy was so manifest that the utterances of the men of those times—even though they were pointed and explicit in regard to the sanctity of the first day of the week, as looked upon by themselves—

could furnish no reliable standard of Christian faith in our day.

The gentleman himself is compelled to admit that his own witness, Tertullian, became, in the second year of the third century, an ardent advocate of the errors, follies, and heresies, of Montanus. Not only so, but the writings of that father are proverbial, among scholars, for the fanciful conceits and the false notions which are so conspicuous upon their pages. Tertullian was a fiery zealot and a bitter partisan, manifestly credulous beyond bounds, and more earnest for his sect than anxious for the reliability of the sources of his information. Zell, in his popular Encyclopedia, speaks of him as follows:—

"After he was past middle age, he embraced the doctrines of Montanus, to which his ardent, sensuous imagination, and ascetic tendencies would incline him. He is said to have been determined to that course by the ill-treatment he received from the Roman clergy. Whether he remained a Montanist till his death, cannot be decided. . . . . They [his works] are characterized by vast learning, profound and comprehensive thought, fiery imagination, and passionate partisanship, leading into exaggeration and sophistry. His style is frequently obscure."

Montanus was a false prophet of the second century, who believed himself to have received, from the Holy Ghost, revelations which were withheld from the apostles; he denied the doctrine of the trinity, the propriety of second marriage, and the forgiveness of certain sins. The disciple of such a man is surely a strange witness to be found in the employ of orthodoxy. Should his appearance, however, be excused, as it is above, by the statement that he was introduced, not because of the reliability of his own opinion, but simply to testify of the usage of his own times; it may be replied, first, that an ardent partisan, a person of strong imagination, and a notorious heretic, is hardly qualified to speak reliably, even in a matter of this nature, since, from the very constitution of his mind, he would almost of necessity allow what he said to be warped by prejudice, or biased by conceptions of interest; secondly, that in the quotation presented from his pen, it is not a little remarkable that, instead of asserting a general usage of Sunday-keeping, he is manifestly finding fault with a large class of his fellow-Christians for not regarding the day in the same light, and observing it with the same rigor, that he did; thirdly, that it is by no means impossible that the very men, whom in his fiery zeal he thus upbraids, were, after all, sounder than himself in the faith, and would, could they be fairly heard upon this subject, vindicate their supposed desecration of the first day, from the same grounds as do the Sabbatarians now, *i. e.*, because they did not look upon it as holy time.

If the above responses are not satisfactory, and if it be insisted that the testimony of the witness shall, after all, be received, then we propose that he be called to the stand once more, and be allowed to fill up the measure of what he has to say upon this subject. We have seen that, according to his opinion, many of his fellow-disciples were lax in their Sunday-keeping habits, and that to one who believed that no labor should be performed upon it, whatever, they treated it very much as men would treat a mere festival occasion. But where did Tertullian and his sympathizers obtain their notions of the manner in which Sunday should be kept? Was it from the Scriptures? We shall see; here is the witness; let him speak for himself:

"As often as the anniversary comes around, we make offerings for the dead as birth-day honors. We count fasting or kneeling in worship on the Lord's day, to be unlawful. We rejoice in the same privilege, also, from Easter to Whitsunday. We feel pained should any wine or bread, though our own, be cast upon the ground. At every forward step and movement, at every going in and out, when we put on our clothes and shoes, when we bathe, when we sit at table, when we light the lamps, on couch, on seat, in all the ordinary actions of daily life, we trace upon the forehead the sign (of the cross). If for these and other such rules, you insist upon having positive Scripture injunctions, you will find none. Tradition will be held forth to you as the originator of them, custom, as their strengthener, and faith, as their observer. That reason will support tradition, and custom, and faith, you will either yourself perceive, or learn from some one who has."—*De Corona*, sects. 3 and 4.

The reader will at once observe that tradition is the foundation which is here laid for that kind of Sunday observance for which Tertullian was so great a stickler. Not only so, but the fact is brought to light, also, that the men whom he represented were in the habit of offering prayers for the dead; of signing themselves with the sign of the cross; and going through other ceremonies, which to us, at the present time, are not only ridiculous in the extreme, but bear upon their face the impress of the man of sin so unmistakably that none will be deceived.

If Tertullian was indeed a fair specimen of the Christian men of his time; if his writings have not been tampered with; and if the opinions of the men of his day, as expressed by himself, should have weight with us in the decision of religious questions, where shall we stop in our acceptance of their creeds? If, because they believed with him in the change of the Sabbath from the seventh to the first day of the week, this fact should have weight with us in bringing us to the same conclusion, independently of Scripture proof, then how can we stop short of their faith in other particulars? such as the acceptance of tradition in doctrinal matters, prayers for the dead, the sign of the cross, etc., etc. In fact, how can we avoid becoming papists ourselves, in the largest sense of the term, since, having gone as far as we have for the purpose of making out Sunday sanctity, we have surrendered nearly all the distinctive principles of Protestantism ?

Of course each individual is at liberty to use his own discretion as to the measure of confidence which he will give to the writings before us; so far as we are concerned, personally, we would not attach to them the slightest weight in the decision of a grave religious question. From the very nature of that which has been already cited, it is manifestly a serious slander upon the true church of the second, and the first part of the third, century, to hold them responsible for the fanciful conceits and destructive errors of this reputed defender of the faith.

Certain it is, that if Tertullian is correctly reported, his writings are not a safe criterion of the sentiments of the Christians of his age in very many points, and it may be fairly concluded, that among them is that concerning the Sabbath, since what he has said of it finds no warrant in the open Bible, which the men of this day hold in their hands. Not only is what he has written absurd and dangerous in the extreme, but his productions are characterized by the most glaring contradictions. Another has said of him: "It would be wiser for Christianity, retreating upon its genuine records in the New Testament, to disclaim this fierce African, than identify itself with his furious invectives, by unsatisfactory apologies for their unchristian fanaticisms." (Milman, in note on Gibbon's Dec. and Fall of the Rom. Emp., chap. xv.)

We leave him, therefore, with his follies and foibles, his errors and faults, his assertions and contradictions, with those who have a taste for this kind of literature.

With the case of Origen it will not be necessary that much time should be consumed. Mr. Mosheim has well remarked of him, that had "the justice of his judgment been equal to the immensity of his genius, the fervor of his piety, his indefatigable patience, his extensive erudition, and his other eminent and superior talents, all encomium must have fallen short of his merits." Unfortunately, however, with an erudition which was truly remarkable, he united a credulity almost without parallel. So numerous and so grave were the errors of his personal faith, that his individual opinions, unsupported by facts and arguments, are utterly worthless in the decision of any theological proposition. Having adopted the mystical system of interpreting the Scriptures, he reached conclusions utterly unsound and preposterous in many cases.

That this is so, the orthodox reader will at once perceive, when we state, first, that he was a believer in the pre-existence of the human soul, and that souls were condemned to animate mortal bodies, because of sins committed in a preexistent state; secondly, that he was a Restorationist, and believed in the final universal salvation of all men, after enduring long periods of punishment. Nor does the advocacy of such sentiments furnish the only difficulty in the way of his testimony, as drawn from his writings now extant. There would indeed be some satisfaction derived from the study of these documents, fanciful though they might appear to be in many respects, if we could only feel assured that they represented correctly the sentiments of the alleged author.

Unhappily, this is not the case. Those who admire Origen most, while attributing much in what he is said to have written, to that weakness of discrimination which is everywhere so manifest in his productions, are compelled to go beyond this, in order to explain many of the grosser views therein contained, by admitting that they were not his own, but that they are the result of fraud and interpolation.

On this point, another, with great candor and friendly charity, when speaking of the sect known as Origenists, after first stating that "he was a man of great talents, and a most indefatigable student, but having a strong attachment to the Platonic philosophy, and a natural turn to mystical and allegorical interpretations, which led him to corrupt greatly the simplicity of the gospel, declares that these circumstances render it very difficult to ascertain exactly what his real sentiments were." He says, also, "1. Being a man of unquestionable talents and high character, his genuine works were interpolated, and others written under his name, in order to *forge* his sanction to sentiments of which, possibly, he never heard. * * * * 3. Origen had many enemies, who probably attributed to him many things which he did not believe, in order, either to injure his fame, or bring his character under censure."—*Encyc. of Rel. Knowl.*, Art. Origenists.

Having said thus much in reference to the testimony before us, it would be possible to take up the writings of this distinguished father, and show from them that there is room for a difference of opinion as to whether he believed that the so-called Christian Sabbath was indeed to be regarded as of twenty-four hours' duration, merely, or whether it covered alike all days of the week, and the whole of our dispensation. This, however, would be a tedious and unprofitable expenditure of time and labor. We leave the whole question, therefore, respecting the teaching of the works of Origen, as one of no significance in this controversy; first, because if we know anything about what he did believe, he was wholly unreliable, either as a teacher of sound doctrine, or as a representative of the better men of his own time; and, secondly; because what he has written has been so corrupted, that we have no guarantee that it truthfully expresses what he believed.

As we presume the majority of our readers are not particularly interested in reference to which posture was assumed in prayer on the first day of the week, by the early church, and as Peter of Alexandria and the Council of Nice are quoted solely in reference to "this independent question," we shall not discuss the note in which reference is made to them. There remains, therefore, only the case of Cyprian, bishop of Carthage, to occupy us longer. What this author says was written about A. D. 253. It will be observed, that in what is declared by him and the Council, the first day of the week is called the Lord's day; beyond this, his testimony is of no value. It is neither stated that the title was applied by divine authority, nor is it affirmed that this day had superseded in Sabbatic honor the ancient Sabbath of the Lord.

There is, however, in reference to circumcision as something which prefigured the Lord's day, or eighth day, enough of mysticism to furnish us with a clue to the character of the men whose intellectual perceptions were so fine that they could discover in an institution which was administered on the eighth day after the birth of the male child, on whatever day of the week that eighth day might fall, a prefiguring of the distinction which was to be bestowed on the definite first day of the week, which had in it, not eight, but only seven, days, in all. Mr. Mosheim, in alluding to a period in close proximity to that in which Cyprian lived, mentions it as one in " which the greater part of the Christian doctors had been engaged in adopting those vain fictions of Platonic philosophy and popular opinions, which, after the time of Constantine, were confirmed, enlarged, and embellished in various ways," and from which he declares "arose that extravagant veneration for departed saints, and those absurd notions of a certain fire destined to purify separate souls, that then prevailed, and of which the public marks were everywhere to be seen."— *Eccles. Hist.*, Fourth Century, part ii., chap. iii.

It is now time to take a retrospective view of the territory over which we have been passing. Be it remembered that the reader was lured from the contemplation of the Scriptures, with this precious promise, that outside of them were to be found the most convincing proofs that the Lord's day was and had been the proper title of the first day of the week since the resurrection of Christ; but what have we seen? Manifestly, not that which we had anticipated:

First, we have discovered that Ignatius, the first witness introduced, does not mention the Lord's day at all, but simply speaks of the Lord's life.

Secondly, that the epistle of Barnabas was a forgery, made up of the most absurd and ridiculous fancies, and written by an unknown character somewhere, perhaps in the second or third century, though purporting to be the work of the companion of Paul.

Thirdly, that it is becoming more and more a matter of doubt whether that which is attributed to Justin Martyr was ever seen by him, and that he not only does not call the Sunday the Lord's day, but also inculcates in what he says, the Romish heresy respecting the use of water in sacrament, &c., &c.

Fourthly, that Dionysius, bishop of Corinth, and Melito, bishop of Sardis, while indeed they do speak of the Lord's day, do not furnish any clue by which we can determine which day they regarded as such.

Fifthly, that Pliny, a heathen writer, employs neither the term Lord's day nor Sabbath, but simply speaks of a stated day, without identification.

Sixthly, that Irenæus is not properly represented as speaking of the Sunday in the use of the title Lord's day, since that expression, in both the instances alluded to, was the language of Eusebius, who lived in the fourth century, and not of Irenæus, who lived in the second.

Seventhly, that Tertullian, who lived at the close of the second and the commencement of the third century, and who was a wild fanatic of the Montanist school, utterly unworthy to represent the sentiments of his times, is the first witness from whom the gentleman has succeeded in obtaining an unequivocal application of the term, Lord's day, to the first day of the week;

also, that he had connected with it, prayers for the dead, the sign of the cross, &c., &c.

Eighthly, that Origen was a man of great learning; that it was questionable whether he believed in a septenary Sabbath, or in one that covered the whole dispensation; and that, in fact, it is admitted by his friends that his works have become so corrupt as to be utterly untrustworthy in the matter of deciding respecting his real opinions.

Ninthly, that Cyprian and his colleagues addressed us from a point of time too far removed from the period of the alleged change of Sabbaths, and too fully within that of the great apostasy, to be of service in an exegesis of the Scriptures.

Tenthly, that three of the most pointed and satisfactory of the testimonies heretofore employed by first-day writers, are now abandoned as having been the result of mistake in translation, or in the matter of attributing them to the proper persons. Summing up, therefore, in a word we inquire again, What has been gained by this departure? We believe that all must see that it has been an entire failure; for, so far as the Sabbath is concerned, we think the reader will hesitate long before he will leave the Scriptures, in the matter of deciding upon its obligation, in order to build the structure of his faith from such material as we have been handling over.

Also, as to the question of what day John referred to in Rev. 1:10, when he said, "I was in the Spirit on the Lord's day," he will deliberate very much before he will decide that it was the first day of the week, simply because an untrustworthy man, admitted to have been heretical on many points, called it such 200 years after the birth of Christ, while Jehovah himself has given to the seventh day that honor, styling it the "Sabbath of the Lord," "the holy of the Lord, honorable," &c., and while Christ himself has declared in so many words, that he was the Lord of the Sabbath day. Mark 2:27, 28.

STATESMAN'S REPLY.

ARTICLE NINE.

THEORIES OF THE CHRISTIAN SABBATH.

WITH the facts of history before us concerning sacred time for nearly three centuries after the resurrection of Christ—facts drawn from the inspired writers of the New Testament and their immediate successors, we are prepared to consider the different theories of the Christian Sabbath. These theories may be summed up in three. Of one or another of these, all the remaining theories are simply modifications.

The first of these three leading theories is as follows: "The Sabbath was a Jewish institution, and expired with the Jewish dispensation. The Lord's day is not in any proper sense a Sabbath. It has an origin, a reason, and an obligation, not drawn from the fourth commandment, but peculiarly its own, as an institution belonging specially to the New-Testament dispensation.

The second theory, in the order in which we notice these different views, maintains that the observance of the Sabbath, as required under the Old-Testament dispensation, knows no change in any particular. The observance of the seventh day of the week is essential to the proper observance of the Sabbath under the gospel dispensation. The observance of the first day of the week is without divine warrant—a departure from the law of God through the corruptions which crept into the church.

The third theory agrees with the second in maintaining that the Sabbath existed from the beginning, and that it has never been abolished or superseded. It disagrees with the second theory in maintaining that the essential idea of the law of the Sabbath is not the holiness of a portion of time, but the *consecration of a specified proportion of time,* one day in seven; that, in accordance with this, a change of day was admissible; that a change was actually made by divine warrant from the resurrection of Christ; and that the first day of the week, the Lord's day, is the true Christian Sabbath, having its moral sanction in the fourth commandment.

By many of those who hold the first of these theories, the Lord's day is made a purely ecclesiastical institution, without any other warrant for its observance than the action of the church, by whose authority and in whose wisdom, the day is set apart for divine service. By others who accept the same general theory, apostolic authority in the early church is admitted to afford a divine warrant for the observance of the day. In a complete treatise on the Lord's day, a careful discussion of this theory would be required. Its want of any sufficient foundation could be satisfactorily shown by a presentation of the following points : (1.) The declaration of the Lord of the Sabbath is explicit—"The Sabbath was made for man." It was not made for any portion of the human family, but for the race of mankind. (2.) Thus, from the design of its Lord, and the very nature of the institution, the Sabbath cannot be limited to any locality or dispensation. (3.) Accordingly, it was given to man at his creation. (Gen. 3 : 3.) (4.) For the same reason, the law of the Sabbath has its proper place, not among ceremonial, local, or positive enactments, but among the immutable moral precepts of the decalogue. (5.) This law is, therefore, of universal and perpetual obligation upon our race. These points would give room for many articles ; but, inasmuch as on all of them there is entire agreement between our seventh-day Sabbatarian friends and ourselves, we pass to a consideration of the second theory, which they accept as correct.

To make good their case, the advocates of the second theory must show that the seventh day continued to be the Sabbath observed by the church after the resurrection of Christ, just as before; and that, in the observance of the first day, a great departure took place from the original practice of the Christian church. They must not make *bare* statements, but they must furnish proof. Instead of appealing to the letter of the law, and insisting that fact must conform to their interpretation of it, they must accept the facts of history, and put their interpretations to the test. It is more reasonable to conclude that an interpretation of law is wrong, than to reject the attested facts of history, when the interpretation and the facts do not harmonize.

Let us briefly sum up the facts already fully brought to view. Christ himself, after his resurrection, passed by the seventh day, and repeatedly put special honor on the first day of the week. This same day was honored by the Pentecostal gift of the Holy Spirit. Christian congregations met for regular weekly service, not on the seventh day, but on the first day of the week. The inspired apostle Paul pointedly condemned the Judaizing teachers who insisted on the observance by Christians of the seventh-day Sabbath. The early writers, companions of the apostles, and others of the succeeding generations, bear the clearest and most explicit testimony to the same facts—the non-observance of the seventh-day Sabbath, and the stated meetings of Christians for divine service on the first day of the week, the Lord's day. Now, if their theory is correct, how will the seventh-day Sabbatarians explain the fact that Christ himself, the Holy Spirit, inspired apostles, and Christian congregations all through the early church, ignored the seventh day and honored the first? A general and vague statement to the effect that an unwarranted change was made from the original practice of the Christian church will not do here. Was not the practice of the apostles and first organized congregations of Christians the original practice of the Christian church? That practice was, as we have seen, to observe the first day of the week. We repeat what we have already proved at length, viz., that there is not an instance in the Scriptures of the observance of the seventh day by any Christian church, nor of any regard to that day, after Christ's resurrection, by apostles or their fellow-laborers, except as they availed themselves, in their missionary work, of the meetings of Jewish assemblies in Jewish places of worship. "An unwarranted change!" Let those who take such language upon their lips consider that their charge lies at the door of Christ and his Spirit, and the inspired apostles.

But now, for the sake of the argument, let us leave all the testimony of the inspired writers of the New Testament to the first-day Sabbath out of view. Again we have the vague charge of unwarranted change. Perhaps the most definite form of this charge is that which makes the change the work of the little horn in Daniel's prophecy, chapter seven. But will the expounder of Daniel be a little more explicit, and tell us who the historical personage is, and give us the dates and names of history? Does the little horn represent Antiochus Epiphanes? If so, then, of course, his change of the law of the Sabbath must have been before the Christian era. Will our expositor give us some facts just here? If the little horn means the papacy, then, according to the prophecy itself, it did not arise until the Roman Empire, represented by the fourth beast, was broken into ten fragments, represented by the ten horns. The little horn sprang up after these, and its change of the law of the Sabbath must date after the fall of the old empire of Rome. But for centuries before this event, we have the testimony of numerous writers that the Christian churches everywhere observed, not the seventh, but the first, day of the week, the Lord's day. Again we ask for facts, not mere statements and theories.

Leaving this vague attempt to connect the assumed unwarranted change with Daniel's prophecy, we come to what is, if possible, still more vague and indefinite. A change, it is asserted, was made by some particular officer or council of the church, as it became corrupt and began to depart from the practice of the original church of Christ. Who was this officer? or where did this council meet? But we will not make unreasonable demands for historical testimony. Let us grant that such an officer or such a council there was at some time or other. The question then arises, When did the change take place? In the days of Cyprian, A. D. 250? The answer is clear. The change must have been made before his day. Origen and Tertullian, fifty years earlier, knew only the first day of the week, the Lord's day, as the Christian Sabbath. Was the change then made in their day? We might assume that it was, only for the clear testimony of Irenæus and Justin Martyr, carrying us back another half century, and the equally explicit testimony of still earlier writers, carrying us back to the apostles themselves.

Notwithstanding all this dearth of historical testimony as to the existence of the supposed ruler or council, let it be further granted that by some such corrupting authority, at some time a decree changing the day for Sabbath observance was issued. How did the supposed legislators establish their decree? How did they make it effectual over all the different parts of the church? Must we suppose that a change like this was effected in the church, and not a scrap of a record left concerning it? The attempt made by the church to establish a common day for the anniversary of Christ's resurrection gave rise to long and bitter controversy, and led to division. And yet, as Prof. F. D. Maurice has well said, "It is supposed that this far more important change, affecting all the daily relations and circumstances of life, took effect by the decree of some apostle or some ecclesiastical synod, of which no record, no legend, even, is preserved! Or, perhaps, a half-heathen, more than half-heathen, statute of Constantine,* about the *Dies Solis* accomplished what the legislators of the church could not accomplish—succeeded not only in securing its adoption by Athanasians, Arians, Semi-Arians, whose controversies Constantine could never heal, but in securing the allegiance of all the barbarous tribes which accepted the gospel under such various conditions in later times. Can any suppositions make greater demands on our credulity than these?" A Procrustean bed indeed must be that interpretation of the law of the Sabbath which, to conform them to itself, must thus deal with the facts of history and the probabilities of historical evidence.

Just here is the difficulty in the theory of Seventh-day Sabbatarians. They have somehow

---

*The attempt to attribute the change of day to Constantine's decree is hardly worth noticing. It is enough to remember that it was issued in the beginning of the fourth century. No one who knows anything of the writings of Tertullian and Origen, dating back more than a century before Constantine, to say nothing of still earlier writers, will venture to ascribe the change to the Roman Emperor's decree. Besides, the language of the very decree referred to recognizes the honorable character of the first day of the week. It recognizes that day as already "venerable."
—*The Christian.*

got lodged in their mind the idea that the last one of the seven days of the week is the sacred day, the observance of which is absolutely essential to the proper keeping of the Sabbath. What has already been proved from history, inspired and uninspired, is sufficient to show that this theory is unworthy of men who, like Christ and his apostles, would grasp the true significance of the law of the Sabbath. But as so much stress is laid upon the question of time, we shall devote our next article to this crucial and very practical point.

A REJOINDER.

"THEORIES OF THE CHRISTIAN SABBATH."

THE thoughtful reader need not be told that the article which he has just read, entitled, "Theories of the Christian Sabbath," has advanced the discussion of the question before us in no material respect. The space devoted so generously to the consideration of theories, in regard to the unsoundness of which there is no difference of opinion between the gentleman and myself, is thrown away, so far as the present argument is concerned. While this is true, however, if it serves no other purpose, it has at least made it clear that, if the gentleman fails to make out his case in the end, it will not be because he has not had ample room for the presentation and elaboration of facts and arguments, since one who was crippled in his effort by a lack of space would hardly be willing to devote so much time and attention to subjects foreign to the present issue.

That which is said with reference to these theories might also be repeated in reference to the statement and restatement of points which it is claimed have been proved. Of course, it is the prerogative of any writer to conduct his own argument in his own way. All that we would call attention to is the fact that the line of policy pursued, in these things, is of a nature to satisfy even the most casual observer, that one who felt that he had resources upon which to draw, without limit, would not compel us to pass again and again over the same ground. There is, however, an apology which might properly be offered in the case of the gentleman, for calling our attention to these trivial points so repeatedly, which is found in the fact that his articles were written before our rejoinders were in print. We believe that, were not this the case, and had he perused what has been said in reply to them, we should be spared the monotony of answering them again. However, lest we should seem to avoid them, it will only be necessary that we say enough, bearing upon each point, to revive, in the mind of one who has followed us thus far, the fuller consideration given to all of them heretofore.

To the statement that Sabbatarians, in order

to make good their case, must make their views harmonize with the facts of history, it is enough to say that, if it is meant by this, the facts of sacred history, as contained in the Bible, this we have already done; for before it can be urged that the opposite is true, as we have elsewhere seen, it must be shown that there is some transaction found in the sacred record which is in conflict with our interpretation of the law. This has not been done; for not only has it been made to appear that the Sabbath law is explicit in its requirement of the observance of the seventh day of the week, but also that there is not a single case of its violation, by a good man, to be found in the inspired pages.

Nor is this all; we have gone beyond this, and proved, by the record, that the opposite was true of the Sunday, since upon it Christ and two of his disciples, on the day of his resurrection, as well as Paul and Luke and others at a subsequent period, did perform upon it labor, which the gentleman himself has not attempted, and will not undertake, to harmonize with any just conception of intelligent Sabbath-keeping. So far as it regards the absence of any mention of meetings of Christians on the Sabbath, it is sufficient to say, as we have already done, that, as in the history given, the account relates largely to missionary trips, where there was no church as yet developed, and, consequently, no possibility of separate meetings, such a record would be out of the question; also, that the argument is only a negative one, and really can have no force, until it can be demonstrated that God's plan is first to command, and then show, in every instance what the commandment means, by practical illustrations furnished from the history of his people; a doctrine which is not only unsound and untrue, but absurd in the extreme.

If, on the other hand, the gentleman means to be understood as insisting that the history of the church since the close of the canon of inspiration must be made to teach the faith which we hold as one which has always been entertained by the church, and therefore sound, we repudiate, in the name of Protestantism, this most pernicious view, and in all matters of practical duty, such as Sabbath-keeping, we decide according to the written word. To the first source (church history), the gentleman has appealed, and if every candid man and woman who has witnessed his effort has not been disgusted with the source to which he has applied, then we know of nothing which would be calculated to create in him this condition of mind.

With the summary, in which it is claimed that Christ, and the apostles, and the Holy Spirit, and the early church, did repeatedly honor the first day of the week, we will not weary the reader here. We have disproved every one of these points, and we trust to the intelligence of those whom we are addressing, in the confident belief that what has been said, in the absence of even an attempt at refutation, needs not to be reproduced here.

We had barely mentioned, in our original articles, that Seventh-day Adventists held to the opinion that the pope of Rome had been instrumental in bringing about the change of the Sabbath. No effort was made to develop the argument on that point, since we did not dare to presume that room would be granted for the perfecting of the work; in fact, what was said was uttered rather with a view to calling the attention of the curious to our published works upon that subject, than for any other purpose. Now, however, this point is made to assume a prominence which does not really belong to it, in an argument so largely doctrinal rather than historic.

With this, nevertheless, we have no fault to find. Nothing is more satisfactory than the awakening of a spirit of investigation on all branches of this great subject; at the same time, we submit that the attitude of the gentleman must be very unsatisfactory to himself, since he will readily perceive that to an opponent, chafing under a denial of the privilege of answering him in the columns of his own paper, this whole affair wears the aspect of an empty bravado. "Tell us," says the editor, and he repeats his invitation again and again, "Whom did this little horn represent? Was it Antiochus? or the pope? If the latter, then how, and when, and where, did he bring about the transition?"

But we reply, Whom do you mean, sir, by the term, "us"? Truly, you would not require us to come to Philadelphia to enlighten you personally upon that point. Certainly, you are not particularly anxious that we should write a series of articles for the benefit of the readers of the *Review*, on a matter with which they are as familiar as they are with the history of their own country; but if, indeed, you had in your mind the readers of the *Statesman*, then it may be inquired again, How has it been possible for us to reach them, under the circumstances? since, throwing your forces behind the wall of your editorial prerogative, and closing against us the gate of possibility, you have shut us out from all access to them. Gladly would we have availed ourselves of the opportunity of doing that which we have been denied the privilege of attempting before the men, many of whom, we believe, would have been glad to follow this matter to the end; but as this cannot be done, a brief reply will be made here.

The first inquiry, relating, as it does, to the point whether Antiochus Epiphanes or the pope, was meant by the "little horn," in the seventh of Daniel, need not consume time. It has been urged by some that the "little horn," of Dan. 8: 9, applied to the former character. We believe the papists still insist upon this; but the gentleman, upon reflection—if in what he has said he has confounded the two—will not seriously argue against the almost universal admission of Protestant writers, that the power brought to view in the seventh chapter of Daniel's prophecy, is that of the papacy. In fact, reasoning as he does himself, most satisfactorily, that it could not arise until after the appearance of the original ten, which represented the final breaking up of the Roman Empire into ten parts, he more than intimates his personal conviction that it could not represent Antiochus Epiphanes, who reigned one hundred and seventy-five years before Christ, since the Roman Empire was not partitioned among the barbarians who invaded it, until A. D. 483, more than six hundred years after the death of the Syrian king.

The following, from a standard authority, will serve to show an almost universal agreement on this subject; and with its presentation we pass to the investigation of questions more difficult, and more worthy of our reflection. "Among Protestant writers, this ('the little horn,' of Dan. 7:8) is considered to be the popedom."—*A. Clarke, Com. in loco.*

"To none can this ('He shall speak great words against the Most High') apply so well, and so fully, as to the popes of Rome."—*Idem*, v. 25.

The real point of debate, as intimated above, is the question whether the Roman Catholic church has been instrumental in bringing about the change of the Sabbath. The gentleman errs in asserting that we have anywhere stated that such a change was brought about by any particular officer or council. This we have never urged, nor does it accord with the view held by us. The "little horn" represented, not one, merely, but a whole line of priest-kings, who were to extend from the time of their rise, to the Judgment, and the setting up of the kingdom of God. Of this line of rulers, it is stated—not that they should really succeed in bringing about an actual change in the requirements of the law of God—but that they should "*think*" to accomplish this end. It is also said that, for a time, times, and dividing of time (1260 years), the saints of God and the law of God should be delivered into their hands. Not, indeed, that God would forsake either his people or his law, utterly, but that, for the period in question, they should be permitted to pursue a course destructive to the one, and antagonistic to the other. In other words, that they should put to death the saints, and presume to alter the commandments of God.

These specifications are simply introduced by way of identification. It is not said that the power indicated should spring into life suddenly, and without a previous stage of development; nor is it declared that the principles which were to characterize it in its mature life should be wholly peculiar to itself. Other powers, such as pagan Rome, might have persecuted the people of God before the rise of the papacy, as they unquestionably did. Other men might have begun the work of tampering with the law of God, long before the days of the hierarchy, and might have prepared to its hands the materials necessary to the accomplishment of the final blasphemous work of the man of sin.

In the days of Paul, "the mystery of iniquity began to work," and from that point, its history was one of gradual development. Some of the most destructive heresies afterward incorporated into the faith of papists, it is well understood, were fully fledged, and quite generally accepted, before the installation of the first pope. So, too, concerning the first-day Sabbath. There can be little doubt that before the bishop of Rome became the "Corrector of Heretics," in A. D. 538, or entered the chair of St. Peter, the Sunday had come to be regarded, by many, as the rival, if not the superior, of the ancient Sabbath. Just how extensively the sentiment prevailed, however, it is hard to determine from church history, because, as has been shown in a previous article, the sources of our information have been so corrupted by unprincipled Romanists, that it is difficult to arrive at the facts in the case.

One thing is certain; there was a mighty struggle on this question, the gentleman to the contrary, notwithstanding, which has left the marks of its existence in the records of the past. Clear down to the rise of Roman Catholicism, there were men who were strenuous for the observance of the seventh day, and rejecters of its rival. Doubtless the Sunday, by slow degrees, had worked itself into almost universal acceptance as a festival resting upon human, and not divine, authority; but the Sabbath of the Lord still continued in the faith of many, especially in the East, as a day to be sacredly devoted to the worship of God. On this point, Neander, the learned church historian, has given distinct and unequivocal utterance :—

"The festival of Sunday, like all other festivals, was only a human ordinance, and it was far from the intention of the apostles to establish a divine command in this respect; far from them and from the early apostolic church to transfer the laws of the Sabbath to Sunday. Perhaps at the end of the second century, a false application of this kind had begun to take place; for men appear, by that time, to have considered laboring on Sunday as a sin."—*Rose's Translation of Neander*, p. 186.*

Giesler also remarks as follows: "While the Christians of Palestine, who kept the whole Jewish law, celebrated, of course, all the Jewish festivals, the heathen converts observed only the Sabbath, and in remembrance of the closing scenes of our Saviour's life, the passover, though

---

* For the extracts given in this connection, the reader is referred to "Sabbath and Sunday," by A. H. Lewis, and to "The History of the Sabbath," by J. N. Andrews.

without the Jewish superstitions. Besides these, the Sunday as the day of our Saviour's resurrection, was devoted to religious worship."—*Church Hist., Apostolic Age to A. D. 70.*

Lyman Coleman, in his "Ancient Christianity Exemplified," testifies as follows: "The observance of the Lord's day as the first day of the week was at first introduced as a separate institution. Both this and the Jewish Sabbath were kept for some time; finally, the latter passed wholly over into the former, which now took the place of the ancient Sabbath of the Israelites. But their Sabbath, the last day of the week, was strictly kept in connection with that of the first day for a long time after the overthrow of the temple and its worship. Down even to the fifth century, the observance of the Jewish Sabbath was continued in the Christian church, but with a rigor and solemnity gradually diminishing, until it was wholly discontinued. * * * Both were observed in the Christian church down to the fifth century, with this difference, that in the eastern church, both days were regarded as joyful occasions; but in the western, the Jewish Sabbath was kept as a fast." Chap. 26, sect. 2.

Wm. Twisse, whose antique style comports with that of the period in which he wrote, most pointedly declares the same fact in a work entitled, "The Morality of the Fourth Commandment:" "Yet for some hundred years in the primitive church, not the Lord's day only, but the seventh day also, was religiously observed, not by Ebion and Cerinthus only, but by pious Christians also, as Baronius writeth and Gomaius confesseth, and Rivut also." Page 9, London, 1641.

Morer, in speaking of the early Christians, remarks of them as follows: " The primitive Christians had a great veneration for the Sabbath, and spent the day in devotion and sermons, and it is not to be doubted but they derived the practice from the apostles themselves."—*Morer's Lord's Day*, p. 189.

Edward Brerewood, professor in Gresham College, London, writes: " The ancient Sabbath did remain, and was observed by the Christians of the east church above three hundred years after our Saviour's death, and besides that, no other day, for more hundred years than I spoke of before, was known in the church by the name of the Sabbath." Page 77, ed. 1631.

Prof. Stuart, in speaking of the period between A. D. 321 and the council of Laodicea, A. D. 364, furnishes the following interesting statement, which discloses the historic fact concerning the ebb and flow of discussion on this subject in the early church : " The practice of it [the keeping of the Sabbath], was continued by Christians who were jealous for the honor of the Mosaic law, and finally became, as we have seen, predominant throughout Christendom. It was supposed at length that the fourth commandment did require the observance of the seventh-day Sabbath [not merely a seventh part of time], and reasoning as Christians of the present day are wont to do, viz., that *all* which belongs to the ten commandments was immutable and perpetual, the churches in general came gradually to regard the seventh-day Sabbath as altogether sacred."—*Appendix to Gurney's Hist. of Sabbath*, pp. 115, 116.

Concerning the same council, Prynne has made a similar historic record; "The seventh-day Sabbath was solemnized by Christ, the apostles, and primitive Christians, till the Laodicean Council did, in a manner, quite abolish the observance of it. * * * The Council of Laodicea, A. D. 364, first settled the observance of the Lord's day, and prohibited keeping of the Jewish Sabbath, under an anathema."—*Dissertation on the Lord's Sabbath*, pp. 33, 44, ed. 1633.

In alluding to the differences in practice between the eastern and the western churches, Neander distinctly sets forth the resolute animosity of the latter to the ancient Sabbath of the Lord, and the manner in which they sought to bring it into disrepute, while elevating the Sunday into favor. He says: "In the western churches, particularly the Roman, where opposition to Judaism was the prevailing tendency, this very opposition produced the custom of celebrating the Saturday as a fast day. This difference of customs would, of course, be striking, where members of the Oriental church spent their Sabbath day in the western church."—*Hist. Chris. Rel.*

and Church, First Three Centuries. Rose's trans., p. 186.

Peter Heylyn also marks the peculiar favor shown to the first day of the week in the western church; and while he declares at one time that it was near "nine hundred years from the Saviour's birth before restraint of husbandry on this day [Sunday] had been first thought of in the east," he elsewhere records the fact that in the fifth and sixth centuries general unanimity respecting the exaltation to divine honor was reached. He writes: "The faithful, being united more than ever before, became more uniform in matters of devotion, and in that uniformity did agree together to give the Lord's day all the honors of a holy festival, yet this was not done all at once, but by degrees, the fifth and sixth centuries being fully spent before it came unto that hight which has since continued. The emperors and the prelates in these times had the same affections, both earnest to advance this day above all others; and to the edicts of the one, and to the ecclesiastical constitutions of the others, it stands indebted for many of those privileges and exemptions which it still enjoyeth."—*Hist. Sab.*, part 2, chap. 4, sect. 1.

Thus it has been proved, by citations from men who have possessed the resources, as well as the disposition, to make themselves acquainted with the history of the first centuries of the Christian church, first, that the first day of the week was looked upon for a long time as a merely human institution; secondly, that the Edenic Sabbath was for centuries after the crucifixion of Christ quite generally celebrated; thirdly, that prejudice against it seems to have been strongest and to have originated earliest at Rome, where, in order to bring it into odium, it was made a day of fasting, while the Sunday was treated as a festival; fourthly, that after a struggle, which extended through hundreds of years, the ancient Sabbath was finally quite generally repudiated, and the Sunday, through the united efforts of prelates, councils, and emperors, was enthroned and enforced upon all.

Into the details of this long and varying conflict, in which victory seems first to have favored the one side and then the other, we are restricted by the limits of our communication from entering. The intelligent reader can readily fill in the outlines which have been given, and will not be slow to perceive that the contest, from the very nature of things, must have been one of intense interest and heated debate. If he would satisfy himself most fully that the gentleman is mistaken in saying that it has left no traces, we refer him for a more full discussion to the authorities quoted.

Changing now the point of view, we will come to the present time. We return once more to the charge that the church of Rome, availing itself of the condition of things which preceded its rise, has consummated the terrible work which was begun with the great apostasy, long before the papacy proper was fully developed. In prosecuting the labor thus entered upon, the reader is invited to pause a moment and decide upon certain principles which ought to govern in the decision of the question. He will remember that if he has been educated in the observance of Sunday, he will be in danger of requiring more testimony than could reasonably be demanded, since his education, and personal interest, and standing, would all incline him to a conservatism which needs to be guarded with a jealous care, lest it should result in a bias which would terminate in the rejection of sufficient light.

All that we ask him to do is to treat this subject the same as he would any other matter of fact. To illustrate: If the body of a murdered man were discovered upon the street, and if there should be found in the community one whose character was bad in every respect, concerning whom those who knew him best had given warning; if on the garments of this suspicious personage blood stains were found; if, in the meantime, a careful examination of the wounds should show that they had been inflicted by a weapon peculiar to the notorious individual; and if, in addition to the foregoing, he should step forward and frankly confess that he had done the deed, no court in the world would hesitate to inflict the penalty of the law, because of any doubt regarding the guilt of the offending party. Now applying the same principles to the case in hand, if every one can be shown to hold good in every particular, then consistency demands that they should produce a conviction equally clear and strong with that in the mind of the court, in determining in the case of the homicide upon the infliction of punishment.

But is it true that the charge against the Roman Catholic church can be made out as conclusively as that against the individual mentioned above? Let us see. The first point there brought forward was the unquestionable fact that the man had been murdered. This was the starting point of the whole affair. That which answers to it in the case before us is the fact that the change of the Sabbath has been made out beyond reasonable doubt; for God commanded the observance of the seventh day, while, somehow, Christendom is generally observing the first, though utterly incapable of furnishing Scripture warrant for the change.

The second point was that respecting the bad reputation of a certain character in the community—its parallel in the persons of the popes is found in the fact that, as we have seen, their rise and history were symbolized centuries before their appearance under the type of the "little horn" of the seventh of Daniel, by one who never errs in his analysis of character, and who declared of the "man of sin" that he should "think to change times and laws," and that they should be given into his hands for "a time and times and the dividing of time," thus proving that this blasphemous power who was to open his mouth in blasphemy against God is capable of attempting the transfer of God's holy Sabbath to a day different from that pointed out in the commandment.

The third point, which related to blood stains upon the garments of the suspected person, finds its counterpart in the teachings of Romanism, most clearly. We learn, in the writings of Moses, that the blood is the life of the individual. This, however, is not more true than it is that the fourth commandment is the life of the Sabbatic institution. If you mar that commandment, you mar the Sabbath in the same ratio. If you destroy that commandment, you destroy the Sabbath. But the assumed ability to alter this precept as well as others of the decalogue is one of the very crimes of which Rome has been guilty, by which she has blotched all over in the most loathsome manner the garments of a once spotless Christianity, and a profoundly reverent faith. That this is so will become manifest when we present a copy of the decalogue as it has been mutilated by the Romish church in the exercise of a pretended divine right to accomplish such a work. For this purpose we append the ten commandments as they stand in Butler's catechism.*

---

*The commandments as given above are supposed to be re-

"1. I am the Lord thy God. Thou shalt not have strange gods before me, &c. 2. Thou shalt not take the name of the Lord thy God in vain. 3. Remember that thou keep holy the Sabbath day. 4. Honor thy father and thy mother. 5. Thou shalt not kill. 6. Thou shalt not commit adultery. 7. Thou shalt not steal. 8. Thou shalt not bear false witness against thy neighbor. 9. Thou shalt not covet thy neighbor's wife. 10. Thou shalt not covet thy neighbor's goods."

Here it will be seen that the second commandment is dropped out altogether, and that the tenth is divided; a portion of it retaining its ancient number, and the remaining portion of it being numbered as the ninth commandment, thereby making the complement of the original ten, which would have been reduced to nine by ignoring the one against image worship. It will also be perceived that with the exception of the words, "Remember that thou keep holy the Sabbath day," the fourth commandment is left out entirely. True, it may be that in the Douay Bible the original commandments are allowed to remain intact, but we shall see hereafter that the above arrangement is not accidental, and that the power to make these changes is unhesitatingly claimed.

The fourth point was that concerning the form

peated by the individual Romanist in response to the injunction, "Say the ten commandments of God."

and nature of the wound, whereby it was discovered that it was made with a weapon precisely such as one possessed by the suspected party. The correspondence in this particular will be found in the boundary of the new Sabbath; in its beginning and ending, occurring as they do at twelve o'clock, midnight, are the unmistakable marks of the hand of one who most assuredly did not live at Jerusalem, and who left upon the creature of his own power the badge of its origin at Rome.

The Jews, as we have seen heretofore, by the agreement of commentators and scholars generally, as well as by the testimony of the Bible, commenced and ended their days with the setting of the sun. At Rome, on the other hand, as well as in other parts of the world, the day began as we now begin the Sunday—at midnight. In this, it is made apparent that some one has been tampering with a day which it is claimed was hallowed by Christ eighteen hundred years ago; since, if it had originated at that time and in that place, it would have conformed in its beginning and ending to the weekly Sabbath, the day of Pentecost, and the other days in the Jewish calendar. The presumption concerning whom this person is, is already made out. The certainty respecting it will be established under the next heading.

The fifth point cited above was the confession of the culprit. Under ordinary circumstances, this alone would have made a conviction inevitable. Answering to it in the fullest degree are the oft-repeated declarations of Romanists, that they have changed the Sabbath from the seventh to the first day of the week, and that they had the ability and the right thus to do. Respecting these assumptions, we might introduce quotations almost without number, but we must content ourselves with a few brief but pointed ones.*

Ques. "What are the days which the church commands to be kept holy?"

"*Ans.* 1. The Sundays, or our Lord's day, which we observe by apostolical tradition instead of the Sabbath. 2. The feasts of our Lord's nativity, or Christmas day; his circumcision, or New Year's day; the Epiphany, or twelfth day; Easter day, or the day of our Lord's resurrection, with the Monday following," &c.

"*Ques.* What was the reason why the weekly Sabbath was changed from the Saturday to the Sunday?"

"*Ans.* Because our Lord fully accomplished the work of our redemption by rising from the dead on Sunday and by sending down the Holy Ghost on Sunday; as therefore the work of our redemption was a greater work than that of our creation, the primitive *church* thought the day in which this work was completely finished was

---

* The following citations will be found in a small tract published at the "*Review* and *Herald*" Office, entitled, "Who Changed the Sabbath?"

more worthy her religious observation than that in which God rested from creation, and should be properly called the Lord's day."

"*Ques.* But has the church power to make any alterations in the commandments of God?"

"*Ans.* The commandments of God, as far as they contain his eternal law, are unalterable and indispensable, but as to whatever was only ceremonial they cease to oblige, since the Mosaic law was abrogated by Christ's death; hence, as far as the commandment obliges us to set aside some part of our time for the worship and service of our Creator, it is an unalterable and unchangeable precept of the eternal law in which the church cannot dispense. But, forasmuch as it prescribes the seventh day in particular for this purpose, it is no more than a ceremonial precept of the old law which obligeth not Christians, and therefore, instead of the seventh day and other festivals appointed by the old law, the *church* has prescribed the Sundays and holidays to be set apart for God's worship, and these we are now obliged to keep in consequence of God's commandment, instead of the ancient Sabbath."

"*Ques.* What warrant have you for keeping the Sunday preferable to the ancient Sabbath, which was the Saturday?"

"*Ans.* We have for it the authority of the Catholic church and apostolic tradition."

"*Ques.* Does the Scripture anywhere command the Sunday to be kept for the Sabbath?"

"*Ans.* The Scripture commands us to hear the church (Matt. 18:17, Luke 10:16), and to hold fast the traditions of the apostles. 2 Thess. 2:15. But the Scriptures do not in particular mention this change of the Sabbath. John speaks of the Lord's day (Rev. 1:10); but he does not tell us what day of the week this was, much less does he tell us that this day was to take the place of the Sabbath ordained in the commandment; * * * * so that truly the best authority we have for this, is the testimony and ordinance of the church. And, therefore, those who pretend to be so religious of the Sunday, whilst they take no notice of the festivals ordained by the same church authority, show that they act by humor, and not by reason and religion, since Sundays and holy days all stand upon the same foundation, viz., the ordinance of the church."—*Cath. Christian Instructed,* pp. 209–211.

"*Ques.* Have you any other way of proving that the church has power to institute festivals of precept?"

"*Ans.* Had she not such power, she could not have done that in which all modern religionists agree with her—she could not have substituted the observance of Sunday, the first day of the week, for the observance of Saturday, the seventh day, a change for which there is no scripture authority."—*Doctrinal Catechism.*

"*Ques.* If keeping the Sunday be a church

precept, why is it numbered in the decalogue, which are the commandments of God and the law of nature?"

"*Ans.* Because the substance, or chief part of it, namely, that the day be set apart for the service of God, is of divine right and of the law of nature; though the determining this particular day, Sunday, rather than Saturday, be a church ordinance and precept."—*Abridgment of Chris. Doc.,* pp. 57, 59.

Thus much for the connection of the papacy with the change of the Sabbath. The reader, repudiating the claim for apostolical tradition, which is of no value with Protestants, and rejecting as fallacious the assumed antiquity of the Roman Catholic church, will discover that there still remains the bold assumption of the ability on the part of that church to change the Sabbath, and also of the historic fact that it has done so. Mr. Gilfillan, while, of course, from his standpoint rejecting the notion that the pope has either in reality changed, or even possessed the ability to change, the divinely appointed day of rest, frankly acknowledges that he arrogates to himself the power so to do, in the following language:—

"Rome, professing to retain, has yet corrupted every doctrine, institution, and law of Jesus Christ, recognizing for example, the mediator between God and man, but associating with him many other intercessors; avowing adherence to the Scripture, but the Scripture as supplemented and made void by the writings and traditions of men; and, in short, without discarding the Lord's day, adding a number of encumbering holidays, giving them in many instances an honor equal and even superior to God's own day, and claiming for the 'Vicar of Christ' lordship even of the Sabbath."—*The Sabbath*, p. 457.

Into the details respecting the fasts; the decrees of councils; the bulls of popes: the myths concerning the calamities which have befallen those laboring on the Sunday; the forgery of an epistle in its interests, which it was claimed fell from Heaven; and the astounding miracles with which the hierarchy has accomplished the prodigious task of making the transfer, we are not permitted to enter here, nor will it be required that we should do so. Any person acquainted with the arts usually employed at Rome will readily perceive the methods which she has called to her assistance. All that a reasonable man could possibly ask is found in the transition from one day to another, in the fact that the law of God was to be tampered with by a persecuting power which was to continue its oppressions of the saints of God for twelve hundred and sixty years, and in the further consideration that no persecuting power except that of Rome has ever continued for that length of time.

Concerning the decree of Constantine, the only place which we assign to it in the controversy between the friends of the Lord's Sabbath and its rival, is that which it holds because of its having made the transition easy. The first day of the week being the one generally observed by the heathen and by this decree enforced by statute, had in its favor the practice and sympathy of the masses of men. This law, though passed by a heathen, and in the interest of the heathen religion, was, as would naturally have been the case, of great service to those who subsequently favored the change of day, since it gave to their effort not only the color, but also the material advantage, of legality; by it, men, under certain circumstances, were compelled to celebrate the day of the sun even though they had previously regarded that of the Lord. This, of course, was burdensome, and worked greatly to the advantage of the heathen festival.

One of two views must be taken of the statute of Constantine: If it were Christian, then it proves that Sunday observance, at the time of its passage, was exceedingly lax, since by its terms only men in the cities and towns were prohibited from laboring upon it, while those in the country were by it allowed and encouraged to carry on the vocations of the farm. If, on the other hand, it were heathen in its origin, then the suggestion that it recognizes the venerableness of the day of the sun, even at so early a period as that of its promulgation, is entirely without force, since it thereby becomes manifest that it received this dignifying appellation, not because it had long been venerated by the disciples of our Lord, but because from time immemorial it had been honored by the heathen—a doubtful compliment to the Christian Sabbath.

STATESMAN'S REPLY.

ARTICLE TEN.

THE PRINCIPLE AS TO TIME IN SABBATH OBSERVANCE.

OUR readers will recollect that the chief difference between the second and the third theories of the Christian Sabbath, as we stated them in our last issue, is in reference to the question of time. Seventh-day Sabbatarians, on the one hand, maintain that the last one of the seven days of the week is *the* sacred day, and that the observance of this very day is absolutely essential to the proper observance of the Sabbath of the Lord, and the keeping of the fourth commandment. On the other hand, we set forth what we believe to be the true theory of the Christian Sabbath, according to which the essential idea of the law of the Sabbath is the consecration to God of an appointed proportion of time—one day in seven, and not the essential holiness of any particular day.

We have already seen that the interpretation of the fourth commandment which insists on the essential holiness of the last day of the week would convict the risen Lord, and his inspired apostles, and the whole church of Christ, even in its purest days, of the violation of that precept of the divine law. But let us now examine a few practical points in connection with this second theory.

1. If the seventh day of the week is to be rigidly adhered to, as the law of the fourth commandment, it must be the seventh from the creation, in regular weekly succession. Will any seventh-day Sabbatarian venture to affirm that, through all the changes of our race, through all the breaks of history, through the bondage in Egypt, and the repeated captivities of God's ancient people, to say nothing of the miracles in connection with Joshua's victory, and Hezekiah's sickness, the unbroken succession of the weekly divisions of time has been maintained? Does the last day of our week answer, in an exact numbering of days, to the seventh day on which God rested after completing the work of creation? The interpretation which we are now considering demands this conformity to the fourth commandment in its letter. He would be a bold man indeed, who would affirm that his seventh day in this nineteenth century is the exact day which his own view of the law of the Sabbath would require him to keep holy. Our present first day may correspond to the original seventh day. Who knows?

2. But admit that these essentially holy twenty-four hours, at the close of each week, may be marked without doubt, how can all Christians in different parts of the world keep them? How can men in different longitudes and latitudes so

mark off the week as to have it end with this intrinsically holy portion of time? The difference in local time in different parts of the earth is a fact familiar to every school-boy. The circumference of the earth, for the convenience of calculation, is divided into three hundred and sixty degrees. As the sun appears to make a circuit round the earth every time the earth rotates on its axis, that is, every twenty-four hours, the apparent motion of the sun from east to west will be fifteen degrees each hour. Let it be noon of the seventh day at any given point in our land, and it will be sunset ninety degrees east, and sunrise ninety degrees west. At what point of the earth's surface shall men claim the right to have the seventh or holy day begin with their sunset or their midnight, and demand that all others east and west shall measure their holy day from so many hours before or after their own midnight or sunset, as their portion may require?

Or, again, in extreme northern and southern latitudes, where perpetual day and constant night alternate with the annual revolution of the earth, how shall the seventh day be marked? How shall this essentially holy day of twenty-four hours be known? As God, in his infinite wisdom, has seen fit to make our earth, and ordain the laws of its diurnal revolution on its axis, and its annual orbit round the sun, it is simply impossible for the inhabitants of the world to keep holy the same identical period of time. The interpretation of the law of the Sabbath at which we are looking is in conflict, therefore, with the laws of the solar system.

3. Our seventh-day friend, perhaps, retreats to

his last refuge. There is no portion of absolute time essentially holy. That was never meant. Very well, then, what is meant? Why, that each one in his own longitude or latitude should observe the seventh day as it is measured by his own local time. We apprehend that, in some latitudes, the seventh day, measured by local time, running through some thousands of hours, would be a weariness to the strictest even of seventh-day Sabbatarians. But we will leave these extreme cases. They must keep holy the appointed proportion—one-seventh of their time. That must be the law of the Sabbath to them. But in the belt of the earth nearer the equator, local time, measured by the natural division of days, must be followed.

Now, let it be said, we have no desire to treat a serious subject lightly. But our friends insist on an interpretation of the fourth commandment which can hardly be treated seriously. We can scarcely blame Dr. Geo. Junkin for employing this shaft of ridicule. He says, substantially, suppose all our seventh-day Sabbatarians (and their number is not an insuperable objection to the experiment), having labored six days, according to the commandment, come to the night of Friday. By an excusable artifice, sponges, saturated with a powerful anæsthetic agent, are held to their noses, and they are laid up, in perfect unconsciousness, for a whole day beyond the close of their usual time of sleep. They awake, supposing it to be the seventh day of the week, as to them, as conscious intelligent beings, and subjects of law, it certainly would be to all intents and purposes. But in fact, by the actual measurement of time, it is the first day of the week.

Might there not be in this way a practical solution of the whole difficulty?

But the actual rising and the setting of the sun may be insisted on whether our seventh-day advocates are conscious or not. Suppose, then, that one of them takes the now rather popular trip of a tour round the world. Going west at the rate of, say thirty degrees a week, starting from New York, he would lengthen each of his days from sunrise to sunrise—supposing the sun to rise at six o'clock, local time, all along the belt of his course—a little over seventeen minutes; and thus, keeping his own count of time, and observing every seventh solar day, on his return to New York at the end of twelve weeks, his seventh-day Sabbath would really be the first day of the week. Though he might not be *mentally* converted to the first-day theory of the Christian Sabbath, he would at least be *physically* converted, and would either be compelled to accept the change, or make a week of six solar days to harmonize in Sabbath observance with his seventh-day brethren at home, or take to his journeying again, and complete the circuit of the earth in the opposite direction, in order to maintain unbroken the succession of weeks of seven days each, and have his Sabbath fall on the one and only day which will suit his interpretation of the fourth commandment.

If, instead of going by the west, our traveler should go by the east, journeying at the same rate of thirty degrees each week, he would diminish the length of each of his days a little over seventeen minutes, and on arriving once more at New York, at the end of twelve even weeks by the time of that city, but twelve weeks and one day by his own time, his seventh-day Sabbath would fall on the sixth day of the week, and we would have a new order of Sabbatarians.

The reason of the diversity is obvious. The trip around the world, according to the supposed rate of travel, would occupy just twelve weeks, or eighty-four days of twenty-four hours each, measured by local time at New York. The total number of hours, reckoning each day twenty-four even hours, would be 2,016. The traveler, proceeding westward at the rate of thirty degrees a week, would add to each day's length just seventeen and one-seventh minutes—making each day from sunrise to sunrise, reckoning this always at six o'clock, local time, twenty-four hours, seventeen and one-seventeenth minutes long. He would, therefore, in the whole number of hours of his trip, 2,016, see the sun rise only eighty-three instead of eighty-four times. Going east, he would shorten each day's length, reducing it from sunrise to sunrise, to twenty-three hours and forty-two and six-seventh minutes. In this case, the whole number of hours, 2,016, would divide up into eighty-five solar days. To one remaining at New York, there would be eighty-four solar days; to the one going west around the world, the same absolute time would be summed up in eighty-three solar days; and to the one going east, it would extend itself to eighty-five solar days. Thus at the close of every trip round the world, the Christian traveler or sailor must readjust the reckoning of his days, in order to observe the Lord's day with his brethren at home. When our Constitution shall have been amended, and a true Christian regard shall be shown to all citizens, if our seventh-day friends feel grievously oppressed by the Sabbath laws, which will then be no dead letter, we shall do our utmost to have the national government provide a number of comfortable vessels, and give our friends a gratuitous trip round the world. We shall take care that the officers are instructed not to sail by the east; for our seventh-day Sabbatarians would then go away only to come home and be sixth-day Sabbatarians. Due care will be taken to have them proceed in the right direction, and to induce them on their return to stay at home, and government's oppression of them by Sabbath laws will then forevermore have ceased.

In all seriousness, we ask, How can a thoughtful man, in view of the fact of the earth's revolution round the sun, and its effect on the measurement of time, hold to the second theory of the Christian Sabbath? We have a matter of fact to record just here. In 1790, nine mutineers from the English vessel, the Bounty, along with six men and twelve women from Tahiti, landed on what is known as Pitcairn's island in the Pacific Ocean. John Adams, one of the mutineers, after the violent death of the other men, was converted by reading a copy of the Bible, and became a true Christian. Keeping his own count of the days, he observed the weekly Sabbath, with the community which was growing up, and which he was at great pains to instruct in the Christian religion. Some time after, an English vessel visited the islands, keeping their count of the days. The officers and crew of this vessel landed at the island on Saturday, but, to their astonishment, found a Christian community keeping the Christian Sabbath. The original settlers and the visitors had gone to the island in different directions. Did the sailors, who kept one day, not observe the Sabbath? Or did the islanders, who kept another day, violate the fourth precept of the decalogue?

Two colonies of seventh-day advocates might leave the same port, one going east and the other west, and might locate on islands on the same parallel of longitude, but on different parallels of latitude. Each, keeping its own record of time, would be found, on settling in their permanent home, to be observing a different day as the weekly Sabbath. Would either colony admit that it was in the wrong? If they were to live apart, each might properly observe its own day; if together, would it matter which day might be observed?

Thus the principle as to time in Sabbath observance insists, not on the essential holiness of any twenty-four hours in themselves, but on the dedication to God of one day in seven, one seventh of the time as nearly as that proportion can be measured by the most convenient means available. This, the third theory does, while it accepts all the facts of history. With one more article, in favor of the third theory of the Christian Sabbath, we shall close this whole discussion.

A REJOINDER.

"THE PRINCIPLE AS TO TIME IN SABBATH OBSERVANCE."

WERE it not true that we had long since ceased to be surprised at anything which an individual could say when opposing the claims of the Lord's Sabbath, after having received the light concerning them, our astonishment at the position taken by the gentleman of the *Statesman*, in the foregoing article, would have no bounds.

To one who has followed him thus far in an elaborate argument, running through a series of nine communications, all for the purpose of establishing, from both Scripture and history, the change of the Sabbath from the seventh to the first day of the week, and the obligation under which all men are now placed to observe the latter instead of the former, it will be extremely difficult to explain, on grounds honorable to himself, this sudden repudiation of all which he has said in the past, while endeavoring to defend the newly found theory of the observance of one day in seven, to the exclusion of any definite day whatever.

In his second article, he says, "We are concerned here and now simply with the transfer of the Sabbath from the seventh to the first day of the week." In the third article, when speaking of apostolic times, he remarks again, " It was also seen that while the observance of the seventh day was not continued, another day of the week, the first, took its place as the stated day for religious assemblies and services." Farther on, he writes again, as follows : " On the last seventh day on which the disciples rested, according to the commandment, the Lord himself is lying in the tomb. The glory of the seventh day dies out with the fading light of that day, throughout the whole of which the grave claimed the body of the Redeemer. But the glory of the Sabbath of the Lord survives. It receives fresh luster from the added glories of the Lord of the Sabbath. 'The Stone which the builders refused has become the head of the corner.' It is very early in the morning, the first day of the week. Again, 'God said, Let there be light; and there was light.' The Sun of Righteousness has risen with healing in his wings. This is the day which the Lord has made ; we will rejoice and be glad in it. The first day of the week has become the Lord's day."

But we must cease from our quotations, for there is no limit to expressions synonymous with the above. Not only so, but were additional proof necessary, by more ample extracts, it could be made to appear that the whole theory of his defense, as already declared, has rested entirely upon the change of the day from the seventh, which was observed till the death of Christ, to the first, which was honored especially by our Lord, by his personal appearance to the disciples on the first and second Sundays following the resurrection, and by the outpouring of the Holy Spirit on the day of Pentecost, with the especial view of teaching the disciples that it had become holy time; also, that they, grasping the moral of the lesson imparted by example, if not by positive precept, inculcated the doctrine of the change, and made it binding upon all.

If we are right in this, and the reader who has followed the debate thus far will unhesitatingly admit that such are the facts, then, of course, the gentleman is arrayed against himself in a manner most distasteful, no doubt, to his personal feelings, as well as disastrous to his polished logic; for to the mind of the merest school-boy it must be apparent that a change of Sabbath from one day of the week to another, involves the definiteness of the day thus honored; *i. e.*, if the first day of the week is now the Christian Sabbath because of the nature of events which transpired upon it in particular, then, of course, it occupies that position to the exclusion of all other days; but this utterly demolishes the seventh-part-of-time theory, which the gentleman has adopted, the very essence of which is, that there is now no superiority in days, and the individual is left free to choose any one which may best accord with his tastes or subserve his interests.

Here, then, we come to a dead halt. Which shall we believe, the nine articles of the gentleman, or the tenth, which is in direct conflict with their teachings? Should we go by the bulk of the testimony, then we must decide that there is a definite day, according to the conviction of our opponent. But if he still holds to that doctrine, then that which he has said against the seventh-day Sabbath, on the ground that the earth is round, and, therefore, that the Edenic Sabbath could not be kept in all portions of it, is deprived of all its force. For, assuredly, if he believes that God now requires all men to honor the first day of the week, the world over, then he must admit that it is possible for them to do so.

But if it is possible for men both to find and to celebrate the first day of the week, on a round world, then, beyond all dispute, the same process which will enable them to do this, will also qualify them to locate and to observe the seventh-day Sabbath. For it is just as certain as mathematical demonstration can make it, that in a week consisting of seven days, having found the first of the number, in order to discover the last, you have but to take the one which preceded the known day, or, if you please, count forward six days from the one already established, and you have the last day of the week to which it belongs.

So, too, with every objection urged in the communication. The one in regard to the difficulties which would be experienced in an attempt to keep the Sabbath of the commandment at the poles, is just as fatal to the first day as it is to the seventh. All this talk, also, in regard to the impossibility of preserving a correct count, and of the lengthening and shortening of the days, as the traveler passes from the east to the west, if it has any force at all, or even the semblance of force, must be met and answered equally by the observers of the so-called Christian Sabbath, with those of the Sabbath of the Lord. This being true, we might pause right here, and roll the burden onto the opposition. Having raised the dust which is blinding the eyes of the ignorant, yet conscientious, it would be but substantial justice for Sabbatarians to fall back and say to them, Take the field, gentlemen, and wrest from the hand of the infidel and the atheist the weapons with which you have armed them to be employed against you in the very work in which you are engaged; for, be it remembered that the children of this world are wiser in their generation than the children of light, and they will readily perceive the advantage which they have gained by such doctrines and difficulties as those to which the gentleman has called their attention.

This, however, we shall not do, but shall ourselves, in due time, strike at the very root of the error, in the interest of a definite and universal day of holy rest. Before entering upon this work, nevertheless, there is a matter which concerns Sabbatarians most deeply, to which attention should be directed.

The gentleman and his friends are pressing upon the nation the necessity of the Constitutional Amendment—contrary to his former declaration, in which he said there was no necessary connection between the Sabbath and the amendment. He now justifies our strictures upon the disingenuousness of his argument, by deliberately stating, in the article before us, with an air of triumphant exultation, that, the amendment once secured, the Sabbath laws in this country will then cease to be a dead letter. By this, he means, of course, that they will be carried into operation. But what are those Sabbath laws? They are laws enforcing the first day of the week, in nearly every State in the Union.

Now, we believe that what the gentleman says will be fulfilled; but right here is the proper place to offer a solemn protest. Will the gentleman fine and imprison my brethren and myself for disregarding the first day of the week, after having conscientiously kept the seventh? If so, we ask for the logic by which such a course could be justified, on the ground that the seventh-part-of-time theory is correct? Now, mark it, the object of the amendment is to make the Bible the fountain of national law. All the enactments of the Congress and all the decisions of the judiciary are to be in harmony with it. If, therefore, Sabbath laws are passed, they must be such as the Scriptures would warrant; for the Sabbath, be it remembered, which this movement seeks to enforce, is the one which the Bible teaches.

But, according to the last theory, the day which God now requires to be observed is not any one in particular, but simply one in seven, the individual being left to make the selection of the one which he prefers thus to honor. Now, therefore, it is submitted that if God has given to man this prerogative of choice, then he has done so because this course was the one which commended itself to infinite wisdom, and no person or set of persons has a right to come between the creature and the Creator, depriving the former of rights which the latter has guaranteed to him. If the Bible Sabbath is indeed an indefinite one, we say to these gentlemen, Hands off; in the name of religion and the Bible you shall not perform a work which will do violence to a large class of conscientious citizens, and which, according to your own argument, is contrary to the doctrine of the Christian Sabbath, as laid down in the word of God. Be consistent with yourselves and your views of Scripture.

If, indeed, you are sincere in believing that Sabbatarians violate no divine law in the keeping of the seventh day, then we say to you in the name of charity, Why not allow them, so long as they are Christian men and women, and obedient citizens, to carry out their convictions of duty, without compelling them, by the appliances of persecuting legislation, to keep the particular first-day Sabbath which indeed you have chosen for yourselves, but for which you have now ceased to claim any special divine honor? To force them, either to disregard their own convictions of duty, or to keep two days holy, would be an act of despotism but one remove from that terrible bigotry which, in the Inquisition, resorted to the rack and the thumbscrew; not, indeed, to make men better Christians or better citizens, but to coerce them into the acceptance of institutions for which there was no divine authority.

But we must pass to the consideration of other points. To the objection that the seventh day may have been lost since creation, and that he is a bold man who would affirm his ability to locate it now, it may be replied that, while Sabbatarians claim for themselves no unusual amount of courage, they do insist that it is an easy matter to demonstrate the succession of weeks, and the proper place of the original seventh day in the septenary cycle at the present time. The way in which this may be done is as follows: At the creation of the world, God blessed and sanctified the seventh day, because that on it he had rested. At the exodus from Egypt, he gave to the people a written law, enforcing the Sabbatic observance of the day on which he had originally ceased from his labors. On the sixth, Moses said to the people, "To-morrow is the rest of the holy Sabbath unto the Lord." For forty years subsequent to this, God marked out this day from the others by causing that no manna should fall upon it whatever, whereas it fell upon every other one of the seven.

Thus we have the authority of God himself, who assuredly could not mistake, that the people of Israel, in the outset, had committed to them the original seventh day, since God not only gave them a Sabbath, but also, according to the reason of the commandment, the Sabbath of the Lord. Descending the line of history to the days of Christ, we find him declaring that he had kept his Father's commandments (John 15:10). But one of these commandments was that relating to the Sabbath; in order, therefore, to the proper observance of it, Christ must have been able to decide which day in the week it was. That this was the case, none will dispute. Thus the day is located in his time satisfactorily, since he kept the same one which the Jews regarded, and which preceded the day of his resurrection. From that time to this, we have the general agreement of Jews, Christians, and heathen, in regard to the precise place in the week of both the first and the seventh day. Surely, this is all which could be demanded in order to reach reasonable certainty.

The difficulty which the gentleman finds in harmonizing the will of God, as expressed in the law of nature and that of a definite Sabbath for the people living near the poles, is apparently possessed of some force. It is, however, not peculiar to him. These barren wastes of ice and snow, though far removed from our civilization, are apparently destined to figure as largely in the spiritual world as they do in that of scientific research; not only on the Sabbath question, but also in that of baptism, it has a part to act. Think, says the advocate of sprinkling, as a shudder runs through his whole system, think of an immersion administered in the regions of eternal ice. Then having suitably impressed his auditors with the physical difficulties in the way of Bible baptism, he concludes that God never could have ordained immersion as the only method, since it is impracticable in the extreme north, and God surely would have commanded a form of ordinance which could be carried out in all parts of the world.

In harmony with this line of deduction is the difficulty stated by our friend. Chiming in with the theory that the laws of nature and the law of God must run harmoniously together, it is shown that at the poles the days and nights are six months long; and, therefore, that a twenty-four hour Sabbath, definitely located upon the last day of the week, is out of the question. The conclusion drawn is that, as the theory of the seventh-day Sabbatarians is in conflict with the ordinance of nature in these portions of the globe, it must be contrary to the original design of God.

But pause a moment; suppose we should grant that in the region in question there are men who cannot keep the seventh-day Sabbath as originally ordained, does that prove of necessity that it ought not to be hallowed in those portions of the world where there is no difficulty in the way of its observance? We think not. To illustrate: Were a man to pass his life in a coal mine, hundreds of feet beneath the surface, laboring continually, and never seeing the sun at all, would he, therefore, be exempted from the definite Sabbath? You answer, No. But why is this reply returned? Manifestly, because the difficulty is not with God and his laws, or the sun, but with the individual who has voluntarily placed himself under abnormal circumstances. In other words, he has located himself where the God of nature never designed that he should, and, in so doing, he has himself created a difficulty which he himself can remove.

So, too, with the Northman. If he finds it impossible to keep a Sabbath which is most perfectly adapted to the wants of mankind, it is simply because he has placed himself in a region which God has declared waste and uninhabitable as emphatically as can be done by nature speaking through the language of eternal ice and snow, and the disappearance for six months in a year of that great luminary whose light and heat are so indispensable to the comfort and advancement of the race. But, if this is true, then the argument from the conflict between the law of the God of nature and that of revelation, concerning a definite day of rest, loses all of its force; for the whole trouble arises, not from any want of adaptation on the part of such a rest to the circumstances of those who are where God would have them located, but from a disregard, in the first place, on the part of the nations in question, of the manifest law of prohibition to the settlement of regions which were designed to remain unoccupied.

Their relief can be found in one of two directions: They can, in the interest of their own progress, retrace their steps to localities where the more advanced portion of the race feel the genial influence of a diurnal sun; or, should they insist upon remaining in the bleak regions of their choice, it is possible for them, according to the accounts of travelers, to mark by the variations of the twilight, even in their six months' night, the boundaries of the Sabbath and the week days as they come and go to those residing in more temperate regions.

It is now time to grapple with the theory that it is impossible for those traveling around the world and those living in different portions of it to keep one and the same day. The first thing to be settled is the matter of what is meant by the expression, "the same day." Upon this point, the gentleman has wasted many words. We have never insisted upon the identical hours.

All that we demand is that the same day should be observed throughout the habitable globe, *i. e.*, each individual should celebrate in his own particular locality the seventh day of the week as it comes to him in its passage round the earth—to use the language of common parlance.

Whether this can be done or not is a question which involves the wisdom of God; for, granting that he gave the fourth commandment as a Sabbath law, and the regulations concerning the Sabbath, as found in the books of Moses, there is no room for dispute that he understood the statute to enforce the keeping of a definite day, and not merely one-seventh part of time. In the sixteenth chapter of Exodus, where the Sabbath is first introduced, is found an excellent opportunity to test this matter. He there marks out the day which he had hallowed as the one which followed the sixth, and the only one on which no manna fell. For forty years, also, this practice of separating the day of his rest by a weekly miracle from all others was continued. But why should he have done this if there was no choice, and if the keeping of the seventh part of time was all that was necessary? Nay, more, why did he make it absolutely impossible for a man to celebrate any other day but the seventh day of the week? That he did so, we can prove in a few words.

We will suppose that a person entertaining

the sentiments of the gentleman should have attempted to carry them out in the forty years during which God led the people in the wilderness; also, that his first experiment was that of Sunday rest. In this he would have failed utterly. Do you ask, How? I answer that God had decreed that no manna should fall on the seventh day (Ex. 16:26), and that the manna which was to be eaten on the Sabbath should be gathered on the day before (Ex. 16:5). It would therefore have been impossible for the individual in question to provide food for his Sunday rest. But, disgusted with this kind of Sabbath-keeping, suppose he should have tried, in order, Monday, Tuesday, Wednesday, Thursday, and Friday, the result would not have varied materially. On Sunday, there was an utter absence of all food; on the other days, that which had been previously gathered, instead of being fit for use, would have been found corrupted and changed into loathsome worms, since God had told the people that only the manna which was gathered on the sixth day should be kept until the day following; and some of them, having made the experiment of disobeying in the particular in question, found the result as cited above (Ex. 16:19, 20). On the other hand, should the same individual have decided finally to consecrate the seventh day of the week, he would have found no difficulty whatever. Gathering his double portion of the manna on the sixth day, by a miracle of God it would have been preserved pure and wholesome through the last day of the week.

But how can this be accounted for on the hypothesis that no particular day was chosen by the Lord? If, indeed, he had adopted the indefinite plan, and had left the people to choose for themselves, it is certain that he did this because it was the best method. But if it were the best method, and if it were in accordance with his view of the statute, then, assuredly, he would not have stultified himself and mocked the people by first granting them a privilege and then, by his providence, preventing them from carrying it out.

Should it be suggested that this law was confined to the land of Palestine and to the Jews in its operation, I answer; first, that at the time spoken of the people were in Arabia, not in Judea, and that even should that be granted, which is not true, viz., that the fourth commandment related simply to the Hebrews, this does not affect the question at all, for no one will insist that Jews were only obliged by it when in Judea. Wherever they might be, they were required to keep the Sabbath, whether in bondage in Assyria, or traversing the known world in quest of gain. From Spain to India, from Scythia to Africa, this law was designed to apply and did apply for hundreds of years before it will be even claimed that it was abolished. This being true, it is established beyond question that God himself imposed upon men, traversing the whole of the eastern continent, a uniform day of worship.

Do you inquire when they commenced it? I answer, At sunset, agreeably to the direction in Lev. 23 : 32. Did they go eastward to the Pacific, or westward to the Atlantic, they were required to commence their rest at that hour. Was it impossible for them to do so? He that says so charges God with folly. Were they capable of carrying out the requirement? Then, at least on the eastern continent, the definite day was a practicable thing. God knew how his people would be scattered; he gave them the institution of the Sabbath, adapted to whatever circumstances they might be placed in; he marked out that Sabbath from the rest of the week, and in the outset settled beyond controversy the question that it was not movable in its nature. Therefore, he who would accept the theory which we have been considering and repudiate the one which we indorse, must do it in the face of God's explanatory providence, in the teeth of his written law, and against the practice of his people, Israel, who for centuries have had no difficulty in finding the Sabbath in every latitude.

So much for the law and its history, making clear, as it does, that our opponents do not understand the possibilities of the case as God looks upon them. We will now proceed to the consideration of the difficulties which they discover in the realization of our theory.

It is claimed that, in going around the world eastward, a day is gained; and in going around westward, a day is lost, to the traveler. From these premises it is argued that a definite day cannot be kept. Has it ever occurred to the gentleman that his own theory would be somewhat disturbed by the same trip? Mark it, it is exactly one-seventh part of time which is to be kept. It will hardly be urged that all the old watches in the land are reliable enough to be trusted in a journey of this length, and, besides, suppose we had lived in a period when such timepieces were not known, then what? Oh! says the objector, we would have gone by the sun. Then you agree with us, after all, that the sun presents the most available method of marking the day; but remember, now, that you are on your journey round the earth, westward; you travel six days, each one considerably lengthened out by the fact that you are going with the sun; you stop and rest on the seventh day, which you call the Sabbath. Unfortunately, however, as you have been lying still, it is considerably shorter than your six days of work; by this means you have cheated the Lord out of one-seventh of the whole time which all of the six days had in excess over the one on which you rested. Traveling eastward, the opposite would be true, and your days of rest would be longer than your days of labor, and would not, therefore, represent one-seventh part of time.

Again, we might show by argument the complete anarchy into which the community would be thrown by the realization of this doctrine, that each man for himself is at liberty to fix upon his weekly Sabbath. Nothing would be easier to prove than that it would seriously obstruct your courts of justice; that it would render stated worship impossible; in fine, that it would bring confusion into every walk in life.

Do you reply that you will obviate the difficulty by legislative enactment, and that you will make this whole nation, from New York to San Francisco, regard the Sunday for the sake of uniformity and good order? I answer; first, have you then improved upon God's great plan? Did he not know that a definite day would be the best, and would he not have been likely to give it to us? Secondly, then you admit that it is, after all, possible to keep one and the same day across the whole of this continent; for were this not true it would be idle for you to attempt to produce uniformity by legislation. But putting this concession of yours in regard to the western, alongside of God's enforcement of a definite day for centuries, on the whole of the eastern, continent, the circuit of the globe is made, and the possibility of keeping a definite Sabbath on both hemispheres is established.

Before me lies the draft of an electrical clock,

which is styled, "The clock of all nations." The design is an ingenious one, and serves to show at a glance the difference in time between prominent cities in all parts of the globe. For this purpose, a central dial is drafted, representing the meridian of New York. The hands on this dial indicate the precise hour of noon. Around this central figure are arranged twenty additional dials, on each one of which is marked by the hands the time of day as it will exist in the cities named, commencing on the east of New York with Pekin, and terminating to the west of it with San Francisco. By it, you perceive at a glance the precise variation of time in the different longitudes to which these cities belong.

For example, while the clock of New York indicates twelve, noon, the one in Pekin indicates twenty minutes before one in the morning; the one in Rome, fifteen minutes to six P. M.; the one in London, five minutes of five P. M.; and so on until you reach New York, where it is twelve M. Then passing westward of that point, where the time is, of course, slower, the dial for Chicago marks seven minutes past eleven A. M.; that of St. Louis, five minutes of eleven A. M.; that in San Francisco, fifteen minutes before nine A. M. By this means, the variation between Pekin and San Francisco is shown to be about sixteen hours, or nearly two-thirds of one whole day. By the same method, the reader will at once discern that it is possible to locate the commencement of the day at any one of these points in its passage around the world.

In order to do this, let it be supposed that the day begins when it did in Bible times, with the setting of the sun. It is, if you please, Sunday at Pekin, and those who keep that day commence to celebrate it at sunset. Now, if we would ascertain just when the citizens of Rome would enter upon a like service, it is only necessary to determine how long it would take the sunset to travel the distance separating these two cities. By consulting the draft in question, we find that the time at Rome is six hours and fifty-five minutes slower than that at Pekin. This being the case, the sunset would reach them, and they would enter upon the first day of the week just six hours and fifty-five minutes after those dwelling on the meridian of Pekin have done so.

So we might go through the whole list. As the world revolves upon its axis, it would bring London to the same point where the people of Rome saw the sun sink in the west and entered upon the Sunday, just fifty minutes subsequent to that event. The citizens of New York would begin their Sunday, also, with the sunset, four hours and fifty-five minutes after those of London did so; and those of Chicago, fifty-five minutes later than those of New York; and those of San Francisco, two hours and twenty minutes subsequent to those of Chicago. All, however, would be hallowing the same day, though not, for a portion of the time, the same hours.* Each, in his own proper locality, would commence to keep the day when it reached him, and continue to keep it until by a complete revolution of the earth he is brought around to the commencement of another day, as indicated by another decline of the sun. This is as God would have it.

In the passage from Egypt to Palestine there was a variation of some minutes; but there was no change in the time of commencing the Sabbath. From even to even shall you keep your Sabbaths, was the divine edict, and his people, in going eastward or westward, obeyed this injunction. In doing so they needed no time-piece; nor would the traveler at the present time. In every habitable region, according to God's plan, the great luminary of heaven visibly marks the boundaries of sacred time. The day began in the east, and travels to the west. A complete revolution of the earth brings it, with its com-

---

* By consulting the figures given above, the reader will be able to demonstrate, not only the fact that the inhabitants along the line from Pekin to San Francisco, can hallow the same day, but also that the day which they hallow will be identical in some of its hours. For example: It was shown that the people of Rome commence their day six hours and fifty-five minutes later than do those of Pekin. Deducting these six hours and fifty-five minutes from twenty-four hours, we have left seventeen hours and five minutes as the period of time during which the citizens of these two cities would be celebrating the Sabbath in common. Applying the same principle to other cities, we find that London and Pekin would worship together for sixteen hours and fifteen minutes; New York and Pekin, eleven hours and twenty minutes; Chicago and Pekin, ten hours and twenty-five minutes; San Francisco and Pekin, eight hours and five minutes.

plement of light and darkness, to the home of every man, no matter as to the meridian of longitude in which he lives. It is the same day, in the Bible sense, as that kept by the Christian thousands of miles to the east of him, though it may not begin at exactly the same moment.

Practically, this question has no real significance whatever. Though it may puzzle the brain of one who has not before him the facts, it has been settled forever in a most remarkable manner by the usage of mankind. The fact is beyond cavil that, from the extreme eastern boundary of the eastern continent to the extreme western verge of the western continent, there is such a perfect agreement upon this point that each day of the week, commencing on the western shore of the Pacific, continues its course across Asia, Europe, and America, until it arrives at the eastern shore of the same sea. So true is this that, were there a line of churches surmounted with bells, in hearing distance of each other, they could ring in the commencement of any day; say at Yokohama in Japan, and its march could be made known along the whole line from that place to San Francisco by a like practice in each of the churches, without a solitary break until the last bell on the Pacific coast had announced its arrival there. Whether it be admitted that it can be done or not, it is a fact that the Christians from China to California do observe the same Sabbath or Sunday all along the line between the two points.

Should it be replied that, although there is a uniform reckoning of the days to those passing from San Francisco eastward to China, or from China westward to San Francisco, that, nevertheless, should they cross the Pacific Ocean from San Francisco westward to China, or from China eastward to San Francisco, it would be necessary for them in the first case to add a day, and in the last, to drop one, in order to make their time harmonize with that of the people in these two countries, the reply is, that this is very true. It does not, however, prove that there is no definite day which can be kept alike by the inhabitants of the two continents; for in order to the keeping of the same day on a round world there must somewhere be a day-line, in other words, there must be a point where the day begins. In crossing that line the same result would ensue as that claimed in the passage from California to China *via* the Pacific, *i. e.*, a day must be either dropped or added in the reckoning of the individual making the transit.

We have already seen that God's plan was to measure the days by the setting of the sun. This being the case, the fourth day, on which the sun was made, commenced at the precise point where at the time of its creation it would have appeared to a person to the east of it as sinking out of sight in the west. The day commencing at that point passed around the earth until every portion of it had in succession witnessed the setting of the sun on the fifth day. The only difficulty that remains in the case, consequently, is that of deciding where the day-line should be located. As already discovered, the practice of nations has fixed it in the Pacific Ocean. It is not a little remarkable that sailors change their reckoning while crossing that ocean backward or forward, and circumnavigate the globe at will without the slightest confusion. The only instance which has been cited in which any trouble has occurred, or any confusion of date has arisen, is that of Pitcairn's Island, in which they failed to make the change under consideration.* Had they done this, they would have found themselves in harmony with the great mass of men living on the same meridian with their insignificant island.

The only matter of debate which remains is that concerning the proper location of the day-line. Has there or has there not been a mistake made in fixing upon the place where it belongs? Certain it is that the providence of God seems to harmonize with the present arrangement. Man commenced his existence in the east. The progress of empire has been westward. Emigration has carried with it a harmonious system of

---

* The gentleman might have cited the case of Alaska, also, as a parallel to that of Pitcairn's Island. The inhabitants of this region, like those of the island mentioned, sailed eastward to this continent across the Pacific Ocean, and failed to drop the required day in their reckoning. The result was, that when we purchased that territory, they were found to be keeping Saturday instead of Sunday. We believe, however, that the mistake is now rectified.

counting the days, by which they have been recognized as beginning on the eastern, and traveling to the western, continent. Especially is this true of the Christian world.

But, again, is there not, aside from this providential arrangement and from the universal opinion that the day does begin in the east, as well as the fact that scientific men have established the point of changing the reckoning somewhere in the Pacific Ocean, some additional reason for supposing that God would choose this locality for the beginning of the day? We answer, There is. Should the day-line run through any continent or large body of land, it will be readily perceived that it would produce great confusion, since, on the one side of it, though imaginary in its character, individuals would be keeping the seventh day of the week, while on the other, their neighbors in close proximity to them would not yet have made their exit from the sixth.

To avoid this difficulty, therefore, the only remedy which could be found would consist in the employment of some great natural boundary, such as a range of mountains or an expanse of water, by which those on one side of the day-line would be so separated as to prevent the disorder which must arise from constant and uninterrupted intercommunication. That there is any range of mountains stretching northward and southward from pole to pole which would answer the purpose in question, no one will insist. The only resource left, consequently, is that of those vast bodies of water called seas or oceans.

Turning now to the one which is known as the Atlantic Ocean, it is found that the day-line could not be run through it without intercepting some habitable portion of the globe. The only resource which remains is found in the Pacific Ocean, which, as has been seen, has been selected by the mass of mankind as a suitable place in which to make those changes that would be necessary in case the day-line was actually located therein. Happily, an examination of a large globe will prove that a line drawn from Behring's Straits southward across the latitudes which are available for the homes of mankind will not touch any portions of land whatever, or at least if it strikes any they would be so insignificant in their character that they would not be worthy of mention.

With these remarks, the subject of the day-line is dismissed with the conviction that the necessity of its existence, the fact that it must be found in the Pacific Ocean if anywhere, and the uniform recognition in practice, if not in theory, by all nations, of its location in that sea, unite in furnishing a combination of facts which render assurance justifiable in the mind of one who does not insist upon more testimony than he ought to demand.

There remain now but two matters in the article of the gentleman which need to be disposed of. These are found in the contemptuous sneer at the insignificance of the numbers of Sabbatarians, and the witticisms, if such they may be called, which are indulged in in the employment of the suggestion concerning the use of the sponges saturated with stupefying chemicals and the gratuitous trip around the world, which it is proposed to give them.

To answer these sallies to the satisfaction of some would be impossible, while with others, possessing the power of logical discrimination and knowing that the office of mere wit is most frequently that of diverting the attention from a course of reasoning which it is felt cannot be met, such an effort would be uncalled for. The paucity in numbers is the same old, threadbare objection which every great reform has been compelled to meet since the world began. While the administration of narcotics and the trip round the world would be just as fatal to the exact observer of the seventh part of time as it would to one celebrating a definite day, even though it were admitted that the consequences of such a journey would be as claimed by the writer.

But besides all this, it will be discovered that the basis of the whole transaction, both in the case of the sponge and the vessel, is fraud, deceit, and force. Stupefy a man with narcotics for twenty-four hours; or nail him down under the hatches of a circumnavigating vessel; break the compass; send him round the world; let the whole community conspire to falsify the facts in the case; do not let him know where he has been; falsify the truth regarding the day observed by first-day keepers; and then, forsooth, you have changed the practice, if not convinced the judgment, of a little handful of conscientious, definite Sabbath-day keepers. Wonderful, gentlemen! Wonderful in the extreme! What results for such prodigious efforts! Alas, for truth, when it must pass such an ordeal as this! We blush, but not for ourselves. We would almost be willing to inhale the anæsthetic or run the hazard of the voyage at sea, taking our chances respecting the proper preservation of the Heaven-appointed day of rest, if, by so doing, we might prevent our brethren of the Amendment school, for whose welfare we have the most earnest desire, from making so sorry a show of the low estimate which they place upon the importance of employing in a controversy like this, arguments which appeal only to the Christian's head and heart, instead of those which appeal to the baser faculties of the mind.

A summary of the ground traveled in this rejoinder would run somewhat as follows:—

1. That in adopting the seventh-part-of-time theory, the gentleman has abandoned the definite first day which he sought to establish in the first nine of his articles.

2. That the seventh-part-of-time theory is just as fatal to the Sunday as it is to the Sabbath.

3. That it overturns the practicability of the proposed Amendment, since it seeks to enforce a definite day, and since, according to it, Sabbatarians have a Bible right to observe the seventh day in the exercise of a divinely given choice of days.

4. That it is possible to establish the identity of the last day of the week at the present time with that upon which God rested at the completion of the creation; from the providential manner in which God pointed it out in the exodus from Egypt; the fact that Christ and his disciples kept the Sabbath according to the commandment; the general agreement among Jews, Christians, and heathen concerning its place in the week from that time to this.

5. That the objection concerning the conflict between a definite Sabbath and the laws of nature at the poles does not array the God of nature against himself, or our version of his commandment, since the trouble does not imply any want of foresight on the part of the Deity, but rather a disregard of the plainest teachings of both providence and nature on the part of those who have placed themselves where it was never designed that men should locate.

6. That if a definite day is impossible, then the wisdom of God is impeached, since, both by the letter of the commandment and by his providential interpretation of it for forty years, that is the very thing which it inculcates.

7. That a definite day can be kept on the

eastern continent, since this had been done for hundreds of years before the change of the law will be even claimed.

8. That a definite day can be observed on the western continent, since this is the very object which the Amendment is designed to secure.

9. That the trip around the world would render it as impossible to keep an exact seventh part of time as it would a definite seventh day.

10. That the seventh-part-of-time theory would introduce into society the direst confusion, defeating even the administration of justice.

11. That, practically, the whole world from the extreme east to the extreme west does keep a definite day.

12. That the loss and gain of time creates no disturbance except in the crossing of the Pacific Ocean.

13. That with a definite day, there must be a day-line.

14. That that day-line is, by the uniform practice of nations, and the providence of God, which renders it impossible that it should exist anywhere else, drawn through the Pacific Ocean.

15. That it only remains for us to do just what we are doing and have been doing for centuries in order to prove by actual demonstration that all the difficulties in the way of a definite Sabbath can be readily disposed of by those who are desirous of keeping the law of God as it reads.

STATESMAN'S REPLY.

ARTICLE ELEVEN.

THE TRUE THEORY OF THE CHRISTIAN SABBATH.

THE third theory of the Christian Sabbath, in the order in which we have been considering the different theories, affirms that the Sabbath was instituted at the creation of man, and that it has never been abolished or superseded. This theory further maintains that the essential idea of the law of the Sabbath is not the holiness of any particular portion of time, but the consecration of a specified proportion of time, viz., one day in seven; that, in accordance with this essential idea of the Sabbath, a change of day was admissible; that a change was actually made by divine warrant, on account of, and dating from, the resurrection of Christ; and that the first day of the week, the Lord's day, is the true Christian Sabbath, having its moral sanction in the fourth commandment.

Enough has already been written in these columns, in disproving the opposing theories, to show that this theory of the Sabbath is the true one. Two things being admitted, there appears to be no escape from this theory. Let it be admitted, first, that God instituted the Sabbath for all mankind, and that its law is of unchanging as well as universal application. This is readily conceded by those with whom we are now in discussion. Then, in the second place, let it be admitted that the inspired apostles, under the guidance of Christ and his Spirit, and with their manifest approbation, ceased to observe the seventh day, and actually observed the first day of the week. This our opponents are very loth to admit. But the testimony given by us at considerable length is simply overwhelming and incontrovertible. The third theory, and it alone, harmonizes the immutable law of the Sabbath with the actual change of day.

In further confirmation of the correctness of this theory, it remains for us, in concluding this discussion, to show that this third theory accords with the fourth commandment, and meets every aspect of the design of the institution of the Sabbath.

The principal feature of the design of the Sabbath is the setting forth of God's sovereign control, as creator, of man and the time of man, as God's creature. Called into being by the Creator, and made lord over the irrational and material creation, man was taught that his time was to be used for God's honor. It was a trust from the Creator; and that man might not forget this, one-seventh of the time in regular recurrence was marked out to be consecrated specially to the Lord of all. This is the very idea in the commemoration of the work of creation. It is to keep alive the knowledge of God as the Creator and Sovereign Ruler of man. To commemorate the creation, is to keep before the mind, week by week, the duty of using our time for the honor of the Author and Upholder of our being.

Nor is the example of God's resting the seventh day made insignificant by this theory of the Christian Sabbath. "In six days God made the heavens and the earth, and rested the seventh day." God's people in different parts of the world do and must begin their work at different times, and yet in each locality they labor six days and rest the seventh. It is the proportion of time which is the law of the commandment, enforced by the divine example; and hence the Christian Sabbath, in the true import of the commandment, is as really the seventh day as the Jewish Sabbath. The Christian labors six days, and not the seventh, according to the divine example and the divine command.

In this way, also, the true theory of the Christian Sabbath meets the design of the institution as it was intended to arrest the current of the outward life and lead up the soul to unseen and eternal verities. And here there is a most important argument for the change of the day for Sabbath observance. It is most reasonable to believe that, if there be any work which more gloriously manifests the perfections of God, and serves better to turn the thoughts of men to things above, than the work of creation, the day which commemorates such a work would be the appropriate time for Sabbath observance.

So far as the essential idea of the Sabbath connects itself with a particular day, the argument is of great weight in favor of a change from the seventh to the first day of the week. The weekly division is the main thing, let the week begin when it may. It may begin on what we now call the third, or fourth, or any other, day. It will matter little. But as the first day, in our enumeration of the days, will always bring to mind the great work of redemption, accomplished by the Saviour, who on the first day of the week rose from the dead, the observance of this day as the Sabbath best answers one of the principal designs of that institution.

And then, how fittingly does the observance of the first day, the day of the Lord's resurrection, correspond to the design of the Sabbath as a foretaste of the heavenly rest—the *Sabbatismos* or Sabbath-keeping that remains for the people of God. Rejoicing here on the Christian Sabbath in what our Redeemer has done for us, we look forward with joyful anticipations to the many mansions which he has gone before us to prepare, that we may be "forever with the Lord."

> "Bright shadows of true rest; some shoots of bliss;
>   Heaven once a week;
> The next world's gladness prepossessed in this,
>   A day to seek
>
> Eternity in time; the steps by which
>   We climb above all ages; lamps that light
> Man through his heap of dark days; and the rich
>   And full redemption of the whole week's flight.
>
> 'The milky way chalked out with suns; a clue
>   That guides through evening hours; and in full story
> A taste of Heaven on earth; a pledge and cue
>   Of a full feast; and the out-courts of glory.'"

A REJOINDER.

"THE TRUE THEORY OF THE CHRISTIAN SABBATH."

It is a peculiarity of this discussion that we are prevented, in our rejoinders, from anticipating the positions which our opponent has in store for us. Were it possible to proceed upon principles of consistency, in debate, and conclude that he, having adopted such and such views, would continue to maintain them steadily for the future, there would be a sort of satisfaction found in preparing material to be employed hereafter. But we have learned, by actual experience, that in this debate such anticipatory action would be labor lost. For example: In the last reply, which had to do with the seventh-part-of-time theory, we had intended to show that, were it true, and that, were the observance of one day in seven all that is now required, even then Sabbatarians stood upon a footing as safe as that of their opponents, since the observance of the seventh day answered to the keeping of one-seventh part of time, equally with that of the celebration of the first day of the week.

Being prevented by want of space from indulging in these reflections, we laid them over for another week, supposing that they would come in play equally well at this time. Alas! what a mistake! We should have struck when the iron was hot. Unfortunately, we are not now confronting the no-day-in-particular doctrine, as we were then; but it is the "Lord's day" again, the first day of an indefinite week, "a particular, definite day, enforced by the command and the example of Christ and the apostles," which once more stands before us. How it is that we have been borne so rapidly over the space which separates these antagonistic positions, the reader will have to decide for himself; for we confess to a perfect want of ability, on our own part, to render him any assistance. Without the slightest attempt at logical deduction, we are first informed that the essential idea in Sabbath observance is not that of the keeping of a particular day, but the consecration of one day in the week, allowing the week to begin wherever it may. This, we are told, would suitably commemorate God's rest at the creation of the world; and, also, that if, in addition, we make the day of our rest identical with the first day of the week, we can thereby celebrate both creation and redemption. For this very purpose, we are informed, the Sabbath commandment was changed, so as to admit of the introduction of a new day.

But pause a moment. Has the gentleman told us just what change was made? Has he told us what words were stricken out? and how it now reads? The reader has not forgotten that this is the very thing the opposition were challenged to perform. He will perceive that this, also, is the very thing which the gentleman has failed to accomplish, and cannot hereafter do, since the reply under review is the last of his series. If it be said that he has cited us to the fourth commandment, as given in the twentieth of Exodus, as containing the law as it now reads, then he is self-condemned; for he admits that the phraseology of that commandment did enforce a definite day, and that, the last day of the week.

But once more: Passing over the absurdity of claiming a change in the law, where there is no ability to produce the statute as amended, let us go back from Sinai to Eden, along with the gentleman, and see if we cannot find, independent of the commandment, evidence that the creation Sabbath was not a portable institution, to be trundled about at the caprice of any and every individual. Mark it, now, it is granted that what is called the Jewish Sabbath law enforced the keeping of the seventh day, and admitted of no other as a substitute. But whence is this conclusion drawn? Undeniably, from the words, "The seventh day is the Sabbath of the Lord thy God; in it thou shalt not do any work."

But where has the gentleman learned that the creation Sabbath was enjoined in the use of language less explicit and limited in its meaning than are the words of the decalogue? If he knows anything about the original decree of Jehovah, and the limitations with which he guarded the Sabbath in the outset, he, like ourselves, is compelled to go to the sacred record for information. If, in going there, he has been able to find anything which would prove that the Edenic Sabbath was less fixed in its character than that of Sinai, then he has made some progress. The only scripture which will throw any light upon the subject will be found in Gen. 2:1–3.

Unhappily for the gentleman, however, it is fatal to his conception that the original Sabbath varied in any way from that of the Jews—so-called. In the account of its institution, the language employed is almost precisely the same with that subsequently traced upon the tables of stone. It is there declared that God sanctified (*i. e.*, set apart to a holy use) the *seventh day*. The reason for this action is the fact that he had rested upon it. Now, it will be observed that it was the "*seventh day*" that God blessed and sanctified, and no other. It is submitted, therefore, as the gentleman concedes, that the same expression (*i. e.*, the seventh day), when employed in the commandment given to Moses, did locate the Sabbath institution immovably upon the last day of the week, until the law was changed; that the same language, when employed originally, must have produced the same result; in other words, if the command to keep the seventh day, as given on Mount Sinai, held the people strictly to the observance of the last day of the week, so, too, Jehovah, in the beginning, restricted the whole race to a Sabbath which was, equally with the other, the seventh, and, therefore, the last day of the week.

In order to avoid this conclusion, it will be required that, by some means, he should be able to show that the same terms which were employed by God, at one time, have a different meaning from that attached to them, as employed by him at another time. Not only so, the Sabbath in Genesis, like that in Exodus, is further limited and defined by two additional facts. First, it was the day on which God rested; secondly, it was the day which he blessed because he had rested upon it. Therefore, before any other day could be substituted for it, these two things must be true of it, as matter of history. This, however, can never be the case, as it regards any day of the week, save the last; consequently, he who celebrates any other is not celebrating the one which God imposed in the beginning. So much for the definiteness of the Sabbath which was given to Adam.

Should it be replied that what has been remarked is correct, and that it is not argued that any one was at liberty to keep any other day than the seventh of the week, until Christ changed the law, and thereby authorized them so to do, we reply, Very good; that brings us back again to the original proposition, which is, Did he make such a change? If he did, then it is just as important that we should have clear and conclusive evidence that such an alteration was made by him, as it is that we should have the abundant testimony which we now possess that a definite Sabbath was originally given to mankind.

All this speculation in regard to what might have been done with perfect consistency under a given state of facts is worse than idle. What we demand is this—What *has been* done? Instead of concluding that Christ did a certain thing because it would have been right so to do, first show us, by actual Scripture quotation, that he really performed the work in question, and the consistency of his action will take care of itself. A theology which has no broader, firmer basis than individual conception of the propriety of certain occurrences which may never have taken place at all, is not worth the paper on which it is drawn out. This, nevertheless, is the very material with which we are dealing.

Eleven articles, ostensibly written to afford divine authority for the change of days, are concluded; and, from beginning to end, there is not found in them a "Thus saith the Lord" for the transfer. Again and again it is inferred that such and such transactions meant so-and-so. Again and again it is concluded that such and such things are admissible, not because of any scriptural warrant, but because they seem good in the eyes of those with whose practice they best conform. The reason why this is so, the reader will readily perceive. It is found, not in the fact that the learned gentleman who represents the opposition is insensible to the superiority of positive Bible statements over individual surmise, but in the necessity under which he is placed, to employ the only material which he has at hand. Meeting him, therefore, where he is, let us prove the unreliability of such deductions as he is indulging in by actual test. The points which he is attempting to establish are these: 1. The original idea of the Sabbath can be met by the observance of the first day of the week, as well as by that of the last. 2. That the commemoration of Christ's resurrection can only be suitably carried out by hallowing the first day of every week.

Now, as to the first of these propositions, it will only be safe to decide that it is correct after giving it mature reflection. We have already seen that God's original plan for preserving the memory of creation week was that of setting apart the last day of each subsequent week for the imitation, on our part, of his rest thereon. To say, therefore, that it would have answered just as well to allow the individual to take any other day—say the first day of the week—for this purpose, is to argue that God acted without cause in making the selection which he did and enforcing it for four thousand years. If the question were one of indifference, why did he not leave the day unfixed? Why not allow them then to commemorate his rest on the first day, as the gentleman would have done now, arguing that the ends of the original Sabbath would, in this way, be fully met. Certain it is that no good reason can be assigned why it would now be more proper to commemorate the rest of Jehovah by a variable Sabbath than it has been heretofore. This being true, the gentleman's logic is found to be unsound, or else the action of the Deity was inconsiderate.

Turning, now, to the second proposition, the reader will be instantly struck with its unqualified antagonism to the first point which is sought to be made out.

Remember, now, that the gentleman is arguing stoutly for first-day sanctity. He is not so particular when the week begins, but it must have just seven days, and the first of them must be devoted to the commemoration of the Lord's resurrection. Should you ask him why he is thus particular in the selection of the first day of the week, he would reply, "Why, that is the day on which the Lord arose, and it is his resurrection, as the crowning act in the work of redemption, which we seek to honor." But, reader, would it not occur to you, immediately, that this is a repudiation of all which he has said concerning the Edenic Sabbath? Now, mark it; what God demands, is, that we should honor the seventh day of the week, as the one which he rested upon, blessed, and sanctified. If, therefore, the rest, the blessing, and the sanctification of that day can be suitably remembered by the observance of another day differing from it, then the assumption that an event is most impressively handed down by the dedication, for this purpose, of the very day on which it transpired, is unsound.

But if this assumption be unsound, then all of the gentleman's talk in regard to the necessity for a change of days, in order to the suitable commemoration of the resurrection of Christ and the completion of the work of redemption, is without force. For, assuredly, if he is right in supposing that God's rest in Eden, on the seventh day, can be commemorated as well on the first day as on the seventh, then the same principle will hold good in regard to the events which transpired on the first day of the week, *i. e.*, they can be kept in remembrance by the hallowing of the seventh day as well as by that of the first. But this being true, his argument for the necessity of the change of Sabbaths is gone, and his philosophy of the change proved to be unsound. The only purpose which it has served in this controversy has been the revelation of that which is really the conviction of its author, as it is that of men generally, that there is no time in which great transactions can be so suitably commemorated as that of the day on which they took place. When the nation wishes to celebrate the anniversary of its independence, it sets apart for this purpose the fourth of July, which answers exactly to the day of the month on which the Declaration of Independence was made. Substitute for this another day, and you have marred the impressiveness of the occasion.

So, too, with God's rest on creation week; it must be so celebrated that all the associations connected with it will be calculated to lead the mind back to its origin and object. Turn it around, as the gentleman proposes to do, *i. e.*, substitute the first day of the week in the place of the last, and you have precisely reversed God's order. You have put the rest-day first, and cause the six laboring days to follow; whereas, God, knowing that rest was only needed *after* labor, worked six days and then rested the seventh, not because he was weary, but because he desired to put on the record for us an example to be strictly followed. The gentleman, however, without the slightest warrant, has, with a rash hand, laid hold of the divine procedure, and now says that the order pursued was not necessary to the inculcation of the great lessons which God designed to impart.

To this, I reply, 1. That God's actions are never superfluous. 2. That, if we err at all, it is safer to err on the side of the divine example. 3. That if the idea of God's working six days is in any way connected with a proper Sabbath rest, then it is indispensable that the Sabbath should follow, and not precede, the working portion of the week. 4. That if the rest of God, merely, is the object which we should keep before our minds by a proper regard for the Sabbatic institution, the gentleman has himself shown, by the logic which he has employed, that the only suitable period for the keeping of that rest is found in that portion of the week on which God ceased from his labors.

The remark of the gentleman that the work of redemption furnishes a subject worthy of being remembered by observance with Sabbatic honor of the day on which it was completed, is worthy of passing notice. The idea which he advances is one which is quite prevalent, and employed with great satisfaction by clergymen generally, when controverting the claims of God's ancient rest-day. The strength of the position lies in the fact that it distinguishes between redemption and creation, assuming, perhaps correctly, that the latter is more exalted than the former. Having won the assent of the mind to this proposition, the reader is quietly carried over to conclusions much less obvious than the first. Almost unconsciously he is led to decide, with his instructor, that, since redemption is a greater work than creation, it ought, therefore, to be honored by a day of rest.

Now we shall not enter into this matter largely, but we simply suggest that either this decision is the result of human, or else it is the product of divine, wisdom. If it is human wisdom, then its teachings should be followed with extreme caution. If it is divine wisdom, then they can be obeyed with the most implicit confidence. Just at this point, therefore, it is all-important that the test be applied. Has Jehovah ever said that the commemoration of creation week had become less desirable on account of the possible redemption of a fallen race, by the death of his Son? The most careful reader of the Bible has failed to find any such language; in fine, the intimation that such is really the fact is rather a reflection upon the Deity himself, since, from it, it might be inferred that the glory of his work had been dimmed by the fall of the race.

But, again, if the Lord has not said that he would not have the memory of creation cherished still, has he ever said that he would have the work of redemption signalized by a weekly rest? Once more the student of the Scriptures unhesitatingly answers in the negative; but if God has failed to make this declaration, who shall presume to put words in his mouth, and read the thoughts of his mind, as those having authority so to do? The man who will undertake to do it is venturing upon ground which lies hard by that of blasphemy. God never neglects to say that which ought to be said; he never calls upon any man to go beyond his commandments, for in them, says Solomon (Eccl. 12:13), is found the whole duty of man.

Furthermore, were we to reason upon this matter at all, every consideration would lead us to the conclusion that the inference of our opponents is not correct. In the first place, redemption is not yet fully completed in the case of any individual. In the second place, the Scripture says we have (are to have) redemption through his *blood* (Col. 1:14). But his blood, it is generally supposed, was shed upon Friday, and, therefore, it is not impossible that the hallowing of that day would more suitably commemorate redemption than that of any other day. In the third place, it was proved at length in a former article, that if creation was suitably commemorated by a day of rest, redemption, which is an event entirely opposite in its character, would naturally be celebrated by some institution of an entirely different nature. In other words, the Sabbath inculcates cessation from labor by the indulgence of inaction, while all the events connected with the resurrection of Christ rendered inactivity impossible.

But finally, we are not left, in a matter of this significance, to the unreliable decisions of the human mind. Not only is it true that God has never appointed a day of septenary inactivity, as the Heaven-chosen memorial of the resurrection of the divine Son of God; but it is also true that God himself, in the exercise of a wisdom which will hardly be impugned by finite beings, has selected an institution entirely different from that under consideration for the illustration of that phase of the work of redemption which was seen in the resurrection of Christ.

Says the great apostle to the Gentiles: "Therefore we are buried with him by baptism into death; that like as Christ was raised up from the dead by the glory of the Father, even so we also should walk in newness of life. For if we have been planted together in the likeness of his death, we shall be also in the likeness of his resurrection." Rom. 6:4, 5. "Buried with him in baptism, wherein also we are risen with him through the faith of the operation of God, who hath raised him from the dead." Col. 2:12.

Baptism, that is, Bible baptism, or the immersion of the individual beneath the water, most forcibly commemorates the death of our Lord. As the administrator lowers the body of the passive subject beneath the yielding wave, by the very necessity of the case, breathing is, for the time, suspended, and the person, as nearly as may be while in life, as he lies motionless in the hands of the individual to whom he has committed himself in the exercise of an act of faith, shadows forth the death and burial of his Lord in a most impressive manner. As he rises, also, from that position, and, proceeding to the shore, unites once more with the throng of living beings who surround him, he most forcibly illustrates the coming back again of our Lord from death and the grave to a life of infinite activity and glory.

All, therefore, which is necessary in order to the remembering, by outward expression, of that most glorious event, which gave back to the disciples, from the nations of the dead, the body of the beloved Master, is that we go forward in the fulfillment of an ordinance which has been provided for that purpose, and which sets forth the events which are thought worthy of a memento in a manner as superior to that in which it could be done by mere inaction, as God's conception of what would be suitable under such circumstances is higher than that of man. The wonder is that any one should have lost sight of the original design of an institution which is remarkably expressive of the purpose for which it was created. In fact, had not the same power which has changed the Sabbath also tampered with the ordinance of baptism by changing the original form into one less expressive of its historic associations, we believe that the view which is now passing under consideration never could have suggested itself to any mind.

But, reader, it is now time that our labor should be drawn to a close. In the providence of God, we have walked together over the territory devoted to the great and important Sabbath question. With pleasure, we are about to lay down our pen for the last time, and submit the whole matter to you for the pronouncing of the final verdict of your individual judgment. As we do so, it is with feelings of most profound gratitude to God for a truth which, while there is underlying it a cross so heavy that it cannot be lifted by human strength unaided, is, nevertheless, so plain that its mere statement is its most complete demonstration. Were it not true that society is at present so organized that the keeping of the seventh day involves social, political, and pecuniary sacrifice, much greater than he is aware of who has not considered the matter, we would not hesitate to say that a complete and speedy revolution could be wrought upon this subject in a brief space of time. Never, in the history of any reformation which has heretofore occurred, were men covered with a more complete panoply of defense, and armed with more destructive weapons of offense, than are God's commandment-keeping people at the present period. The only mystery connected with the subject is, that, being as plain as it is, the fact of the change should not have attracted universal attention before.

Traversing again the ground over which we have come with the gentleman who has managed the opposition in this debate, the poverty of his resources is most striking. In all that he has said, he has proved nothing which has in any way relieved his case, nor can his failure be attributed to any lack of capacity on his part. In the handling of the material with which he has had to do, he has displayed not a little ingenuity. The arguments which he has employed and the positions which he has taken are those of the orthodox ministry generally at the present time. His failure is entirely attributable to the natural weakness of the position which he has sought to defend. His was indeed a hard task. He felt the moral necessity of a Sabbath, as a Christian man; and, finding the religious world keeping the first day of the week, he sought to defend this practice from the Bible stand-point. But, alas for his cause! The more he has appealed to this source, the more certain has it become that the Bible, and the usages of Christendom in this matter, can never be harmonized. In its pages we find the most ample authority for a day of rest, but none for the one which is generally honored as such. The record in brief stands as follows:—

1. There is a Sabbath.
2. That Sabbath is the seventh, and not the first, day of the week, for the following reasons:—

(1.) In the beginning God rested on the seventh day, thereby laying the foundation for its Sabbatic honor (Gen. 2:3); whereas, he never rested upon the first day.

(2.) He blessed the seventh day; whereas, he never blessed the first day.

(3.) He sanctified the seventh day, or devoted it to a religious use; whereas, he never sanctified the first day.

(4.) The day of his rest, his blessing, and his sanctification, he commanded to be kept holy, in a law of perpetual obligation; whereas, he never commanded the observance of the first day.

(5.) The Lord Jesus Christ recognized the obligation of the seventh day by a life-long custom of observing it (Luke 4 : 16); whereas, the Lord Jesus Christ never rested upon the first day of the week; but always treated it as a secular day.

(6.) He also recognized its perpetuity forty years after his death, when speaking of events connected with the destruction of Jerusalem, by instructing his disciples to pray that their flight might not occur thereon (Matt. 24 : 20); whereas, he never spoke of the first day as one to be honored in the future, nor, indeed, so far as we know, did he ever take it upon his lips at all.

(7.) It is the day which the holy women kept, according to the commandment, after the crucifixion of our Lord (Luke 23 : 56); whereas, there is no account that any good man has ever rested upon the first day out of regard for its sanctity.

(8.) It is the day on which Paul, as his manner was, taught in the synagogue (Acts 17 : 2); whereas, Paul never made the first day of the week, habitually, one of public teaching, a thing which he would have been sure to do had he looked upon it as sacred to the Lord.

(9.) Being mentioned fifty-six times in the New Testament, it is in all these instances called the Sabbath; whereas, the first day is mentioned eight times in the New Testament, and in every case it is called, simply, the first day of the week.

(10.) In the year of our Lord 95, it is spoken of by John as the Lord's day (Rev. 1 : 10); whereas, the first day is in no case mentioned in the use of a sacred title.

(11.) It is mentioned not only as the Sabbath, but it is also spoken of as the next Sabbath, and every Sabbath, thus proving that it had no rival (Acts 13:4; 15:21); whereas, the day before the first, and the sixth day after it, being spoken of as the Sabbath, it (*i. e.*, the first day,) is classed with the other days of the week.

(12.) In the Acts of the Apostles, and, in fine, in the whole canon of the New Testament, there is not a single transaction which is related as having occurred upon the seventh day in the least incompatible with the notion that it continued to be regarded as holy time, while the law which enforces its observance is inculcated in the clearest and most emphatic terms (Matt. 5:17–19; Rom. 3:31; Jas. 2:8–12); whereas, the first day was one on which Christ indulged in travel on the highway in company with others, after his resurrection, without informing them of its character or rebuking them for sin. It is also a day on which two of the disciples walked the distance of fifteen miles on one occasion, while on another, Paul performed the journey of nineteen and one-half miles on foot, while Luke and seven companions worked the vessel around the headland for a much greater distance (Luke 24:13, 29; Acts 20:1–13.)

In view of the above, the whole question of obligation may be summed up in the following words: Shall we keep a day which God has commanded, which Christ inculcated, and which holy men regarded from the opening until the close of the canon of Scripture? or shall we disregard that, putting in its place one which neither God, nor Christ, nor a holy angel, nor an inspired man, ever, anywhere, under any circumstances, enjoined, and which, in addition, God and Christ, and holy men and women, are everywhere in the sacred word brought to view as treating in a manner such as they would only treat a day of secular character?

In fine, it is simply the same old test applied once more to human action, which has in all ages been the measure of moral character, *i. e.*, Shall we obey God? or shall we not? Shall we gratify our own inclination and have our own way by pertinaciously persisting in a course of action for which we have no Scripture warrant? or shall we take the Bible in one hand and, accepting its doctrines as the words of life, follow them to their legitimate consequences in our daily walk? Says John, "This is the love of God, that ye keep his commandments." Says James, "Show me your faith without works, and I will show you my faith by my works."

Sublime sentiments, indeed! In them is expressed the moving, controlling principle of every Christian heart. Oh! that all men in the ages of the past had held to the noble purpose of taking God at his word, believing that he meant just what he said, and walking out with a noble courage upon their confidence in his wisdom to legislate, and his right to command. Had they done so; had they been willing to be taught instead of going uninstructed; had they submitted to be led instead of insisting upon independent action, how much misery would have been spared our kind! Take, for example, the case of Eve— God exempted one tree in the garden from the rest, saying, "Thou shalt not eat of it; for in the day that thou eatest thereof thou shalt surely die." Unhappily, the mother of all living ventured to deviate from the command of God in what appeared to her an unimportant particular, and, as the result, a race was plunged into the terrible consequences of rebellion.

It would seem as if this should have been enough to teach all, that it is only safe to do just what God requires in small, as well as great, things. Alas! however, this has not been the case. Nadab and Abihu, with the example of Eve before them, contrary to the directions of the Lord, ventured to substitute natural fire for the hallowed fire of the altar. To them, there was no apparent difference; but in a moment the curse of God fell upon them and they were borne lifeless, and without the honors of an ordinary funeral service, away from the camp of Israel. Uzzah, despising the commandment of the Lord, by which the Levites alone were to touch the ark, in an unguarded moment, reached out his hand to steady it, and God made a breach upon him in the presence of the people. Uzzah fell lifeless before the ark which contained the same law which is under consideration. It was not the ark that sanctified the law; but, rather, the law that sanctified the ark.

If, therefore, God was so jealous of that which was merely the vehicle of the ten words spoken by his voice and written by his finger, how must he feel in regard to those words themselves? In them, is found the embodiment of the whole duty of man. With them, God now tests, as he has always tested, the characters of men. "Know ye not," says Paul, "his servants ye are to whom ye obey; whether of sin unto death, or of obedience unto righteousness?"

True, it may be, that we can transgress that law at the present time without suffering the *visible* displeasure of God, as did those whom, in the past, he set forth as examples of his wrath. But let us not deceive ourselves on this account; God is no respecter of persons. Moral character is what he admires, exact obedience is what he demands. In his providence, at the present time, it is our fortune to live in an epoch when great light is shining upon the long dishonored and mutilated Sabbath commandment. A worldly church, having departed from the simplicity of gospel teaching and gospel method for the propagation of truth, has called to her aid the elements of force and the appliances of law. Closing their eyes to light, ample in itself for all the purposes of duty and doctrine, they have entered upon a crusade, determining to venture the experiment, so oft repeated, of enforcing, as doctrines, the commandments of men.

The end of this matter God knows, and has pointed out in his word. With outward success they may meet; but it will be at the terrible cost of that vital godliness which is alone found where the arm of God is made the arm of our strength. For those who, in the past, have ignorantly broken the law of Jehovah, God has ample forgiveness; but for those who, in the face of God's providential dealings, and in diametrical opposition to the plain teachings of his word, to which their attention is being called, shall still persist, not only in disobedience, but, also, in acts of oppression against those who prefer the narrow and rugged path of Bible fidelity, there can be nothing in reserve but the terrible displeasure of him whose right it is to command.

Reader, whoever you may be, and whatever may have been your past convictions and life, we turn to you in a final appeal. As you revere God, as you love Christ and his precious word, we exhort you in this matter to seek wisdom from the only true source. Be not discouraged by the disparity in numbers, neither tremble before the hosts which may frown upon you in the coming contest. "The Lord, he is God.' Under the shadow of his wing we can safely abide. No nobler destiny was ever vouchsafed to the obedient among the children of men, than is prepared for those who shall prove their fealty to the God of Heaven by a noble testimony to their love for him, by the keeping of his holy Sabbath, under circumstances, in the near future, which shall indeed try the souls of men.

May God grant that both reader and writer, nay more, also our opponent in this discussion—toward whom we entertain none but the kindliest feelings—also, all, everywhere, who are indeed the children of the living God and the brethren of our blessed Lord, may come to see eye to eye in this matter, so that, finally, we shall be brought safely through the perils of this last great conflict, which the true church is to endure, and stand victorious over all our enemies upon the Mount Zion of our God, there to sing the song of a deliverance complete and eternal, in a world where, from one new moon to another, and from one Sabbath to another, all flesh shall come to worship before the Lord. (Isa. 66 : 23.)

INDEX OF POINTS DISCUSSED.

PART FIRST:

ELD. LITTLEJOHN'S ARTICLES IN THE STATESMAN.

ARTICLE ONE.
PAGE.
Tendency toward Sabbath Discussion, ... 5
Various Views concerning Reform, ... 6
Inquiry as to Proper Action, ... 13

ARTICLE TWO.
Religious View of Sabbath Reform, ... 16
Sabbath Commandment, ... 19
Has this Law been Changed? 22

ARTICLE THREE.
Reasons for Sunday Observance Examined, ... 28
The Resurrection, ... 30
Example of Christ, ... 32

ARTICLE FOUR.
Texts on First Day of the Week, ... 36
They do Not Prove its Sacredness, ... 39
The Meeting of John 20:19, Considered, ... 42

ARTICLE FIVE.
John 20:26, Examined, ... 48
Act of Worship does Not Consecrate the Day, ... 50
1 Cor. 16:2, Examined, ... 54

ARTICLE SIX.

Acts 20:7, Examined,	57
Acts 2:1, Considered,	63
Pentecost Not First Day, but Fiftieth Day,	64
Rev. 1:10, Examined,	66
Proposed Amendment of the Constitution Not in Harmony with Bible Truth,	68

ARTICLE SEVEN.

Bible View of the Sabbath,	71
The Law Changed by the Catholic Power,	76
Position of Seventh-day Adventists,	79
Proposed Amendment Dangerous to our Liberties,	83

PART SECOND:

REPLIES AND REJOINDERS.

REPLY ONE.

Seventh-day Sabbatarianism and the Christian Amendment,	87
Supposed Action of Missionaries,	89
The Proposed Amendment Expresses only Fundamental Principles,	91

FIRST REJOINDER.

Amendment Not Related merely to Principles, but to Sunday in Particular,	96
Supposition of Missionary Action Examined,	103

REPLY TWO.

The Seventh Day Not Observed by the Early Christian
    Church, ... 107
Examination of New-Testament Proofs, ... 108

SECOND REJOINDER.

Our Common Ground, ... 116
The Seventh Day, only, the Sabbath in the New Testa-
    ment, ... 119
No Effort Has been Made to Place Sunday upon Precept, 124
Consideration of Col. 2: 14–17, ... 125
Rom. 14: 5, Examined, ... 129
Survey of the Ground Passed Over, ... 131

REPLY THREE.

Testimony of the Gospels for the First-day Sabbath, ... 133
Resurrection of Christ, ... 134
John 20, ... 136

THIRD REJOINDER.

No Evidence of First-day Sacredness, ... 140
The Gospels do Not Call First Day the Sabbath, ... 150

REPLY FOUR.

Argument for the First-day Sabbath from the Gift of the
    Holy Spirit on the Day of Pentecost, ... 154
Authors Differing Concerning the Day of the Week, ... 155
Argument for the First Day, ... 156

FOURTH REJOINDER.

Value of Testimony—First-day Keepers Witnessing that
    Pentecost Fell on the Sabbath, ... 163
No Reason Stated, nor Commandment Found, for First-
    day Sabbath, ... 172

REPLY FIVE.

First-day Sabbath at Troas, ... 177
The Reckoning of Time Considered, ... 179

FIFTH REJOINDER.

No Custom Found in Acts 20, ... 183
Argument for Change of Time Considered, ... 191
Evidence of Acts 20 Favorable to the Sabbath, ... 201

REPLY SIX.

Testimony of Paul and John to the First-day Sabbath, 202
Examination of 1 Cor. 16: 2, ... 203
Of Rev. 1: 10, ... 205

SIXTH REJOINDER.

1 Cor. 16: 2, ... 207
— Testimony of J. W. Morton, ... 207
— Concession of Albert Barnes, ... 209
— Paul's Plan of Systematic Beneficence, ... 211
— Devotion at Home, ... 214
Rev. 1: 10, ... 219
— The Sabbath is the Lord's Day, ... 220
— Christ Lord of the Sabbath, ... 221
— No Proof Given that First Day is the Lord's Day, 222

REPLY SEVEN.

Testimony of the Early Fathers to the First-day Sabbath, ... 225
Testimony of Ignatius, ... 225
Errors of Dr. Dwight, etc., Corrected, ... 227
Barnabas and Justin Martyr, ... 228
Dionysius, ... 229
Pliny, ... 230

SEVENTH REJOINDER.

Value of Traditional Testimony, ... 231
Ignatius, ... 235
Barnabas, ... 239
Justin Martyr, ... 243
What Justin Martyr Believed, ... 246
Dionysius, Melito, Pliny, ... 250
Deficiency of Testimony for First-day as a Sabbath, ... 253

REPLY EIGHT.

Patristic Testimony to the First-day Sabbath, ... 254
Irenæus, ... 254
Errors of Dr. Dwight and Others in Quoting this Father, 256
Tertullian, Origen, Cyprian, ... 257

EIGHTH REJOINDER.

The Apostasy, ... 261
Testimony of Irenæus, ... 262
Of Tertullian, ... 267
Of Origen, ... 273
Of Cyprian, ... 276
Summary View of the Case, ... 277

REPLY NINE.

Theories of the Christian Sabbath, ... 280
Claim of an Unwarranted Change of the Sabbath Considered, ... 284

NINTH REJOINDER.

No Advance Ground Taken, ... 287
Harmony of Sabbath Law and Sacred History, ... 289
Roman Apostasy and Change of Sabbath, ... 293
Seventh-day Sabbath in the Early Church, ... 296
Testimony of Romanists, ... 304

REPLY TEN.

The Principle as to Time in Sabbath Observance, ... 313
One Day in Seven, not the Seventh Day, Required, ... 313
Difficulties of Keeping Definite Day, ... 314

TENTH REJOINDER.

Inconsistency of the *Statesman's* Positions, ... 321
No-Definite-Day Argument Fatal to First Day, and to
 any Sabbath, ... 325
Inconsistency of his Position on Necessity of Legislation, 326
Difficulties of Sabbath-Keeping Considered, ... 329
Absurdity of the Theory of an Indefinite Day, ... 333
Definite Time Around the World, ... 339
Summary, ... 348

REPLY ELEVEN.

The True Theory of the Christian Sabbath, ... 351
First Day of the Week the True Christian Sabbath, ... 351
A Memorial of Redemption, ... 353

ELEVENTH REJOINDER.

Inconsistency of the Replies, ... 355
No Amendment of Sabbath Law Produced, ... 356
A Gospel Memorial of the Resurrection, ... 367
Sabbath Keeping Involves Sacrifice, ... 369
Summary of Evidence for the Sabbath, ... 371
The Commandment, or Tradition? 374
Conclusion, ... 377

CATALOGUE

Of Books, Pamphlets, Tracts, &c., Issued by the Seventh-Day Adventist Publishing Association,
Battle Creek, Mich.

HYMNS AND TUNES; 320 pages of hymns, 96 pages of music; in plain morocco, $1.00.

A COMPLETE HISTORY OF THE SABBATH AND FIRST DAY OF THE WEEK. By J. N. Andrews. $1.00.

THE SPIRIT OF PROPHECY, Vols. 1 & 2. By Ellen G. White, Each $1.00.

THE CONSTITUTIONAL AMENDMENT: or The Sunday, The Sabbath, The Change, and The Restitution. A Discussion between W. H. Littlejohn and the Editor of the *Christian Statesman*. Bound, $1.00. Paper, 40 cts. First Part, 10 cts

THOUGHTS ON THE REVELATION, critical and practical. By U. Smith. 328 pp., $1.00.

THOUGHTS ON THE BOOK OF DANIEL, critical and practical. By U. Smith. Bound, $1.00; condensed edition, paper, 35 cts.

THE NATURE AND DESTINY OF MAN. By U. Smith. 384 pp., bound, $1.00, paper, 40 cts.

LIFE INCIDENTS, in connection with the great Advent movement. By Eld. James White. 373 pp., $1.00.

AUTOBIOGRAPHY OF ELD. JOSEPH BATES, with portrait of the author. 318 pp., $1.00.

HOW TO LIVE: comprising a series of articles on Health, and how to preserve it, with various recipes for cooking healthful food, &c. 400 pp., $1.00.

SABBATH READINGS; or Moral and Religious Reading for Youth and Children. 400 pp., 60 cts.; in five pamphlets, 50 cts.

APPEAL TO YOUTH: Address at the Funeral of Henry N. White; also a brief narrative of his life, &c. 96 pp., muslin, 40 cts.; paper covers, 10 cts.

THE GAME OF LIFE, with notes. Three illustrations 5x6

inches each, representing Satan playing with man for his soul. In board, 50 cts., in paper, 30 cts.

THE UNITED STATES IN PROPHECY. By U. Smith. Bound, 40 cts.; paper, 20 cts.

HYMNS AND SPIRITUAL SONGS for Camp-meetings and other Religious Gatherings. Compiled by Eld. James White. 196 pp. Bound, 50 cts., paper, 25 cts.

REFUTATION OF THE AGE TO COME. By J. H. Waggoner. Price 20 cts.

PROGRESSIVE BIBLE LESSONS FOR CHILDREN; for Sabbath Schools and Families. G. H. Bell. Bound, 35 cts., paper, 25 cts.

THE ADVENT KEEPSAKE; comprising a text of Scripture for each day of the year, on the subjects of the Second Advent, the Resurrection, &c. Plain muslin, 25 cts.; gilt. 40 cts.

A SOLEMN APPEAL relative to Solitary Vice, and the Abuses and Excesses of the Marriage Relation. Edited by Eld. James White. Muslin, 50 cts.; paper, 30 cts.

AN APPEAL to the Working Men and Women, in the Ranks of Seventh-day Adventists. By James White. 172 pp., bound, 40 cts.; paper covers, 25 cts.

SERMONS ON THE SABBATH AND LAW; embracing an outline of the Biblical and Secular History of the Sabbath for 6000 years. By J. N. Andrews. 25 cts.

THE STATE OF THE DEAD. By U. Smith. 224 pp., 25 cts.

HISTORY of the Doctrine of the Immortality of the Soul. By D. M. Canright. 25 cts.

DISCUSSION ON THE SABBATH QUESTION, between Elds. Lane and Barnaby. 25 cts.

THE ATONEMENT; an Examination of a Remedial System in the light of Nature and Revelation. By J. H. Waggoner. 20 cts.

OUR FAITH AND HOPE. Nos. 1 & 2 —Sermons on the Advent, &c. By James White. Each 20 cts.

THE NATURE AND TENDENCY OF MODERN SPIRITUALISM. By J. H. Waggoner. 20 cts.

THE BIBLE FROM HEAVEN; or, a dissertation on the Evidences of Christianity 20 cts.

CATALOGUE OF PUBLICATIONS.

DISCUSSION ON THE SABBATH QUESTION, between Elds. Grant and Cornell. 20 cts.

REVIEW OF OBJECTIONS TO THE VISIONS. U. Smith, 20 cts.

COMPLETE TESTIMONY OF THE FATHERS, concerning the Sabbath and First Day of the Week. By J. N. Andrews. 15 cts.

THE DESTINY OF THE WICKED. By U. Smith. 15 cts.

THE MINISTRATION OF ANGELS; and the Origin, History, and Destiny of Satan. By D. M. Canright. 15 cts.

THE MESSAGES OF REV. 14, particularly the Third Angel's Message and Two-Horned Beast. By J. N. Andrews. 15 cts.

THE RESURRECTION OF THE UNJUST; a Vindication of the Doctrine. By J. H. Waggoner. 15 cts.

THE SANCTUARY AND TWENTY-THREE HUNDRED DAYS. By J. N. Andrews. 10 cts.

THE SAINTS' INHERITANCE, or, The Earth made New. By J. N. Loughborough. 10 cts.

THE SEVENTH PART OF TIME; a sermon on the Sabbath Question. By W. H. Littlejohn. 10 cts.

REVIEW OF GILFILLAN, and other authors, on the Sabbath. By T. B. Brown. 10 cts.

THE SEVEN TRUMPETS; an Exposition of Rev. 8 and 9. 10 cts.

THE DATE OF THE SEVENTY WEEKS OF DAN. 9 established. By J. N. Andrews. 10 cts.

THE TRUTH FOUND; the Nature and Obligation of the Sabbath of the Fourth Commandment. By J. H. Waggoner. 10 cts.

VINDICATION OF THE TRUE SABBATH. By J. W. Morton. 10 cts.

SUNDAY SEVENTH-DAY EXAMINED. A Refutation of the Teachings of Mede, Jennings, Akers, and Fuller. By J. N. Andrews. 10 cts.

MATTHEW TWENTY-FOUR; a full Exposition of the chapter. By James White. 10 cts.

THE POSITION AND WORK OF THE TRUE PEOPLE OF GOD under the Third Angel's Message. By W. H. Littlejohn. 10 cts.

AN APPEAL TO THE BAPTISTS, from the Seventh-day Baptists, for the Restoration of the Bible Sabbath. 10 cts.

MILTON ON THE STATE OF THE DEAD. 5 cts.

FOUR-CENT TRACTS: The Two Covenants—The Law and the Gospel—The Seventh Part of Time—Who Changed the Sabbath?—Celestial Railroad—Samuel and the Witch of Endor—The Ten Commandments not Abolished—Address to the Baptists.

THREE-CENT TRACTS: The Kingdom—Scripture References—Much in Little—The End of the Wicked—Infidel Cavils Considered—Spiritualism a Satanic Delusion—The Lost Time Question.

TWO-CENT TRACTS: The Sufferings of Christ—Seven Reasons for Sunday-Keeping Examined—Sabbath by Elihu—The Rich Man and Lazarus—The Second Advent—Definite Seventh Day—Argument on Sabbaton—Clerical Slander—Departing and Being with Christ—Fundamental Principles of S. D. Adventists—The Millennium.

ONE-CENT TRACTS: Appeal on Immortality—Brief Thoughts on Immortality—Thoughts for the Candid—Sign of the Day of God—The Two Laws—Geology and the Bible—The Perfection of the Ten Commandments—The Coming of the Lord—Without Excuse.

CHARTS: THE PROPHETIC, AND LAW OF GOD, CHARTS, painted and mounted, such as are used by our preachers, each $1.50. The two charts, on cloth, unpainted, by mail, with key, without rollers, $2.50.

The Way of Life. This is an Allegorical Picture, showing the way of Life and Salvation through Jesus Christ from Paradise Lost to Paradise Restored. By Eld. M. G. Kellogg. The size of this instructive and beautiful picture is 19x24 inches. Price, post-paid, $1.00.

Works in Other Languages.

The Association also publishes the *Advent Tidende*, Danish monthly, at $1.00 per year, and works on some of the above-named subjects in the German, French, Danish, and Holland languages.

☞ Any of the foregoing works will be sent by mail to any part of the United States, post-paid, on receipt of the prices above stated. A Full Catalogue of our various Publications will be furnished GRATIS, on application.

*** Address, REVIEW & HERALD,
BATTLE CREEK, MICH.

PERIODICALS.

The Advent Review & Herald of the Sabbath, weekly. This sheet is an earnest exponent of the Prophecies, and treats largely upon the Signs of the Times, Second Advent of Christ, Harmony of the Law and the Gospel, the Sabbath of the Lord, and, What we Must do to be Saved. Terms, $2.00 a year in advance.

The Youth's Instructor, monthly. This is a high-toned, practical sheet, devoted to moral and religious instruction, adapted to the wants of youth and children. It is the largest and the best youth's paper published in America. Terms, 50 cts. a year, in advance.

The Health Reformer. This is a live Journal, devoted to an Exposition of the Laws of Human Life, and the application of those laws in the Preservation of Health, and the Treatment of Disease. The *Reformer* will contain, each issue, thirty-two pages of reading matter, from able and earnest pens, devoted to real, practical life, to physical, moral, and mental improvement. Its publishers are determined that it shall be the best Health Journal in the land.

Terms, $1.00 a year, in advance. Address, Health Reformer, Battle Creek, Mich.

BOOKS FROM OTHER PUBLISHERS.

Future Punishment, by H. H. Dobney, Baptist minister of England. The Scriptural Doctrine of Future Punishment, with an Appendix, containing the "State of the Dead," by John Milton, author of "Paradise Lost," extracted from his "Treatise on Christian Doctrine."

This is a very able and critical work. It should be read by every one who is interested in the immortality subject. It is also

one of the best works upon the subject to put into the hands of candid ministers, and other persons of mind.
Price, post-paid, $1.00.

THE VOICE OF THE CHURCH, on the Coming and Kingdom of the Redeemer ; or, a History of the Doctrine of the Reign of Christ on Earth. By D. T. Taylor. A very valuable work, highly indorsed on both sides of the Atlantic.
Price, post-paid, $1.00.

The Great Reformation, by Martin, 5 Vols.,	$ 7.00
D'Aubigne's History of the Reformation, 5 Vols,	4.50
Scripture Biography,	4.50
Cruden's Concordance, sheep,	2 00
" " muslin,	1 50
Bible Dictionary, sheep,	2.00
" " muslin,	1.50
Cole's Concordance,	1.50
Prince of the House of David,	2.00
Pillar of Fire,	2.00
Throne of David,	2.00
The Court and Camp of David,	1.50
The Old Red House,	1.50
Higher Christian Life,	1.50
Pilgrim's Progress, large type,	1.25
" " small "	.60
Biography of George Whitefield,	1.25
History of English Puritans,	1.25
Story of a Pocket Bible,	1.25
Captain Russell's Watchword,	1.25
The Upward Path,	1 25
Ellen Dacre,	1.25
The Brother's Choice,	1.15
Climbing the Mountain,	1.15
The Two Books,	1.15
Awakening of Italy,	1.00

CATALOGUE OF PUBLICATIONS.

White Foreigners,	1.00
Lady Huntington,	1.00
Young Man's Counselor,	1.00
Young Lady's Counselor,	1.00
Paul Venner,	1.00
Among the Alps,	1.00
Poems of Home Life,	.80
Edith Somers,	.80
Nuts for Boys to Crack,	.80
Anecdotes for the Family,	.75
Pictorial Narratives,	.60
Bertie's Birthday Present,	.60
Songs for Little Ones,	.60
Memoir of Dr. Payson,	.60
Mirage of Life,	.60
Huguenots of France,	.50
The Boy Patriot,	.50
Springtime of Life,	.50
May Coverly,	.50
Glen Cabin,	.50
The Old, Old Story, cloth, gilt,	.50
Poems by Rebekah Smith,	.50
Charlotte Elizabeth,	.40
Save the Erring,	.40
Blanche Gamond,	.40
My Brother Ben,	.40
Hannah's Path,	.35
Star of Bethlehem,	.30
Father's Letters to a Daughter,	.30

☞ A more full Catalogue of books of this nature, for sale at this Office, can be had on application.

Address, REVIEW & HERALD,
BATTLE CREEK, MICH.

HEALTH REFORM PUBLICATIONS.

Good Health, and How to Preserve It. A brief treatise on the various hygienic agents and conditions which are essential for the preservation of health. Just the thing for a person who wishes to learn how to avoid disease. Pamphlet, price, post paid, 10 cents.

Disease and Drugs. Nature and Cause of Disease. and So-called "Action" of Drugs. This is a clear and comprehensive exposition of the nature and true cause of disease, and also exposes the absurdity and falsity of drug medication. Pamphlet. Price, 10 cents.

The Bath: Its Use and Application. A full description of the various baths employed in the hygienic treatment of disease, together with the manner of applying them, and the diseases to which they are severally adapted. Pamphlet. Price, post-paid, 15 cents.

Hydropathic Encyclopedia. Trall. Price, post-paid, $4.50.

Uterine Diseases and Displacements. Trall. Price, post paid, $3.00.

Science of Human Life. By Sylvester Graham, M. D. Price, post-paid, $3.00.

Domestic Practice. Johnson. Price, post-paid, $1.75.

Hand Book of Health—Physiology and Hygiene. Price, post-paid, 75 cents; paper cover, 40 cents

Water Cure in Chronic Diseases. By J. M. Gully, M. D. Price, post-paid, $1.75.

Cure of Consumption. Dr. Work. Price, post-paid, 30 cts.

The Hygienic System. By R. T. Trall, M. D. Recently published at the Office of the HEALTH REFORMER. It is just the work for the time, and should be read by the million. Price, post-paid, 15 cents.

The Health and Diseases of Women. By R. T. Trall, M. D. A work of great value. Price, post-paid, 15 cents.

Tobacco-Using. A philosophical exposition of the Effects of Tobacco on the Human System. By R. T. Trall, M. D. Price, post-paid, 15 cents.

Valuable Pamphlet. Containing three of the most important of Graham's twenty-five Lectures on the Science of Human Life—eighth, the Organs and their Uses; thirteenth, Man's Physical Nature and the Structure of His Teeth; fourteenth, the Dietetic Character of Man. Price, post-paid, 35 cts.

Address,   Health Reformer, *Battle Creek, Mich*

www.ingramcontent.com/pod-product-compliance
Lightning Source LLC
Chambersburg PA
CBHW032015220426
43664CB00006B/250